The Textual Life of Airports

Reading the Culture of Flight

Christopher Schaberg

B L O O M S B U R Y

NEW YORK · LONDON · NEW DELHI · SYDNEY

Contents

Acknowledgements

This book has involved so many people who listened to my airport theories, and who shared with me their own stories of flight. I could not possibly name everyone who steered me toward an airport scene in a book, or suggested a piece of airport art worth looking into. Thinking about the textual life of airports has truly been an experiment in finding signs of literariness in everyday conversation and in ordinary objects.

Thanks especially to Caren Kaplan, Colin Milburn, Timothy Morton, and Scott Shershow at UC Davis for reading and commenting on many early drafts of this project; and to John Marx, who originally suggested the phrase "the textual life of airports" as a description for what I was up to in this book. Ken Wissoker gave me excellent advice when the book project was in a conceptual stage. Kara Thompson has been a steadfast friend and collaborator, offering brilliant feedback, lively imagination, and kind encouragement throughout the book's development. Mark Yakich urged me to write my own stories of working at the airport; these narratives led me down unexpected and fruitful paths. Randy Malamud gave the book an enthusiastic and detailed reader report—his was an incredibly insightful and spirited outside perspective on the project. Thanks to Terra Durio, my savvy research assistant during the 2010–11 academic year. Great thanks to Andrew Maxwell for his work on the index. I could always count on Greg Keeler to help me bust through writing blocks. I am indebted to Zane Schwaiger for being a fantastic reader of the entire manuscript as the book neared completion. Abundant thanks go to Haaris Naqvi, my editor at Continuum, for being keen, intrepid, and helpful throughout the process, from my first contact with him to final delivery of the manuscript, and at every step in between.

I am grateful to JoAnn Cruz, Dean of Humanities and Natural Sciences at Loyola University New Orleans, for support during the summer of 2010, and to the Loyola Committee on Grants and Leaves for giving me a Faculty Research Grant for the 2010–11 academic year. I'm very thankful to have such wonderful and invigorating colleagues in the Department of English at Loyola. Thanks to my students at UC Davis and Loyola University New Orleans for putting up with my tangential references to airports and the culture of flight in classes ostensibly about literature.

Thanks to the journals *Media Fields*, *Nebula*, and *Western American Literature* for publishing early versions of parts of the project, and to Michael Cornelius who included my essay on the Hardy Boys airport mysteries in his book *The Boy Detectives*.

Susann and Jim Schaberg graciously offered me productive places to write during the summers of 2007, 2010, and 2011.

Finally, my deepest thanks to Lara for endless support and patience throughout the writing process; I promise, no more deliberately planned long layovers.

I have travelled a good deal in Concord . . .
    —Henry David Thoreau, *Walden*

Reprint acknowledgements

Part of Chapter 3 is from *The Boy Detectives: Essays on the Hardy Boys and Others* © 2010. Edited by Michael G. Cornelius by permission of McFarland & Company, Inc., Box 611, Jefferson NC 28640.

A version of Chapter 8 was originally published in *Nebula* 6(2) July 2009.

My review of *Ordinary Affects*, from which I draw in Chapter 7, was originally published in *Western American Literature* 44(2) Summer 2009.

Chapter 5 "The Airport Screening Complex" appeared in *Media Fields Journal: Media, Labor, Mobility* (2) March 2011.

Leo Cullum's cartoon "I'll Never Make It" © Leo Cullum / The New Yorker Collection / www.cartoonbank.com, reprinted by permission.

Photographs of Ralph Helmick's sculpture Rara Avis by Clements/Howcroft and © Ralph Helmick and Stuart Schechter, reproduced by permission.

"Waiting for a Ride" and "No Shadow" Copyright © 2004 by Gary Snyder from *Danger on Peaks*. Reprinted by permission of Counterpoint.

"Men at Work" © 2011 by Julie Bruck from *MONKEY RANCH* (Brick Books: London, Ontario), forthcoming 2012. Lines cited by permission of the author.

"The Arrivals Gate" lyrics © Ani DiFranco, reprinted by permission of Righteous Babes Records.

"Around the World" *New Yorker* cover © Adrian Tomine, illustration reprinted by permission of the artist.

INTRODUCTION

This is a book about airports. It is a book about the common stories of airports that circulate in everyday life, and about the secret stories of airports—the disturbing, uncomfortable, or smoothed over tales that lie just beneath the surface of these sites. I am interested in how airports encapsulate certain ideas of modern life in the United States: airports are sites where identity is confirmed or questioned; they are spaces of public display; they are contested zones where privacy and national security vie for priority; they are complex factories for the production of patriotism and the privilege of mobility. At the same time, airports can be considered as generic spaces, forgettable and often uncomfortable. They are designed to be passed through, and in rapid fashion; this is what the anthropologist Marc Augé means by the term "non-places." And yet, airports are also enmeshed with matters of place, region, and slow time. These are some of the topics I discuss in the chapters of this book.

This book speculates about the *textuality* of airports. A text is anything that can be *read*: novels and poems certainly, but also artworks, film scenes, and even magazine advertisements that seem utterly ignorable. A text is anything that requires interpretation—whether active or passive, difficult or seemingly simple. For my purposes here, texts correspond to certain stories (cultural, local, or global). I track how stories are spun around airports, and I follow the interpretive threads that unravel in these sites. Some airports stories are *uncertain* stories: they are ambiguous or turn out to be contradictory. I locate these stories both in literature and in the everyday life of airport culture. I focus on how airports *read*, or how they are interpreted, in a range of contexts. These readings and interpretations can tell us a lot about how and why humans travel by air: what beliefs humans invest in flight, and what mysteries still lie beneath the sky, on the ground.

I tend to linger on instances where ideas of air travel become complex, and where plural meanings emerge. For example, Sam Shepard begins the short story "Land of the Living" in an airport with "long, stale lines of humans in limbo."[1] The zoomed out perspective and detached description afford a glimpse of how a species moves and clumps together. Shepard does not simply stage the airport as a convenient setting for character development, but he also suggests that the space itself warrants *reading*: the story occupies the airport as an interpretive region, a place where human subjects are in an uncertain state. Such brief airport appearances are what I collect and puzzle over in this book.

By using the term *textual*, I aim to draw together a range of connotations from how narratives are contained and disseminated, to frameworks of reading and interpretation. In the seminal work *Non-Places: Introduction to an Anthropology of Supermodernity*, Augé claims:

> . . . the real non-places of supermodernity—the ones we inhabit when we are driving down the motorway, wandering through the supermarket or sitting in an airport lounge waiting for the next flight to London or Marseille—have the peculiarity that they are defined partly by the words and *texts* they offer us: their "instructions for use," which may be prescriptive ("Take right-hand lane"), prohibitive ("No smoking") or informative ("You are now entering the Beaujolais region"). Sometimes these are couched in more or less explicit and codified ideograms (on road signs, maps and tourist guides), sometimes in ordinary language. This establishes the traffic conditions of spaces in which individuals are supposed to interact only with *texts* . . .[2]

In this book I follow Augé's directive to look at the *textual* aspects of supermodernity. Specifically, I pay attention to what I call *the textual life of airports*. I find this to be a densely layered and highly reflexive form of existence. It is apparent in the everyday operations of air travel as well as in literary representations of airports, and also in other popular culture depictions of flight.

This book treats literature not merely as one form of cultural representation among others; rather, literature offers a critical point of entry for seeing how airports function culturally, socially, psychologically, philosophically—and finally, ecologically. I argue that airports depend on textuality to a great degree, as much for their straightforward operations (such as the daily performances and narratives that play out all the way from the check-in stand to the departure gate), as for their everyday mysteries and inoperative moments (for instance, how a thousand unique stories can be contained in and canceled out by phrases like "weather delay" and "lost baggage").

While it may seem counterintuitive to turn to literature as a way to investigate airports and survey a broad cultural topos, this book argues that airports have been situated as *the* place to read in contemporary culture. From airport marketed e-reading technologies to the profit margins of airport bookstores, from elaborate identity checks to killing time with light reading—I demonstrate that airports and textual practices are intimately bound together. Somewhat reflexively, then, the book brings careful, literary reading practices to bear on a wide field of interests and disciplines that converge at the airport.

I use literature in order to analyze the textual life of airports, and I show in turn how airports are literary-critical spaces, even when reflected in cultural artifacts that are not literary per se, such as films, art installations, or advertising spots. In the style of Roland Barthes, I treat cultural fragments and literary works as productive and active *texts*. In his classic essay "From Work to Text," Barthes describes a Text (as differentiated from a Work) as "that space . . . where languages circulate." As Barthes goes on to suggest, "the metaphor of the Text is that of the *network*"—"its constitutive movement is that of cutting across."[3] Each of these descriptions gestures to how I treat airports as *textual* spaces—and how I look at airports *in* a host of literary and cultural texts.

I examine many visual texts throughout the book, and my methodological model here comes from Donna Haraway. In *When Species Meet*, Haraway explains her approach this way: "Figures help me grapple inside the flesh of mortal world-making entanglements that I call contact zones."[4] Likewise, I see in the visual culture of airports the "contact zones" where common and uncommon narratives collide, and where cultural trends and unique exceptions commingle. While it may seem odd to think of airports as bodily or fleshy, this is an adjustment in perspective that I try to enact: I focus on visual figures in and of airports to show how airports are entangled with bodies and enactments of "world-making." Haraway goes on to argue that figures "are not representations or didactic illustrations, but rather material–semiotic nodes or knots in which diverse bodies and meanings coshape one another."[5] I am constantly interested in the feedback loops where stories shape airports, and airports shape stories—this is dynamic "coshaping" that exists in the everyday practices of air travel. If Barthes's semiology embraces literature and culture alike through the critical lens of *text*, Haraway's turn to *figures* suggests an accompanying and compatible method for treating the visual culture of flight. Through my readings, I expose airports to be rich and chimerical figures.

When I turn to other linguistic expressions, cultural artifacts, and visual examples that lie beyond the proper realm of the literary, I often attempt to demonstrate how airport tropes and paradoxes circulate beyond the bounds of air travel per se. So, for instance, when the media theorist Lev Manovich offhandedly validates his "Introduction to Info-Aesthetics" by announcing "I spent countless hours in airports," here I would point out how the familiar forms of air travel get insinuated and implicated in a burgeoning new media ecology.[6] Manovich means for his readers to understand that his analyses of information-based social practices are *grounded*, as it were, and embodied in everyday life. Manovich also expects his readers to understand that the experience of waiting in airports is heavily mediated, and dense with information networks. His essay has nothing else to do with air travel, and yet this passing reference to airports indicates an assumption about a common *feeling*. In just this way, the textual life of airports often pops up in indirect references to the culture of flight.

Throughout the book I use the phrase "the culture of flight." I expect this phrase to register in an intentionally imprecise national sense. My textual

examples throughout the book are gleaned primarily from U.S. literature
and culture, and I am interested in the ways that certain American identities
are formed around airports and tropes of flying. As a recent *New York Times*
article about the contemporary state of air travel suggested, "Americans are
willing to tolerate a great number of things at the airport that they would
never stand for in other parts of their lives."[7] There is a sense in this statement that airports depend on a level of tolerance that is particularly unique
to Americans. The culture of flight is about sustained tensions and stubborn
sentiments that *somehow* have to do with being American.

We can see another dimension of the culture of flight in the vaguely
competing license plate logos of Ohio and North Carolina, respectively:
"The Birthplace of Aviation" and "First in Flight." Both slogans allude to
the Wright brothers, yet these license plates locate the origin of flight in
different geographical U.S. locations. Then there is the bumper sticker "If it
isn't a Boeing, I'm not going." This glib rhyme reflects pride in the American
corporation, and suspicion of foreign aircraft manufacturers. It hardly matters here that the national hubris associated with Boeing is undermined by
the reality of jet parts that come from all over the globe; the point is that it
becomes a *textual* attitude about flight. Thus, when I allude to "the culture
of flight" I am referring to a dispersed set of sensibilities, individual feelings, and collective moods circulating around the subject of air travel. This
culture, for obvious reasons, tends to be the most evident, concentrated, and
multifaceted in and around airports.

We might note an earlier indicator of the culture of flight in F. Scott
Fitzgerald's short story "Three Hours between Planes," wherein the main
character Donald Plant utilizes a three-hour layover to rekindle an old
flame. Donald calls his childhood crush Nancy on the phone, and after cor-
dial hellos, Donald mentions that he is ". . . out at the airport—just for a few
hours."[8] Nancy promptly invites Donald over to her house; her husband is
away on a business trip. Donald jumps in a taxi, and the story continues:
"On his way Donald analyzed the conversation. His words 'at the airport'
established that he had retained his position in the upper bourgeoisie."[9]
Here, the airport is signaled to be a word open to interpretation: "airport"
means more than a spatial designation, and carries with it connotations of
privilege and economic structure. The culture of flight thus involves *reading airports* for their symbolic values: airports serve as intermediary yet
interpretively charged points amid the accelerating mobilities of twentieth-
century consumer culture.

The culture of flight is an ongoing phenomenon with a rich history.[10] But
this is also a recently recharged matter: the events of September 11, 2001,
boosted airports and air travel into the headlines of the American news
cycle, and these subjects have stayed in the foreground more or less over
the past ten years, oscillating between being cast, on the one hand, as an
intensely sensitive zone for national security, and, on the other, as a griping
point for economic woes and breaches of individual rights.

Jacques Derrida hints at this aspect of the culture of flight in one of his careful reflections on the events of 9/11. Derrida points out that what happened on September 11, 2001, took place, as it were, *"from the inside*, from forces that [were] apparently without any force of their own but that [were] able to find the means, through ruse and the implementation of *high-tech* knowledge, to get hold of an American weapon in an American city on the ground of an American airport."[11] Derrida recognizes a critical vulnerability inherent in the chain of national icons, and suggests the paradox wherein an American airliner is a suicidal *weapon* by another name. As I indicate throughout this book, the culture of flight necessarily contains its own potential for self-reflexive halts and jolts that arrest or delay flight— sometimes these are violent, as in commercial airliners hijacked, and other times these suspensions are generated out of the routine bustle of overbooked flights or severe weather. These are unsettling problems that I return to throughout the book.

While it is no doubt true that other parts of the world have their own particular cultures of flight (the stringent airport security of Israel comes to mind, or the routinely ramshackle experience of commercial flight throughout Russia, as a friend once narrated it to me), this book aims to show the significantly American ways that the culture of flight is imagined—significant because these ways of imagining flight are often in subtle or outright conflict with coincident notions of selfhood, property, freedom, and mobility associated with American identity. At the same time, I readily concede that the culture of flight spills beyond national boundaries or political lines of demarcation: like consumer culture, the culture of flight is a distributed and shifting arrangement of modalities and mindsets, a pervasive mesh of people and things wrapping the globe.

In the spring of 2001 I took a part-time job working at an airport outside of Bozeman, Montana. I was employed by SkyWest, a regional carrier for United Airlines; my job title was "cross-utilized agent." This meant that because it was a small airport, I learned to do nearly everything: load baggage, create itineraries and issue tickets, check people in for their flights, de-ice the aircraft, push the aircraft back from the gate to the taxiway, and clean the planes at night. In short, I learned what goes on behind the scenes at an airport. It was at once the strangest and the most routine job I'd ever had. Throughout the book, I draw from my work experiences as a way of approaching several aspects of the culture of flight.

For instance, the fact that the airport was in a mountain town made for striking juxtapositions of geologic time and human pursuits, cloudscapes and concrete slabs. And so another concern of this book involves how airports raise environmental questions. I mean this not only in the way that airports actually impact ecosystems, but also how they depend on certain environmental sensibilities and aesthetics—like the way that the Bozeman airport greeted passengers with overtly Western themes, as in the huge grizzly bear sculpture sitting at the bottom of the arrivals stairway, or the cougar frozen in mid-leap over the baggage claim area. As I researched and wrote this book, I increasingly found airports to have odd relationships with ideas of environment. Sometimes airports seem to blur the distinctions between inside and outside, and other times these boundaries are rigidly enforced. Sometimes airports are identifiably "regional," and other times one might feel as though one could be *anywhere*—airports can feel utterly generic (pleasingly or uncomfortably so).

In her book *Flight Maps: Adventures with Nature in Modern America*, Jennifer Price discusses the phenomenon of Nature Company stores and how they sell images and objects that in turn create a profusion of ideas concerning what Nature is and how one can experience it. Price observes: "*Where* have we been looking for nature most often since the 1980s? Not in the 'where' where we generally think of nature as being. It is not surprising that one of the more successful Nature Company stores, while not in a mall, has been in the Pittsburgh Airport."[12] In other words, Price suggests that there are curious conjunctions and ironies between the nowhere of airports and the desire for nature as a genuine place. Throughout this book, I ruminate on instances where airports and concepts of nature overlap, whether ironically or collaboratively, and specifically as these instances reside in literary representations and public art installations.

The chapters of this book are speculative, in the sense that they chart stories about airports from bits of evidence across scattered texts. Each chapter functions as what the political philosopher Jane Bennett might call an "onto-story."[13] The chapters are cumulative tales of being that individually draw many disparate texts, objects, and subjects together. Each chapter sketches a convergence of energies and affects—all around airport themes and scenarios of flight.

Very briefly, then, Chapter 1 takes up the idea of "airport reading." What does it mean to read in an airport, and when are people called on to read the airport itself? This chapter lays out the method of the book, a sort of critical zooming practice of reading airports *as* texts and reading airports *in* texts. Chapter 2 considers airport labor, and examines occasions when passengers (or book readers) are called on to view or interpret the work of air travel—but also when airport workers become active readers of the culture of flight. Chapter 3 discusses how airports provoke expectations for mystery and adventure. Chapter 4 analyzes airport scenes in 9/11 fiction, and demonstrates the key role of airports in narrative commemorations of that day. Chapter 5 advances a theory for what I call "the airport screening complex": this is about the many layers of screens and uses of screening that unfurl within and around the post-9/11 airport. Chapter 6 explores alternative studies of airports, both in fictive situations where an airport becomes a destination in and of itself, and in cases where airports are critically apprehended, or otherwise treated experimentally. Around intersections of airports and environmental aesthetics, Chapter 7 proposes an ecological reading of airports based on scenes and sensations of *waiting*. Building on an eccentric environmental phenomenology of airports, Chapter 8 spins a wild story about the collusions and collisions of avian imagery at airports, human aviation, and actual birdlife. Chapter 9 concludes the book by reflecting on the textuality of the baggage claim, as a cultural trope and as a mundane space of calculation and collection. This is the figure of the endpoint of travel, and it is also a threshold where the textual life of airports blurs into the world beyond.

CHAPTER 1

WHAT IS AIRPORT READING?

Simply books

Once during a layover in the Minneapolis airport, I found myself killing time by wandering the C concourse, and exploring the little offshoots and shops that pepper the long hallway. In an alcove that led to the G gates, I was struck by a store called Simply Books. As it turns out, this is a chain of airport bookstores, run by the retail operator HMS Host and located in seven major U.S. airports.

Figure 1.1 Simply Books at the Minneapolis airport (author's photo)

The idea of an airport bookstore may not sound surprising in the least. But what captivated me was the marketing of this consumer site as a *simple* space. For one thing, the bookstore sold much more than simply books. Magazines, newspapers, and other items geared toward airport distraction were on sale throughout the store. And then, I had to wonder about the strategic location of this bookstore: there is nothing simple about airport consumerism. Framing this shop, there was the stark geometric façade that made the bookstore appear almost temple-like, as if a space unto itself. Of course this aesthetic tactic is commonplace: many airport store thresholds are designed in such a way as to have them pop out of the visual matrix that is a terminal or concourse. At the same time, however, such design should never get in the way of the functional flows of the airport.

In this way, though, there was something about the presentation of Simply Books that seemed to challenge the directional force of the airport. The invitation was to simplicity, to a sort of idealized absorption in *reading*. This rubbed against the multiple demands of the space all around: calls to boarding, intermittent jet engine blasts, the airport CNN network blaring from the ceiling, changing gate information, navigating the architectural whims of the airport . . . . In short, the airport presented itself as an utterly demanding text, with myriad messages and streams of information coming at the reader (or passenger) from numerous directions. Amid all this, the Simply Books store stood out, at once discontiguous with the ambience and intimately a part of it.

Texts within texts

Marc Augé begins *Non-Places: Introduction for an Anthropology of Supermodernity* with a prologue in the form of a story. Augé, pithily and yet with great attention to detail, narrates the journey of generic business traveler Pierre Dupont as he drives to Charles de Gaulle airport, checks in for his flight, passes time before boarding, and, finally, takes off.

Augé's use of narrative is noteworthy as a strategy for an anthropological text on spaces such as airports, as it places the reader in a somewhat unfamiliarly ethnographic perspective concerning the routines of contemporary travel. Furthermore, the narrative becomes reflexive at one moment: this happens when Dupont strolls into the airport "bookshop where he leafed through a couple of magazines before choosing an undemanding book: travel, adventure, spy fiction. Then he resumed his unhurried progress."[1] The "book" in this passage functions as a text within a text. It is an interior object of reading that illuminates how airports work.

In this chapter I look at cases where texts reflect on the textual life of airports. I call this conjunction *airport reading*. Airport reading appears where layers of textuality pile up in the space/time of flight. I look for these instances in order to draw out the narrative underpinnings of airports. The above example from *Non-Places* evinces airport reading, as the prologue of Augé's critical project borrows its aesthetic from part of the subject under scrutiny: at that moment, the story of Dupont preparing for his flight seems suddenly to be curiously like the contents of an undemanding airport novel.

Airport reading can appear in other ways, as well. For instance, consider one of the epigraphs to Walter Kirn's 2001 novel *Up in the Air*:

> Secure your own mask before assisting others.
>
> Northwest Airlines
> *Pre-Flight Instruction*[2]

In this case, Kirn begins a novel about air travel by evoking the textuality of air travel—these are words spoken by a flight attendant prior to takeoff, while one's plane taxis to the runway. This simple allusion to the standardized language of flight suggests, like Augé's redoubled narrative, that there are novelistic dimensions built into the everyday practices of air travel. In other words, air travel depends on a network of stories and meanings—texts that are interpreted by the everyday practices of flight.

As if to further animate this textual life, the opening sentences of *Up in the Air* continue to develop the theme:

> To know me you have to fly with me. Sit down. I'm the aisle, you're the window—trapped. You crack your paperback, last spring's big legal thriller, convinced that what you want is solitude, though I know otherwise: you need to talk. The jaunty male flight attendant brings our drinks: a two percent milk with one ice cube for me, a Wild Turkey for you. It's wet outside, the runways streaked and dark.[3]

The narrator of the novel almost immediately speaks of a novel inside the novel: an interior object of airport reading. This is that disposable variety of entertainment created specifically to be consumed in the in between times of travel. This is what the critic Fredric Jameson calls ". . . so-called paraliterature with its airport paperback categories of the gothic and the romance, the popular biography, the murder mystery and the science fiction or fantasy novel."[4] For Jameson the "airport paperback categories" of genre fiction count as a staple feature of postmodern culture, with their mass audience appeal, their planned obsolescence, and their penchant for pastiche. For Kirn, the object of airport reading initiates a story *about* the routines and rituals of air travel—or what he terms "Airworld."[5]

As I noted with Augé, airport reading both falls under the purview of the subject at hand, and serves as a methodology: his narrative prologue to *Non-Places* initiates a critical anthropological approach to the subject of modern travel. Similarly, the opening sentences from the novel *Up in the Air* suggest a continuum between airport reading material and close observation of the landscape at hand. Kirn's narrator practices an ecology of non-place, detailed from the "jaunty male flight attendant" and specific drinks served, to "the runways streaked and dark." Indeed, *Up in the Air* is a veritable tome of social analyses and spatial ruminations: the main character Ryan Bingham has an ultimate goal of accruing "A million frequent flyer miles. One million."[6] Reading about Bingham's quest is also to read about the culture of flight—not so unlike how a continuation of Augé's tale of Pierre Dupont might read.

What is airport reading?

Let us look closer at the idea of airport reading. One on level, the phrase simply refers to any form of light entertainment to be consumed in the space/time of travel. Airport reading is precisely what Simply Books sells: consumable products, for sure—but also an ideology of certain kinds of consumption. Here is how the website about.com concisely defines it:

> Airport reading needs to be fast paced enough to make your wait fly by and engaging enough to keep your attention from people watching or starring at whatever is playing on the airport news channel. Airport reading shouldn't be too emotionally engaging though (no one wants to break down in tears in a crowded terminal).[7]

Airport reading is precisely that "paperback, last spring's big legal thriller" with which Kirn begins *Up in the Air*. This is a genre of reading material, then; but as we see in this definition, it is also a mindset, and a certain *way* of reading. Airport reading involves a sustained emotional detachment, but it also demands a heightened level of focus that can resist the myriad distractions that wrap airports with a familiar feel: boarding announcements, the roar of jet engines, beeping people movers, and the like. Airport reading has to take up time, but it also must be fast: thus it can make "your wait fly by." Such a book should be "engaging enough" to keep from being distracted by the multimedia spectacle of an airport—but not so "emotionally engaging" that the reader would then become totally absorbed in the ancillary text. In other words, this type of reading depends on the airport itself to have already emerged as a primary text of sorts, a legible space where there are people to watch, planes roaring into the air, and a built-in streaming television network (among many other informational signs, auditory cues, and aestheticized views).

And yet, as we saw in the works of Augé and Kirn, airport reading can also open up to close observation of specific transit spaces and practices of travel. This dimension of airport reading can be witnessed in numerous texts that pass through airport spaces, often as a way to forward commentaries on specific characters or culture at large.

Consider a scene from Lorrie Moore's 2009 novel *A Gate at the Stairs*. At one point fairly early in the novel, the narrative passes through an airport:

"Gate two, upstairs," said the woman at the counter, handing us our boarding passes, and since we only had carry-on bags, we went directly upstairs, except that Sarah, seeing that no people were on the down escalator, decided to try to go up it. "Watch this," she said to me. "This is how you get a little exercise before getting on a plane." And she ran quickly up the moving steps, using it like a treadmill, and waving goofily to me from the middle, as if she were Lucille Ball. "Ma'am, that's the wrong escalator," said someone on the other side, going up, and then because it was taking Sarah so long to get to the top, someone else came riding up and said, "Do you know you're going up the down side?" No one understood what she was doing, and so no one smiled.

"Exercise!" exclaimed Sarah. This burst of eccentricity in her I could see was familiar to herself, and unrestricted.[8]

This brief airport scene forwards a character sketch of Sarah Brink as an offbeat person. But it also *reads* the airport: the terminal must be interpreted as having a vibe of seriousness and strict functionality, against which the narrator can illuminate and reflect on Sarah's "burst of eccentricity." The scene depends on an entirely realistic ambience for the reader to grasp the ironic use of the airport escalator set against the assumed deadpan of most travelers.

The novel's broader subject also draws from the minor airport passage: Sarah's playful session in the airport is completely disjunctive with the mood of post-9/11 air travel, where "no one smiled." Indeed, airports play a key role in post-9/11 U.S. identity, as sites where nationality is confirmed and patriotism is on display.[9]

Moore's novel, then, uses the airport to plant a narrative seed. The intentional misuse of the terminal escalator suggests how the character of Sarah Brink generally swims against the current—and this includes the culture of post-9/11 racial prejudice that is a strong undercurrent in the book.

This passage also mentions the actress Lucille Ball as a referent for Sarah's "goofily" affected act. With this passing comparison, the reader is redirected to a popular culture inter-text, and the airport becomes a place ambient with spectacle value and a capacity for entertainment.[10]

As we can see, the brief airport scene in *A Gate at the Stairs* depends on a bundle of interpretative moves, yet all the while serving simply as a transition space, a textual non-place. Like many of the airport passages I survey in this book, this scene does not stand out—not as a pivotal point in narrative—and it is precisely this ambient, unremarkable quality that contributes to the culture of flight. Airport reading in this respect also consists, then, of broader literary treatments of airport spaces as particular kinds of narrative settings.

I want to stress this literary function of airport reading with another example. A contemporary writer who consistently evokes airports in both ambient and densely (inter)textual ways is Don DeLillo. For instance, the characters in DeLillo's 1997 magnum opus *Underworld* find themselves in and around numerous airports as the narrative struggles through the latter half of a bomb-scar(r)ed twentieth century, determined to arrive, at last, at "Peace."[11]

One passage from *Underworld* is particularly helpful in terms of further unpacking the idea of airport reading:

> Nick was trying to find the magazine he'd been saving to take to Houston. He saved certain kinds of reading for business trips, things he never got around to looking at otherwise, magazines that stacked and nagged and finally went to the sidewalk on the designated day. There was a noise that started, a worldly hum—you began to hear it when you left your carpeted house and rode out to the airport. He wanted something friendly to read in the single sustained drone that marks every mile in a business traveler's day.[12]

Even though the actual airport makes only an indirect appearance in this passage—"rode out to the airport"—it is in fact key to the entire passage.[13] The airport exists on the perimeter of this scene, yet it also lies at the heart of this passage as a space guaranteed for waiting, a reserved time for "certain kinds of reading." The airport functions as a sort of precondition for reading time: a bracketed space that amplifies the "noise" of flight which then must be canceled out by reading. The novel becomes something of a redoubling media form, signaling and routing outlying trajectories of *additional* reading: the novel points out (at) other forms of reading familiar to late-twentieth-century travelers—in particular, "the magazine." To put it simply, in this passage one reads in a novel about how certain kinds of texts are to be read in the space/time of airports.

Extra layers of textuality are also produced by the synaesthetic elements of this passage. DeLillo calls on the reader to imagine a shift in feeling under one's feet, from the texture of carpet to whatever hard ground is supposed to exist at the airport. And the nod to paper recycling ("to the sidewalk on the designated day") alludes to the crinkle of magazine pages—and perhaps even to the materiality of the book in one's hands at the moment of reading. Finally, the acousmatic "single sustained drone" of air travel—"a worldly hum"—is counterposed with the "friendly" feel of reading. In short, this passage requires the reader to take time, while reading, to consider the time of airport reading—what it feels like, from multiple sensory modes.

Time for magazines

I want to follow DeLillo's cue toward magazines to investigate another dimension of airport reading. This is part of the visual culture of flight: how air travel appears in the pages of magazines. In particular, I wish to look at two visual texts that feature airport reading in full effect, with all its interpretive imperatives and convoluted demands for travel, entertainment, and absorption.

In 2006 Sony ran an ad for the Reader (an early e-reading device, to be followed by the more successful Amazon Kindle and Apple iPad, among others) that uses an airport departure lounge as a setting in which to market the device. The fine print of the ad boasts that the Reader can hold "about 80 electronic books" and is "as easy to carry as a slim paperback"—clearly, we are well-entrenched in the milieu of airport reading.

Figure 1.2 "Pick a nice spot for your library" (© 2006 Sony Electronics Inc.)

The ad depicts an empty airport departure lounge, complete with a white, unmarked Boeing 747–400 in the background, framed by floor-to-ceiling windows. Behind the aircraft lies a partly cloudy sky—neither stormy nor crystal clear. Beside a row of standard airport seating, a blue sign is posted on a contextually incongruous construction-zone T-bar post: it shows a nondescript icon of a person reading a book. Note how the T-bar punctures the departure lounge floor: this suggests that the ground of the airport is earthy, almost outside. This environmental intrusion rubs against the idea in the fine print that the airport could be reconceived as a "library."

What is perhaps most striking about this image is the profound emptiness of the airport. This presents a curious paradox: if one needed to resort to the Sony Reader's full book capacity in an airport, it would likely be due to a long delay, which would also mean a jam-packed departure lounge. Yet the Sony departure lounge has been imagined as a silent space, an ideal site for solitary reading—as the fine print reads, "Pick a nice spot for your library." This departure lounge is doubly warped, first as an ironically empty space, and second as a destination for (electronic) book reading.

The layers of textuality are piled high in this ad for the Sony Reader. We are asked to interpret the generic airport space; to translate the eerie emptiness into a library-like ambience; and then to rethink the excruciating time of waiting as a luxurious chance to *read*. We are interpellated to *fly*—then to *wait*—then to *read*. And this prompt toward book reading arrives in the form of a magazine ad: the imaginary library of books functions as a certain wish image for passing time, when in fact, as noted in the passage from *Underworld*, airport waiting is perhaps better suited to time for magazines.

The idea of the book is central to the textual life of airports, but it is a vexed matter, as we noted in the original definition of airport reading. As an object of airport reading, the book trembles on an interesting threshold between deep meaning and utter disposability.

For a second visual example of this threshold, let us look at an illustration by Adrian Tomine that was featured as a *New Yorker* magazine cover in the winter of 2005/2006; this image depicts another departure lounge dedicated to airport reading. The illustration in some ways looks similar to the Sony ad, and in other ways strikes a quite different note.

Figure 1.3 "Around the World" (© Adrian Tomine, reproduced by permission of the artist)

This airport scene is a multicultural fantasyland where everyone is at peace—despite the fact that no one is going anywhere, at least not any-time soon. This departure gate suggests a cosmopolitan dream where every delayed and waiting passenger is reading a book. Unlike the Sony Reader ad, every airport seat is taken; the departure gate is full of passengers. But like the Sony Reader ad, *reading* appears to neutralize the stress and drama of flight—if also, strangely, to accentuate the banality of airport waiting. In both cases, the airport is cast as a predictable space where travel time poten-tially turns into endless waiting.

White bits of snow falling outside Tomine's imaginary airport serve to explain why the departures monitor displays a uniform stream of DELAYED status signs—and miraculously, the passengers are all going with the flow, calmly reading their unmarked (and apparently hardbound) books. The blankness of the book covers suggests a kind of baseline openness to inter-pretation: we can imagine that these texts are *anything*, and that each pas-senger's reading taste is so individual that the only uniform meaning is in the most general *form* of the book. This really is a wish image for airport reading: the illustration certifies the airport as an authentic place through recourse to a somewhat unrelated high-culture material object, as signified by the antique books. The irony here is that airport delays are more widely embraced as time for magazines and other disposable forms of reading/ entertainment—and of course Tomine's illustration appeared *on* a magazine cover, as well. There is, then, a symbolic trembling housed in each of these blank, hardbound books: we know that the books might be abandoned at any moment, were the weather to suddenly clear—for airport reading is always subservient to the primary motive of *flight*.[14]

The serene and serious airport readers in Tomine's scene are set against the pandemonium that is likely occurring beyond the confines of the depar-ture lounge—such as de-icing trucks working overtime, baggage vehicles stuck in the snow, and perishable airplane meals going bad, to name a few. To rephrase two lines of a poem by Wallace Stevens: The passengers are reading. / The airline employees must be working.[15]

Reading Airport: *From text to work*

Up to this point, we have primarily discussed airport reading from the per-spective of waiting passengers: this is material designed for passing time, to be consumed before boarding, while delayed, or in-flight. And yet airport reading often turns on the *work* of airports: the acts, commands, and opera-tions that typify and mobilize the culture of flight. Recall for a moment the passage from *A Gate at the Stairs*, which begins with "the woman at the counter." While workers often seem relegated to the background or periph-ery, the textual life of airports almost always concerns real acts of labor and the imagined roles of airline employees behind the scenes. Of course, for those who work at airports, the spatial practices therein have very different meanings: airport reading becomes less a matter of passing time or consuming media, and more a matter of processing information in order to usher in arrivals and prepare passengers and planes for departure.

In his follow-up book to *Non-Places*, Augé clarifies a critical point in this regard: "What is a place for some may be a non-place for others, and vice versa. An airport, for example, does not have the same status in the eyes of the passenger who hastily crosses through it and an employee who works there everyday."[16] Indeed, as we noted in the *New Yorker* cover above, airport workers always exist in obverse relation to acts of airport reading.

And yet airport reading can also reflect quite explicitly on the non-place as a workspace. Perhaps the quintessential example of this dimension of airport reading arrives in the form of Arthur Hailey's 1968 novel *Airport*—which with its self-reflexive title also happens to perfectly fit the definition of airport reading as "light or undemanding entertainment."[17]

Like Adrian Tomine's *New Yorker* cover illustration, *Airport* is set amid a debilitating winter storm. Unlike Tomine's illustration, however, *Airport* is arranged primarily around the airport workers with all their various tasks, from plowing the runway, to air traffic control, to dealing with unruly passengers as flights are delayed. The main character and hero of the novel is Mel Bakersfeld, the manager of the fictitious Lincoln International Airport. Here is how *Airport* introduces its main character:

> Mel, airport general manager—lean, rangy, and a powerhouse of disciplined energy—was standing by the Snow Control Desk, high in the control tower. He peered out into the darkness. Normally, from this glass-walled room, the entire airport complex—runways, taxi strips, terminals, traffic on the ground and air—was visible like neatly aligned building blocks and models, even at night their shapes and movements well defined by lights.[18]

It is into this elaborate "darkness" of the airport that the novel tunnels, reflecting on the minutiae of air travel and the fickle and determined personalities who make it all happen. The novel itself reproduces the scopic economy of the control tower, seeing into the day-to-day operations of the "runways, taxi strips, terminals, traffic on the ground and air"—in short, all the "shapes and movements well defined by light."

One cannot help but recall here Michel Foucault's incisive formulation of the panoptic disciplinary structure, with its "concerted distribution of bodies, lights, gazes . . . in an arrangement whose internal mechanisms produce the relation in which individuals are caught up."[19] As Foucault famously describes it:

> The Panopticon is a privileged place for experiments on men, and for analyzing with complete certainty the transformations that may be obtained by them. The Panopticon may even provide an apparatus for supervising its own

mechanisms. In this central tower, the director may spy on all the employees that he has under his orders: nurses, doctors, foremen, teachers, warders; he will be able to judge them continuously, alter their behavior, impose upon them the methods he thinks best; and it will even be possible to observe the director himself. An inspector arriving unexpectedly at the centre of the Panopticon will be able to judge at a glance, without anything being concealed from him, how the entire establishment is functioning.[20]

Indeed, the entire plot of *Airport* revolves around Mel Bakersfeld in his "privileged place" of authority, as he watches over the airport, monitoring the various decisions made by other workers, and espousing his views on the contemporaneous conditions of civil aviation and "the methods he thinks best" for the future of flight.

Furthermore, the novel itself aptly extends the panoptic logic, functioning as that added potential for an "inspector" to be able to check in on how the entire system is working: the narrative relays specialized knowledge about the daily routines of air travel, thus placing the *reader* in the position of *inspector*, as it were. And as airport reading proper, the book supports the effective conditions of air travel, including the inevitable delays that will keep planes on the ground, and cause passengers to pull out their paperbacks and settle into the departure lounges, to read.

In other words, *Airport* interweaves multiple threads of textuality: as a suspenseful thriller it fits the definition of airport reading; as a story *about* airports it reflects on and produces knowledge concerning the culture of flight; by focusing on the character of the airport manager, it supervises "its own mechanisms"; finally, the novel reaches a high point of reflexivity by being able to indicate "how the entire establishment is functioning." If a departure lounge is full of passengers reading books like *Airport*, one can deduce that passengers are waiting, and thus that the airport must be *working*: working to keep passengers in anticipation of flight, and working to prepare aircraft for takeoff—against whatever environmental odds.

On top of the logistical drama of the snowstorm, *Airport* adds an unfolding bomb plot. Yet consistently and overwhelmingly throughout the novel, *Airport* is a story about work—about all the necessary labor functions required for airliners to take off and land. At the end of 533 pages and mere hours later—after snow delays, relationship blowouts, suicide attempts, aviation debates, and security threats—we find ourselves back in the panoptic gaze of the airport manager, and nearly everything is seen to be working again. Here are the closing paragraphs of the novel:

Now that the runway was open, he saw, other aircraft were beginning to use it, arriving in a steady stream despite the lateness. A Convair 880 of TWA swept by and landed. Behind it, half a mile out, were the landing lights of another flight approaching. Behind the second, a third was turning in.

> The fact that Mel could see the third set of lights made him aware that the
> cloud base had lifted. He noticed suddenly that the snowfall had stopped; in
> a few places to the south, patches of sky were clearing. With relief, he realized
> the storm was moving on.[21]

The relief with which *Airport* ends is oriented toward the work that air
travel requires. This scene conjures great physical space, with the expanse
of the runway glimpsed in a sort of panorama following a jetliner sweeping
by, and then out to a horizon twice projected, by "half a mile" and then to
a distance "behind" that. The final paragraph yokes Mel's expanded vision
and his awareness of the improving weather conditions, returning us once
again to a Foucauldian observation of the observer. Hailey's potboiler is fascinating in that it flips the perspective of airport reading, from the position
of the passenger to the position of the laborer, whose work has become a
spectacle for the passenger.

As if to literalize this theoretical quality of the novel, at one point Hailey
makes it plain:

> It was a pity, Mel Bakersfeld reflected, that runway snow teams were not more
> on public view. The sight was spectacular and stirring. Even now, in storm
> and darkness, approaching the massed equipment from the rear, the effect was
> impressive. Giant columns of snow cascaded to the right in arcs of a hundred
> and fifty feet. The arcs were framed in vehicle searchlights, and shimmered
> from the added color of some twenty revolving beacons—one on the roof of
> each vehicle in the group.[22]

Mel's suggestion that the work of airports is "spectacular and stirring" inter-
prets the airport as a textual surface, as a "sight" worth reading, a subject
that demands interpretation—but also is open to enjoyment. By rendering
aesthetic the work of runway plowing twice over—first speculatively in the
mind of Mel, then through narrative description—this passage is indicative
of the intimate connections between airport reading and airport labor.

This sentiment can also be witnessed in design plans for airport innova-
tions. For instance, in a "fly-through" video of the new Terminal B of the
Sacramento airport, the narrator explains that as automated people movers
whisk passengers from the terminal to the aircraft gates, the elevated shut-
tles provide "views of the airport activities below."[23] The idea that airport
work should function as entertainment for passengers is an issue that I take
up at length in Chapter 2.

Critical airport reading

I wish to end this chapter by discussing a strain of cultural reflection that
takes airports as a topic to be studied and scrutinized. We might call this

critical airport reading. Yet hardly a distinct mode of viewing airports, such critical readings are often entangled with or embedded in passing mentions and descriptive language. As we saw in Arthur Hailey's *Airport*, the lightest reading can hinge on the heaviest work—and such work has theoretical implications. We noted these implications by evoking Foucault's formulation of panopticism, in terms of how the novel reproduces disciplinary and observational systems in its form as well as in its content. This is not to say that airports are simply or exceptionally carceral sites, but rather that Hailey's novelistic treatment of the work of airports exposes—and opens up to interpretation—operations of power.

As the aviation scholar David Pascoe rightly suggests in his book *Airspaces*, "it is not simply through the basic physical manifestations of airspace that that we can discern the shapes of our modernities; we must also be aware of its *representations*."[24] Pascoe goes on to argue that while air travel is indisputably dependent on strong senses of "cultural identification" and "aesthetic properties," representations of flight are "almost unduly overlooked."[25] Pascoe's book attempts to attend to this critical oversight, and to read the spaces of air travel as they appear in cultural representations.

In this way, Pascoe's project follows up on Augé's observation that "the link between individuals and their surroundings in the space of a non-place is established through the mediation of words, or even texts."[26] Indeed, *Airspaces* reads texts as diverse as the July 2000 crash of the Air France Concorde at Charles de Gaulle airport in Paris; airport sketches and ruminations by the architect Le Corbusier; and the closing airport scene in the film *Casablanca*.[27] Here, then, we encounter another dimension of airport reading: a critical turn toward the subject of flight. This is reflected in Augé's speculative anthropology of supermodernity and in Pascoe's cultural study of airspaces.

Critical airport reading is also evident in popular journalism. For instance, the *New York Times* writer Joe Sharkey's travel column "On The Road" regularly deals with matters of flight, reflecting on the modern predicaments faced by airlines and passengers alike. In one article from 2006, after the liquid bomb scare, Sharkey compares airport security checkpoints to a "theater of the absurd," and mentions Samuel Beckett in jest.[28] Even while Sharkey's columns are more interested in the functional operations of air travel, his recourse to literary form is telling: Sharkey casts the airport as a textual space, a performative site that demands to be interpreted.

In another instance of this popular form of critical airport reading, the *New Yorker* critic Anthony Lane touches on airports in a 2006 article on low-fare European travel. At one point in the article he writes: "Airports are not pleasure palaces. They are strip-lit little dungeons, and, far from being encouraged to linger within them, we should whisk through them as speedily as possible."[29] Lane's loaded metaphor of the "dungeon" suggests a literary texture, a need to render airports figuratively even while describing their most obvious attributes or affects. These rhetorical insinuations imply a link worthy of analysis, even when—or especially when—the textual life of airports seems to appear in passing. This *passing* quality of airports in texts can tend to obfuscate theoretically nuanced ideas. For instance, as I go on to show, the association between airports and carceral structures is a complex matter, alluded to often in cultural representations, but also housing serious questions of just what sort of space airports are.

Indeed, such matters of interpretation are taken up in Brian Edwards's book on airport design, *The Modern Airport Terminal*. Edwards ends the introduction to this book by posing an unresolved (and perhaps irresolvable) issue: "New safety checks, instigated almost universally after 11th September 2001, mean that little passes through to the departure lounge without being subject to an X-ray scan. Speed and security are often in conflict, adding to frustration for passengers and airline staff alike."[30] Lane's adamant call above not to "linger" in airports, and instead move through them "as speedily as possible" is in direct tension with the containing figure of the dungeon. Likewise, Sharkey's comparison of the security checkpoint with a theater of the absurd suggests a certain holding, captivating power of the airport security spectacle: even as the space is devoted to speedy travel, it cannot help but captivate the captive passenger (who is also somewhat paradoxically "in transit"). The dialectic of speed and security is one of the many dramas in the textual life of airports, apparent across a range of representations and historical moments, playing out long before 9/11.

But the tension between speed and security around airports is not always about bomb threats and flying bodies. Often, this tension plays out on the ground in ways that complicate fixed notions of location and meaning, thus highlighting the work of interpretation. For instance, let us consider an eccentric airport appearance in an essay on James Joyce's *Ulysses* by the philosopher Jacques Derrida. I wish to cite the last three paragraphs of this essay in order to demonstrate how Derrida's airport performs a textual role:

> Only another event can sign, can countersign to bring it about that an event has already happened. This event, that we naively call the first event, can only affirm itself in the confirmation of the other: a completely other event.
>
> The other signs. And the *yes* keeps restarting itself, an infinite number of times, even more than, and quite differently from, Mrs. Breen's week of seven *yeses* when she hears Bloom recount to her the story of Marcus Tertius Moses and Dancer Moses (*U*, 437): "MRS. BREEN (*eagerly*) Yes, yes, yes, yes, yes, yes, yes."
>
> I decided to stop here because I almost had an accident just as I was jotting down this last sentence, when, on leaving the airport, I was driving home after the trip to Tokyo.[31]

On one view, we might simply conclude that this passage marks an informal, improvisational way to end a piece of writing: perhaps even more than texting and driving, essay writing and driving don't mix well. The speed required to depart the airport threatens the security of the essay, and vice versa.

But in classic Derridean fashion, this playful gesture is laced with textual nuance: strictly speaking, the "last sentence" cited in this the final paragraph is not the sentence at hand: it is the *prior* long sentence on *Ulysses* to which the last sentence refers. Likewise, the "here" in the final sentence is not *there*: it is above, in the penultimate paragraph. In other words, Derrida's airport sentence functions as a textual relay, redirecting the reader to reconsider the prior (last) sentence, to reinterpret the penultimate as the final paragraph. The closing sentence—Derrida's airport sentence—is a re-mark, a making-explicit of the (abrupt, arguably inconclusive) conclusion of this essay.

For my interests, I take this passage to be a critical (if indirect) airport reading: Derrida evokes the non-place aura of an airport to initiate interpretive work. At the very end of an essay, the almost non sequitur appearance of an airport poses a lingering question about where the work of reading ends. It does not end with the "last sentence"—the work of reading continues in to this final sentence about the airport. In effect, the final paragraph enacts Derrida's theory of the countersignature mentioned in the first paragraph cited above: the conclusion of the essay (the event) requires the countersignature of the near accident (the completely other event) on the way home from the airport.

To conclude his essay on "re-marking" and the untranslatable "yes" in Joyce, Derrida introduces one further aporia: the airport sentence interrupts the conclusion by way of adding an additional point of conclusion—a terminal, as it were, that is not the author's destination in any sense of the word. As Marc Augé's formulation of non-place has it: "Vocabulary has a central role here because it is what weaves the tissue of habits, educates the gaze, informs the landscape."[32] Indeed, Derrida's casual description of leaving the airport is anything but coincidental; rather, this as-if spontaneous narrative reinforces the interpretive issue at stake in Derrida's essay, as well as exposes the textual life of airports.

Deconstruction aside, critical airport reading often hinges on the work of interpretation. This occurs in the most innocent sounding narrative descriptions of airports, such as we see in Alastair Gordon's *Naked Airport: A Cultural History of the World's Most Revolutionary Structure* (2004). Here is Gordon's recollection of his first visit to Eero Saarinen's TWA terminal in New York:

The air was charged with anticipation. Pilots stepped through pools of milky light. Beautiful stewardesses trailed behind them wearing red outfits and perfectly straight stocking seams. The ambient lighting, the flirtatious smiles, the lipstick-red carpet and uniforms, the cushioned benches and steel railings curving around the mezzanine—all conspired on the senses. Even the clock that hung from the ceiling had a suggestive globular shape. We sat in an oversize

conversation pit, beneath a panoramic screen of glass, and watched the service
vehicles scoot between planes. "This is unbelievably cool," said my cousin in a
hushed, almost reverential tone.[33]

For Gordon, the airport appears as a site rife with affects, moods, and signs
to be interpreted. The space overwhelms the senses, and requires the utterance of *coolness*, as if to confirm legibility—or how the airport is to be *read*.
Curiously enough, in Gordon's description the work of interpretation turns
reflexively back to *work*. Gordon's lyrical language centers on the pilots,
the "beautiful stewardesses," and the "service vehicles." This attention to
labor returns us to the elaborate work environment that occupies Hailey's
Airport, and reminds us that far from being about simply books, airport
reading is a dense textual field where idealized spaces, times that require
distraction, and spectacular systems of work all tarry together. It is to this
latter point that I now turn.

CHAPTER 2

WORK IN THE CULTURE OF FLIGHT

Discourses of labor

Working at the airport was like entering a parallel universe. As an airline employee I used a code to access the locked stairwells that circumvented the security checkpoint. I learned to operate the complicated Apollo reservation system for creating flight itineraries. The tarmac was like a lunar landscape: clad in my utility pants that resembled Han Solo's in *Star Wars*, and wearing my airport identification badge, I was free to maneuver the diesel Tugs and baggage carts around the aircraft.

One thing I noticed was that the job involved relatively tacit initiations, whereby employees were gradually trained to use the equipment and issue a range of verbal commands for airport contexts. Thus, one of the earliest tasks I learned was to load luggage, first onto a baggage cart, and then onto the aircraft. This involved learning how to read baggage tags, and how to physically arrange luggage according to size and shape. In other words, the job of loading baggage required a certain quality of textual training.

Later tasks would include issuing calls for boarding, in appropriate (if at times grammatically awkward) airline verbiage. I remember this as an intense exercise in phonic discipline that would soon become routine: clicking the P.A. handset button and making the announcement for a boarding, a delay, or a cancellation. The first few times, my manager or supervisor monitored my announcements carefully—but after I proved myself able to deliver the appropriate information with the right inflections, then the job became utterly unremarkable, routine.

A scene in Chuck Palahniuk's cult novel *Fight Club* (1996) reminds me of this experience, at one point when the main character gets off a flight only to find out that his checked baggage did not arrive:

> There was the airline representative at the gate, and there was the security task force guy to say, ha, your electric razor kept your baggage at Dulles. The task force guy called the baggage handlers Throwers. Then he called them Rampers. To prove things could be worse, the guy told me at least it wasn't a dildo. Then, maybe to make me laugh, the guy said industry slang for flight attendant was Space Waitress. Or Air Mattress. It looked like the guy was wearing a pilot's uniform, white shirt with little epaulets and a blue tie. My luggage had been cleared, he said, and would arrive the next day.[1]

Of note in this passage is the knowledge barrier that the narrator encounters around discourses of labor: baggage handlers are first called one thing, then another—both terms alluding metonymically to the work of the airline workers, first through action (*throwing* bags), then through the surface they move across (the *ramp* refers to the tarmac around the aircraft). The conversation slips to glib sexual humor and further job-related vernacular, but the narrator is effectively blocked from the discursive field even as the "security task force guy" creates an opening through intimations and innuendoes: at the end of the passage, the narrator has no more ability to obtain his luggage, which will purportedly "arrive the next day."

As if to stress this threshold of mystification, the narrator notices that the worker's outfit resembles a pilot's uniform: "white shirt with little epaulets and a blue tie." The narrator can identify this type of garb—but here it is slightly out of context, and the official-looking agent is carrying on in a distinctly unprofessional manner. Nevertheless, the passage concludes by veering back to plain information about the narrator's luggage. Palahniuk represents a social space that involves its own jargon and semiotic codes, reflexively (re)producing the airport as a textual site. The "security task force guy" exists as if in another world, in a workspace whose operative texts and meanings remain coded, if also begging to be translated.[2]

In *Airspaces*, David Pascoe suggests that Arthur Hailey's novel *Airport* reads "more like a handbook of airport operations than popular fiction."[3] Palahniuk's *Fight Club* functions like the obverse of Hailey's *Airport* in this way: in *Airport* the manager oversees all the work and processes of flight, whereas the baggage scene in *Fight Club* offers a mere discursive glimpse of what it nevertheless exposed as an elaborate network of jobs, terminology, and procedures. The airport worker in this scene functions as a barrier and as a screen: an obstacle for the narrator of the story, and an improvised entertainment center indicative of the culture of flight. Strict security protocols and everyday work antics collude at this textual interface.

Anecdote of the airport in The Last Tycoon

In his introduction to *Politics at the Airport*, Mark Salter argues that "to present the airport as a controlled, centralized, panoptic, or orderly space is badly ideological."[4] I take Salter's point entirely, and agree that it is wrong to imagine airports as clearly regulated spaces or as neatly functioning systems. Yet it is worth recalling at this point how Foucault directs his analysis of the Panopticon outward to other working dimensions of society: "Is it surprising that prisons resemble factories, schools, barracks, hospitals, which all resemble prisons?"[5] To this list Foucault might have easily added airports. This is not to say that airports are in any simple way panoptic structures, but rather that they involve and borrow from the complex layering of power and visibility emblematized by the Panopticon.

This expanded view of carceral structures, in fact, is what the environmental psychologist Robert Sommer contributed in his own work on what he calls "hard architecture." In *Tight Spaces: Hard Architecture and How to Humanize It* (1974), Sommer writes: "There is a massive effort today to gain security through steel, concrete, and electronic equipment. The prison has become the model for housing developments, commercial buildings, and even airports."[6] Sommer's phrase "even airports" is suggestive for our project: it imagines that airports *should* exist somehow beyond the heavy pressures and dreary structures of modern society. It is as if airports are supposed to maintain and continue the aura of inspiration and uplift that the corollary airplanes seem to command. And yet, the day-to-day realities of airports are practical, function-oriented, and systematic—with minimal room for imaginative whims or flights of fancy. Certainly, airports rely on a baseline imagination in the form of innovative design and planning for new aircraft models; but the point is that airports allow for an extremely narrow margin of spontaneity or improvisation. (And here again we might recall the ironic escalator play of Sarah Brink in *A Gate at the Stairs*: even that was enough to disturb the terminal order of things.)

Indeed, the literature of flight reflects a constant and widespread realization of airports as depressing spaces, and this awareness is consistently generated in proximity to figures of labor. I am not arguing that the work of airports is in itself depressing, nor am I arguing that all who pass through fictional airports are rendered depressed. Rather, I mean to point out how scenes of airport labor tend to complicate any simple notions of flight. Where we encounter labor in the literature of flight, interpretive difficulties abound—and these difficulties reveal the textual life of airports at work.

To discuss airport labor in a literary context, I now turn to F. Scott Fitzgerald's unfinished novel, published posthumously as *The Last Tycoon*.[7] I demonstrate how Fitzgerald puzzles over the culture of flight and the work of interpretation demanded by airports. Against any easy reading of flight in this novel, I want to suggest that Fitzgerald presents the airport as difficult to read, on many accounts.

Shortly into the story, the narrator Cecelia is en route on a flight from the east coast to Hollywood, where her father is a business partner of the novel's film producer protagonist, Monroe Stahr (who is also on the plane, traveling under the guise of "Mr. Smith"). From within the DC-3 Cecelia exclaims, "The world from an airplane I knew."[8] Cecelia's odd syntax raises any number of questions: Is this a literary allusion to poetic transcendence, a Romantic residue having to do with the wish to wander cloud-like, in the traditions of Wordsworth and Shelley?[9] Does this statement indicate a Modernist convergence of airborne perception and a global epistemology?[10] Or does Cecelia's claim reflect little more than the ramping up of commercial air travel, that by the mid-1930s Americans are regularly traveling by air? Fitzgerald does not draw out this speculative link between domestic air travel and narrative point of view; just as the novel gets underway, Cecelia's flight makes an unscheduled landing due to stormy weather. The aircraft in flight is exchanged for the dreary setting of an airport, and the high-flying passengers are to be unexpectedly "grounded in Nashville."[11]

As the plane makes its descent, Cecelia reflects almost anthropologically on the existence of airports:

> I suppose there has been nothing like airports since the days of the stage-stops—nothing quite as lonely, as somber-silent. The old red-brick depots were built right into the towns they marked—people didn't get off at those isolated stations unless they lived there. But airports lead you way back into history like oases, like the stops on the great trade routes.[12]

It is perhaps surprising and counterintuitive that at this relatively early point in the history of air travel, airports are already depicted as retrograde, gloomy sites. By comparing airports with the older "stage-stops" Cecelia diminishes any sense of grandeur and instead foregrounds a "lonely" and "somber-silent" ambience. Furthermore, the comparison with "oases" is especially intriguing given the novel's primary subject of Hollywood: the airport is cast as a potentially spectral site, particularly if we take this word as an allusion to classic cinematic oases that turn out to be mirages.[13] What this passage conveys strongly is a sense that airports are caught up in history—and this goes somewhat against the future-oriented sensibility more commonly associated with air travel.

Curiously, Arthur Hailey's fictitious airport manager conveys a similar attitude in the late-1960s, even while Mel still believes in and supports idealistic possibilities of flight. Mel reflects: "Less than a lustrum ago, the airport was considered among the world's finest and most modern. [Now] Lincoln International, like a surprising number of other major airports, was close to becoming a whited sepulcher." Even as Mel sees his near-obsolescent airport become bogged down in all sorts of practical and political mires, he still touts "a new era of aviation" based on his theory of flight: "Aviation, Mel Bakersfeld had pointed out, was the only truly successful international undertaking. It transcended ideological boundaries as well as the merely geographic. Because it was a means of intermingling diverse populations at ever-diminishing cost, it offered the most practical means to world understanding yet devised by man."[14]

At once more realistic and less clearly politicized, Fitzgerald's airport has no truck with transcending "ideological boundaries." Rather, the Nashville airport stands as a complex cultural node where class differences are at once real and imagined, materially entrenched and yet possibly ephemeral. To flesh out these matters, I now turn to a particular citation of *The Last Tycoon*.

In *Naked Airport*, Alastair Gordon suggests that "Air travel was a fitting means of transportation for the ambitious characters Fitzgerald depicts in *The Last Tycoon*; it also served as a metaphor for the economic and social gulf that separated the haves and the have-nots."[15] Gordon goes on to offer textual evidence from *The Last Tycoon* for his metaphorical interpretation of class divides. He writes:

> With her plane grounded, Cecelia is struck by the contrast between her glamorous fellow passengers and the common folk milling about the airport grounds: "In the big transcontinental planes we were the coastal rich, who casually alighted from our clouds in mid-America . . . . The young people look at the planes, the older ones look at the passengers with a watchful incredulity . . . ."[16]

Gordon sees the "glamorous" air travelers and the "common folk" as neatly divided by who is worth being watched and who is watching. In Gordon's citation, however, Fitzgerald's sentences have in fact been flipped in order from how they appear in the novel. The entire passage from *The Last Tycoon* (which follows directly after the "great trade routes" sentence, cited above) actually reads this way:

> The sight of air travellers strolling in ones and twos into midnight airports will draw a small crowd any night up to two. The young people look at the planes, the older ones look at the passengers with a watchful incredulity. In the big transcontinental planes we were the coastal rich, who casually alighted from our clouds in mid-America. High adventure might be among us, disguised as a movie star. But mostly it wasn't. And I always wished fervently that we looked more interesting than we did—just as I often have at premieres, when the fans look at you with scornful reproach because you're not a star.[17]

Indeed, Fitzgerald does depict air travel as a "sight" that draws onlookers. Gordon's quotation of this passage, though, places the airplane and airport in a more logical sequence from the standpoint of Cecelia's perspective: the airplane taxis toward the airport, where onlookers gradually become visible. Thus Gordon's central ellipsis serves to reorder the spatio-temporal schema presented in the novel, so that the scene makes more visual sense. But Fitzgerald's evacuation of causality and reversal of logic make for a more complex airport reading: the planes, the passengers, and the crowds are all bound together in a dynamic montage, challenging any as-if static relationships between spectacle/spectator and the "haves"/"have-nots." Furthermore, from whose perspective are the air travelers seen as "the coastal rich, who casually alighted from our clouds in mid-America"? We should recall that this is an unplanned stop, due to a weather delay; the passengers are uncomfortable and annoyed—and at least one of the passengers is suicidal, as we learn a few pages later. It is entirely likely that Cecelia's claim here is sarcastic, an *imaginary* view of air travelers.[18]

Gordon's ellipses also achieve a compelling omission: the last two sentences of the paragraph (omitted by Gordon) utterly complicate the picture:

"High adventure might be among us, disguised as a movie star. *But mostly it wasn't.* And I always wished fervently that we looked more interesting than we did—just as I often have at premieres, when the fans look at you with scornful reproach because you're not a star" (my emphasis). The airport onlookers don't just want to see rich people: they are hoping to see Hollywood stars. This is not just about seeing people who have more money, then, but about being *entertained*. The end of Cecelia's reflection in fact deemphasizes the "social gulf" as easily as it seems to have emphasized it sentences earlier. In fact, the spectacle of the air travelers is exposed as an illusion: these passengers are *not* stars, and they don't even *look* that interesting. Cecelia compares this to Hollywood premieres where celebrity status trumps mere capital value: people don't care as much about seeing the filmmakers or producers—it's the actors that count. This key passage reverses the standard practice of airport reading as an activity for travelers: here, it is the onlookers who seek the light entertainment.

We must also note that the potential "high adventure" imagined here is decidedly *not* the modern phenomenon of air travel—rather, the "high adventure" is a fictitious extension of the celebrities who might be onboard the aircraft. In other words, for Fitzgerald the real drama of the airport is in its capacity for *entertainment*. The airport raises expectations for entertaining fiction, which in this case Cecelia ironically claims to be absent: there are no celebrities on board Cecelia's plane, and yet we are well in the midst of airport fiction. Fitzgerald's airport is set in relation to the simulacral realm of Hollywood, thereby making flight more than just a metaphor for class difference: it is also charged with demands for entertainment.[19]

The bulk of the novel focuses on the tireless labors of the eponymous film tycoon Monroe Stahr, and thus it is precisely the work of entertainment that is the subject of *The Last Tycoon*. Yet this attention to *work* is initiated at the airport. For Fitzgerald the airport represents more than just an occasional non-place: it is also a spectacular workspace. By this I mean that Fitzgerald uses the labor of air travel to introduce and stand as an analog to the intricacies of Hollywood. Here is the scene that evinces this theory:

> The storm had wandered away into Eastern Tennessee and broken against the mountains, and we were taking off in less than an hour. Sleepy-eyed travellers appeared from the hotel, and I dozed for a few minutes on one of those iron maidens they use for couches. Slowly the idea of a perilous journey was recreated out of the debris of our failure: a new stewardess, tall, handsome, flashing dark, exactly like the other except she wore seer-sucker instead of Frenchy red-and-blue, went briskly past us with a suitcase.[20]

This scene begins with a wide view of weather patterns and geography, and quickly zooms in to a narrower time frame and the ambient minutiae of the airport. As Cecelia dozes on the characteristically un-ergonomic seating, she entertains a gradual notion: Cecelia "slowly" becomes aware of the idea that she has been on "a perilous journey."[21]

And yet, the earlier turbulence in the text did not cause significant concern; in fact, Cecelia's earlier record of the plane's descent through the storm comes through an understated observation that verges on kitsch: "The green sign 'Fasten your belts—No smoking' had been on since we first rode into the storm."[22] These ideas of the "perilous journey" and the "debris" of the flight's "failure" are a flagrant attempt to repackage the novel's contents—indeed, they are "recreated" for dramatic, narrative effect. It is as if Fitzgerald is self-referentially highlighting the novel's own artifice. After all, this is not the scene of a plane crash or even an emergency landing: this is a group of groggy, upper-class Hollywood passengers who were stuck for a night in an airport in Tennessee. We might think of this scene as an eccentric Modernist allusion: an ironic anecdote of the airport that, once established, takes "dominion everywhere."[23]

What actually conjures the "idea" of the perilous journey is none other than the spectacular entrance of the labor force: a flashy stewardess. The presentation here is cinematic: the sequence does not follow analytic rationale, but comes together through a phantasm of associations and flitting observations. For what does a flight attendant—coifed, bustling toward the plane, ready for departure—have to do with *peril*? The stewardess on the grounded flight of the night before was barely alarmed by the turbulence; the most extreme measure taken was to offer Cecelia various sedatives: "'—and, dear, do you want some aspirin?' She perched on the side of the seat and rocked precariously to and fro with the June hurricane, '—or a Nembutal?' . . . 'Do you want some gum?'"[24] In fact, the syntax of Cecelia's description of the "new stewardess" mimics her previous description of the first stewardess: "The stewardess—she was tall, handsome, and flashing dark, a type that they seem to run to—."[25] Air travel is presented as a production site of simulation and simulacra. In the airport, the hyperbolic "June hurricane" from the night before that fazed nobody is recast as a "perilous journey," and the laborers are presented as *types*: they are somewhat indistinguishable from one another, copies of copies, with no original reference point or end in sight. Cecelia has already been identified in relation to a world of artifice (i.e., cinema), and the airport expands the context of entertainment via the working trope of stewardesses.[26]

My point here is to show how the appearance of the "new stewardess" prompts narrative entertainment: a melodramatic retelling of the previous night's "perilous journey" is coincident with the "flashing dark" apparition of the stewardess. In *The Last Tycoon*, airport reading as close observation of the details of travel—including the couture of the workforce—is intermingled with exaggerated storytelling about flight. Like Cecelia's sense of airport onlookers who wish to see stars disembarking from planes, the narrative itself embellishes the stormy flight in retrospect. It would seem that working and entertainment are curiously conjoined in this airport reading.

I would thus argue that air travel in *The Last Tycoon* does not serve as a simple metaphor for a clear "social gulf." In fact, what we see around Fitzgerald's airport is a host of identity confusions and uncertain classifications: some of the passengers are flying under assumed names; celebrities may be on the aircraft (or not); the airline employees intermingle with the travelers and command their attention; and the flight, when recollected in tranquility, takes on an ominous mood—it becomes an object of entertainment. Fitzgerald's air travel scenes in *The Last Tycoon* hinge not so much on clear class differences, but rather they muddy the interpretive water around how airports *read*, to different audiences at different times, blurring lines between leisure and labor, utility and entertainment. This generative profusion of meanings evinces how the airport is a site of interpretation.

Hyperreal connections

I have demonstrated that airport reading is partly about entertainment, and often indirectly about the work going on all around flight—whether to pay attention to it, or not. I now look at a contemporary text that further illustrates the airport workspace as overdetermined entertainment zone.

Don DeLillo's 1999 play *Valparaiso* takes as its dramatic subject the routines of air travel and the rhetoric of airlines that, when contextualized as literature, tip over into the absurd. Much of the play centers on the ill-fated trip of Michael Majeski, routine business traveler. Through interviews and monologues, we learn that Majeski departed for Chicago on what he thought was a regional trip to Valparaiso, Indiana, only to be rerouted to the Miami airport, where it seemed that he was in fact headed for Valparaiso, Florida—at last to end up on a wide-body plane en route to Santiago, bound for a final destination of Valparaiso, Chile. As Majeski tells his story, and relates geographic confusion concerning his final destination, his very sense of selfhood and origin become increasingly uncertain, as well.

Here is a condensed sequence of scenes that follow Majeski through his airport of origin, on a mad dash from one flight to another, and finally in the aircraft as it takes off:

> I was standing at the podium in the boarding area preparatory to boarding my flight to Chicago. Passenger X, please present yourself at the podium. . . .
>
> But the ticket woman at the podium happens to glance at my itinerary. The ticket is fine. The flight to Chicago is entered correctly. . . .
>
> She says, "Why are you going to Chicago if your itinerary says Miami?" And she rustles the sheet of paper my company's travel agent attached to the ticket. . . .
>
> I'm standing there shocked. I'd never done this trip before. . . .
>
> I'm shocked senseless and breathless. Is the ticket wrong or is the itinerary wrong? I have no time to find out. She tries to be helpful. There's a Miami flight she can hold if I start running for the gate in about half a second. Or I can board right here for Chicago in a relaxed and civilized manner. . . .
>
> She looks at her screen. She sees Miami. She sees an empty seat. But I am leaning toward Chicago. . . .

I start to run. Then what. I run. I make up my mind and run. She holds Miami
for me and I look at her and run. I run for the gate at the far end of the terminal. I run senselessly and breathlessly. I run past people with carry-on and
people with baggage carts and I run past shuttle buggies filled with people and
carry-on and bulging baggage and interracial babies. . . .

Anonymous people hurrying toward their lives. I'm watching the takeoff on
live video. I'm on the plane, I'm in my seat. There's a monitor on the bulkhead.
I look at the monitor and the plane is taking off. I look out the window and
the plane is taking off. Then what. The plane is taking off outside the cabin
and the plane is taking off inside the cabin. I look at the monitor, I look at the
earth.[27]

Over the course of these airport scenes, Majeski exposes strong links between
the commonplace interpellation of the air traveler ("Passenger X, please
present yourself at the podium.") and the imperative to entertainment, as
evinced by the "live video" of the plane's takeoff. On the one hand, the
scenes reflect ordinary language and the contingencies of everyday travel:
the sudden change of departure gates is commonplace, and the interactions
between passenger and airline employee are rendered in realistic form: "She
tries to be helpful. There's a Miami flight she can hold if I start running for
the gate in about half a second."

And yet, by reproducing the realism of commercial flight, the oddity of
self-referential perception on the in-flight entertainment system becomes
indicative of a conceptual crisis explored in this play. Majeski sees the takeoff represented as a form of entertainment, and then looks out to see "the
earth"—and thus the grounded airport itself becomes an object of entertainment, a potential theater of the absurd. Indeed, as Majeski exclaims in
a later scene:

I felt submissive. I had to submit to the systems. They were all powerful and
all-knowing. If I was sitting in this assigned seat. Think about it. If the computers and metal detectors and uniformed personnel and bomb-sniffing dogs had
allowed me to reach this assigned seat and given me this airline blanket that
I could not rip out of its plastic shroud, then I must belong here. That's how I
was thinking at the time.[28]

DeLillo's Majeski comes to represent a paradoxical, distinctly postmodern
zero level of subjectivity: he is at once the free flying liberal subject and the
determined body whose life is subject to an elaborate orchestration involving
"computers and metal detectors and uniformed personnel and bomb-sniffing
dogs." I use the term *postmodern* here to indicate how DeLillo's airport carries on and extrapolates the *modern* antics of flight as seen in Fitzgerald's
The Last Tycoon—from the privileged passengers "grounded in Nashville"
to the stylized flight attendants. As Jean-François Lyotard puts it, "postmodernism is not modernism at its end, but in a nascent state, and this state is
recurrent." By rehearsing the "rules and categories" of postmodern flight,

DeLillo philosophically investigates the emergent presence and burgeoning presentations of modern air travel.[29]

Indeed, DeLillo puts the language and routines of flight attendants and airport workers explicitly on display, recasting corporate rhetoric to serve as a jumbled and ironical chorus throughout the play. These characters are defined as conveying *hyperreal* messages, another identifier of the postmodern topos of the play. As the stage directions explain it:

> *The Chorus consists of three people in stylish civilian versions of flight-crew uniforms. These outfits are severe, faintly intimidating, mostly black and not necessarily matching. Members wear harsh dark makeup.*
>
> *The Chorus exists in a space separate from the stage proceedings, in a another dimension—an eerie fluorescence that suggests the hyperreality of a filmed TV commercial potentially viewable in a thousand cities, at twenty-second intervals, day and night, for an indefinite period of time.*
>
> *The Chorus recites the longer passages in unison. The middle member alone recites the brief italicized segments while the other two members gesture in the manner of flight attendants miming safety instructions before takeoff.*[30]

We might be reminded somewhat of Fitzgerald's simulacral "flashing dark" stewardesses, here. The flight attendants in *Valparaiso* are neither simply real nor purely unreal: rather, they are *hyperreal*. As Jean Baudrillard describes hyperreality, its features exist in "a universe of simulation"—this is the realm of air travel, a hyperreal workspace.[31] DeLillo's chorus members are caricatures of a type, and their lines are at turns realistic, unnecessarily repetitive, incorrectly juxtaposed, or just ridiculously off topic:

CHORUS
In preparation for departure
Pull the mask toward you
For domestic reservations, press or say *two*
Then place the mask Then place the mask
Has anyone had access
Has anyone ever said to you that shadows
Tend to gather in the dying light of day
If the air system in the cabin suddenly

MEMBER
A video screen attached to your seat
Another pacifying baby treat
That's platinum class on Air Reliance

CHORUS
In the event of a water landing
Has anyone had access to your baggage

Has anyone touched you in a tender place
To inflate the vest
Schwimm westen / Gilets de sauvetage / Chalecos salvavidas
Please make your selection from the following menu
In the event of a vertical descent
Press or say Press or say [32]

Valparaiso exploits the full range of the airport workspace as a miasma of entertainment demands and extreme situations. The chorus is a mash-up of (multilingual) standard safety briefing language ("In preparation for departure"), absurd worst-case scenarios ("vertical descent"), and automated voice commands ("For domestic reservations, press or say *two*")—all these combine to present the airline industry as an elaborate entertainment system, a place rife with hyperreal connections. And yet far from being purely comical, Majeski's disorienting journey ends with a covertly videotaped suicide attempt conflated with a live television murder: the media forms and corporate rhetoric of air travel are shown to be in sinister concert with a broader network of staged entertainment and real violence. *Valparaiso* is a critical pastiche that dramatizes the textual life of airports, where acts of work are seen to be both absurdly entertaining and deeply unsettling.

Reading men at work

We have seen how reflections of airport labor are also reflections *on* this work, in all its functional aspects and entertaining potentialities. Far from relying on any simple opposition between passengers and workers, the textual life of airports involves complex relationships between working, traveling—and reading. I wish to end this chapter by touching briefly on a contemporary poem that considers the airport as a social text awkwardly situated in a matrix of entertainment and work.

Julie Bruck's 2010 poem "Men at Work" literalizes the link between entertainment and airport labor. While waiting for a flight, the speaker of the poem notices the 1980s Australian pop band Men at Work in the departure lounge, and the group "holds everyone's attention." The speaker describes "four brittle pop stars sprawled across / the rigid fibreglass chairs at the airport gate."[33] The band is identified by the material culture of concert tours, including "the stacked electric-guitar cases / draped with black leather jackets"—and this distinctive couture is then asymmetrically mirrored by the sight of "Doug, the portly / Air Canada gate manager in his personalized jacket."[34]

The poem juxtaposes two forms of work: managing the Air Canada gate, and the labor of live pop music (in other words, traveling from town to town). The speaker suggests that the airline employee Doug identifies with the "lassitude" of the "resurrected" rock band; in this way, the work of

airports is seen as weary and repetitive, much like an 80s band called on
to rehearse tired songs, "whose lyrics never did make sense but / which are
laced to a beat that won't let go . . ."[35] These lines recall the role of airline
discourse in DeLillo's *Valparaiso*, where the familiar 'lyrics' of air travel take
on a hyperreal feel.

As the band waits for its flight, a social dynamic unfolds, at once reproducing the pop culture spectacle and diminishing its draw. The speaker's
gaze wavers between the sight of the band and the actual center stage of the
airport work, only to settle on an oddly figured traveling collective. In the
closing lines of the poem, the passengers are propelled "down the carpeted
ramps / of late-night flights on feeder airlines, hips / back in charge of our
strange young bodies / now shaking down runways in rows."[36] The bustle
of the airport is condensed in this moment of boarding and takeoff, the
individual lives of passengers rendered generic in terms of travel routines
and popular knowledge. Whole systems of cultural production and social
classification are consolidated in the departure gate, and *men at work* are
exposed to be all around. As the speaker suggests, even "we clutchers of
boarding passes" become strange laborers, ready to have "abandoned our
carry-ons for tickets / to a midsized arena"—in other words, mass entertainment is registered as an obligation as heavy as personal baggage: thus
"carry-ons for tickets."[37]

For Bruck, then, the postmodern airport operates similarly to how Henri
Lefebvre describes the modern street. This is how the street reads, according
to Lefebvre:

> A site of coming and going, of intrusion, circulation and communication, in
> an astonishing reversal it turns into the mirror image of the things it con-
> nects, more alive than those things. It becomes a microcosm of modern life.
> It plucks from obscurity all that is hidden. It makes life public. It takes away
> its private character and drags it across the stage of an informal theatre,
> where the actors are putting on a play that is also without form. The street
> publishes what happens elsewhere, in secret. It distorts it, but introduces it
> into the social text.[38]

Bruck's airport likewise acts as a "social text," in this case exposing similari-
ties between quite different labor practices: publishing a secret about the
ties between work and entertainment, as it were. Through a spatial arrangement, the airport publishes certain affective symmetries, wherein the "black
leather jackets" appear as distorted versions of the Air Canada jacket, and
the departure lounge becomes the "informal theatre" where men at work
are in full performance mode.

The departure gate indeed becomes a stage—yet somewhat different
from Lefebvre's modern street, Bruck's airport scene seems to accentuate the
form of the play at hand: the roles of pop entertainer and airline employee
alike become formally exaggerated, and seen totally in terms of bodies at

work. Yet if the departure gate has become a "microcosm" of (post)modern life, the poem also complicates this by redoubling the textual play of the airport—suggesting that the social text is legible not by itself, but by (a) literary work.

In this chapter I have attempted to outline links and overlaps between airline labor and airports as stages for (or subjects of) entertainment. This is a matter of how airport work is perceived and performed, and how these perceptions and performances reflect (or reflect on) the habits and routines of the culture of flight. For Julie Bruck, poetic reflection in the airport deduces a certain *something* about work and entertainment in postmodern life. If the connections between airport work and entertainment seem slightly hazy (if also overdetermined), I want to suggest that this mysterious quality is a productive one for the textual life of airports. Chapter 3 takes up this matter by considering a selection of adolescent airport mysteries.

CHAPTER 3

DETECTING THE UNCERTAIN SUBJECT OF AIRPORT MYSTERIES

Armed federal agents and the mystery of flight

When I worked at the airport there was a specific procedure for checking-in passengers who were federal agents and who wanted to fly with their handguns. As I recall, there was a pink form to be filled out by the federal agent, countersigned by the airline worker, and then this form was delivered to the pilot, who could authorize the request. In my experience, these requests were never denied.

Let me clarify, here: this was a privilege not exclusive to Federal Air Marshals. As I was taught, *any* federal agent could request to travel with a concealed weapon. With the airport that I worked at being in Montana, we were much more likely to get Federal Game Wardens flying our routes. Nevertheless, I recall several occasions when such agents would request the pink form and fill out the appropriate information. And so at the departure gate as we prepared to board, there would be one passenger with a conspicuous bulge on the hip or under a jacket flap, a semiautomatic pistol.

I am less concerned here with the efficacy or wisdom of guns on planes, though I did always wonder whether, ethically speaking, if it wasn't wrong to be hiding the fact of a gun on the plane from the other civilian passengers. What is of interest to me about armed federal agents is the presumed mystery of flight that comes along with this accepted practice. For an agent to choose to carry a gun onto a routine commercial flight from Bozeman to Denver, there must be some sneaking suspicion of *at least the possibility* of a mystery or some deception that *might* be taking place on the plane. And this inkling of latent deception then reflexively triggers a need for *detection*, and the potential for *action*—embodied in the armed federal agent.

Of course, such an analysis might strike the reader as naïve in a post-9/11 context, but I am merely pointing out another storyline that permeates the culture of flight: a constant presence of mystery that runs in two ways, both toward the subject with malicious intent, and toward the secret agent who is prepared for such a contingency. (And as the case of United 93 highlighted, given the right circumstances *any* passenger can serve as such an agent.) In their book *Aviopolis*, Gillian Fuller and Ross Harley describe this paradoxical arrangement as such: "The airport is in a constant state of emergency—its structures prepare constantly for disaster."[1] By boarding a flight carrying a concealed weapon, federal agents *produce* the state of emergency that they claim to be protecting the flight *from*.

The uncertain subject of the Hardy Boys airport mysteries

Since their inception, airports have occupied a contested yet tentative spot in the national imagination: these icons of technological progress must be deemed to be secure *and* to be outmoding themselves at every instant. This paradox of progress plays out in cultural representations of airports, such as in Steven Spielberg's 2004 film *The Terminal*, in which the JFK International Terminal stands as a revolving set, at turns utopian and dystopian, open and closed, democratic and fascistic.

This revolving action of airports hinges on what I call the *uncertain subject*. I define this term through an analysis of three Hardy Boys detective stories that are staged in and around airports.

I mean the phrase *uncertain subject* to register in a double sense, referring to the spatiality of the site itself (the airport as a subject), as well as to the concept of the individual for whom this site exists: the mobile, liberal "self" who travels through, works in, and is sometimes delayed by airports. In short, airports function in these mysteries as ambiguous spaces that produce questionable subjects. As the Hardy Boys try to solve mysteries around airports, the stories unfurl into tangential conspiracies and local travesties, and the sites of transit become increasingly immaterial. I demonstrate how the uncertain subject of the Hardy Boys airport mysteries activates and sustains an aura of mystery; by zooming out, we come to view a broader literary critical context in which this boy detective fiction can be understood as participating in and contributing to the textual life of airports.

At the outset, we might note that this is a series with its own uncertain author-subject: the pseudonym "Franklin W. Dixon" standing in for numerous named and unnamed scribes who have written the Hardy Boys since 1927. Frank and Joe Hardy frequently find themselves at airports on their way to solve mysteries, and three books are staged specifically in and around these sites: *The Great Airport Mystery* from 1930, *Hostages of Hate* from 1987, and *Tagged for Terror* from 1993. In these airport adventures, when one looks for the airport, what one usually finds is empty or generic space; when one looks at the subject within or around the airport, one discovers flexible, indeterminate personae who can hold many subject positions in the action of the stories being unfolded. This is the uncertain subject of airports.

The terminal is immaterial in Tagged for Terror

In the 1993 "Casefiles" mystery *Tagged for Terror*, Frank and Joe are dispatched to Atlanta, Georgia, to attend to a rampant baggage theft problem that is plaguing the airline "Eddings Air." En route to Atlanta, in the private jet of the eponymous airline owner Michael Eddings, the Hardy Boys are informed of the situation: "The thefts started large-scale about six months ago. . . . The stolen luggage usually contains valuables like jewelry or cameras. Why we've been hit harder that other airlines, we don't know. Nobody in the industry has reported losses like ours."[2]

The arbitrary targeting of Eddings Air remains a mystery through the end of the story; indeed, *Tagged for Terror* is something of a mystery about a mystery, where the thievery of personal property transforms, without reason, into an abstract terrorist plot that seems to rely on—yet have no direct connection with—accomplices who are low-wage baggage handlers. To solve this meta-mystery, the Hardy Boys go undercover as baggage handlers for Eddings Air. When Joe meets one of his fellow laborers for the first time, wages are among the first thing Joe learns about: "Welcome aboard. The hours are bad, the pay is low, the work is tedious. Other than that, it's a great place to work."[3]

From this sarcastic introduction to the material reality of airport work, the narrative unravels into a terror plot of undisclosed scope—as if to suggest that there are inherent (if hidden) links between low-wage laborers and evil terrorists. This linkage of terrorists and airport wageworkers is mindful of the speculative ties made between food service caterers and the hijackers shortly after 9/11/2001, which conjectured that airport ramp workers who had apparently no relation to al Qaeda had helped to plant weapons on the planes.[4] Furthermore, the lead-in for the sequel of *Tagged for Terror* tells us that this is the first of a series of three mysteries entitled "Ring of Evil," involving a longer storyline in which the terror group "the Assassins are preparing to square off against the ultra secret government agency, the Network."[5] It would seem as if the mundane workspace of the airport serves as a concourse for unrelated—yet structurally associated—plots for political power.

On the other hand, the airport in *Tagged for Terror* is hardly even a distinct site. At one point, Frank ". . . glanced around at the fast-food restaurants, magazine stands, and souvenir shops that turned almost every large airport into a shopping mall."[6] Atlanta's Hartsfield Airport is depicted as an utterly generic location in a consumer culture, merely another place for one-stop-shopping. Even when Frank and Joe are involved in a near-death crash landing, Joe's reaction is to compare the airport emergency protocols with processed food:

A paramedic herded them away from the crippled jet as fire fighters doused the plane with fire-retardant foam that reminded Joe of whipped cream being shot from a spray can. The crash had almost ripped off the right wing. A trail of motor oil and metal fragments led back down the runway to the jet engine, which had been torn from the underside of the wing.[7]

Amid this scene of a serious, airport-specific accident, consumer culture is conjured as a seemingly natural referent. Thus, while the airport is staged as a high-stakes venue for all sorts of intrigue, it also barely stands out against the broad metonymic landscape of which it is merely one part. The airport is essential material for the mystery plot, and yet the airport is generic and misrecognized as *anyplace*: terminal immaterial.

Tagged for Terror hinges on the Hardy Boys' immersion into airport culture. It is accepted as a definite possibility that certain airport laborers are involved with the luggage thefts:

> "Security is pretty tight," Frank pointed out. "Slipping luggage out shouldn't be that easy."
>
> "It might not be that hard for someone who's worked here long enough to be trusted," Joe replied. "Maybe as long as you're wearing an Eddings uniform, you can blend in so nobody'd notice you."[8]

The trusted working base of the airport is always-already suspect. This paranoia threatens to undermine the very logic of the liberal subject, who would seem to hold an inherent trust value when it comes to *work*. In other words, the travelers and workers who comprise the flows of deregulated airports rely on a fundamental logic of trust that glues the personal work ethic to the idea of private property in transit. Yet the Hardy Boys, in their immediate skepticism of this baseline trust (those wearing the right uniforms can therefore be *mis*trusted), unravel the very fabric with which free travel is wrapped. Private property leads to theft, and uniforms are ironically deceptive: the worker might be a terrorist *or* an undercover operative (like the Hardy Boys). Indeed, in the final chase of the story, Joe mistakes two men wearing "nylon jackets" for common travelers—but *they* end up being gun-packing government operatives.[9] By the end of *Tagged for Terror*, identities have been flipped and misperceived to the point that the airport is a darkly comic stage where everybody has something to hide and nobody has a clear destination. The problem of missing luggage fades into the background, and ambient fears of terrorism and misleading identities permeate the inconclusive ending. As Frank says about this airport mystery, ". . . it's over—but not for us."[10]

The (literary) plot thickens: Hostages of Hate

In certain ways, the drama of *Tagged for Terror* is both anticipated and undermined by the earlier *Hostages of Hate*, another paperback "Casefile" published in 1987. This story again forecasts the rhetoric of 9/11 when, at the beginning of the story, what is supposed to be the staged hijacking of a commercial airliner suddenly turns into a real hijacking:

> Frank and Joe stared as if they were watching a movie. The law enforcement officers ran back and forth. Some rushed forward, as if to charge the plane. The Uzi snarled again, stitching a line of broken runway just in front of the police. They stumbled to a stop, falling over themselves in Keystone Kops style.[11]

Recall one of the eerily common responses concerning the World Trade Center strikes of September 11: *It was like watching a movie*. In this passage, the story takes a tonally awkward detour into comic pop culture. The real police officers running from real machine gun fire manage to eclipse the idea of simulation and wind-up as anachronisms on the dark side of a comic moon: an actual, clamorous terrorist strike is equated with a silly, silent show. At the outset of *Hostages of Hate*, the airport tarmac is used to simulate a terrorist attack; the novel revolves around a national seminar on counterterrorism. However, the tarmac converts into the site of a *real* hijacking—and this conversion turns full circle throughout the story, where in the penultimate scenes the Hardy Boys go undercover as terrorists in order to board the hijacked plane and confront the "real" terrorists.

As if to emphasize this indeterminacy of genres and allegiances, the shady terrorist contact that the Hardy Boys first meet up with identifies himself as an ex-U.S. Marine:

> "I can still use my old Marine contacts to get guns for the cause," Lonnie said, settling his bulk behind a desk. "Still got some buddies. Even down in the barracks by the Navy Yard. And, of course, there are my detonation skills. I built the bomb that's in the airplane."[12]

In this bold schema, the U.S. soldier easily becomes a terrorist operative, and the exchange of armaments between national and terrorist "causes" is fluid. Then, so as to lubricate this already slippery slope, as the Hardy Boys carry out their mission and infiltrate the terrorist cell, they undergo increasingly violent confrontations with the law. At one point during an altercation, Frank brutally knocks out a lead government agent, handcuffs him, and leaves him in the backseat of a police cruiser as Frank and Joe escape with a terrorist who (they hope) will lead them to the ringleader. After this encounter, the narrative ruminates on the predicament: "If Frank couldn't free the hostages after all this, he'd probably be better off with the hijackers."[13] The threshold of heroism is success; otherwise, a hero is just a terrorist by another name.

At one point, as Frank and Joe are fleeing the law, the usual monotonous prose of the Hardy Boys series heads down a curiously literary path. Frank and Joe are being chased by federal agents, and they are nearly about to be caught; Frank is trying to figure out a plan of escape, when suddenly:

> Just ahead of him, Joe turned and waved his arm. "This way!" He plunged through an entrance and down an escalator. Frank followed his brother in a broken-field run down the moving steps. Then he knew where they were heading—*into a station for the Metro*, Washington's subway system.[14]

Embedded in this passage are the makings of the classic Modernist poem, Ezra Pound's archetypal experiment in vorticism: "In a Station of the Metro."

It is as if the Hardy Boys story offers a subtle gesture to a quite discordant aesthetic: in the midst of an incredibly suspenseful (if utterly trite) chase scene, the narrative diverges (appropriately enough) into a poetic medita- tion on public transportation. While the Hardy Boys do not linger in this space for long, this passage is nonetheless obliquely intertextual in its word- ing, as though to underscore the *narrative* material at hand: this is a pursuit made of *words*, and the airport continues to exist on the horizon of a *textual* landscape. If *Hostages of Hate* were to be read as a bizarrely protracted experiment in vorticist expression (imagine a witty English major relegated to writing Hardy Boys mysteries), the airport becomes a vaporous funnel through which many unrelated things come rushing.

By the time the Hardy Boys make it back to the airport and sneak their way onto the hijacked plane pretending to be fellow terrorist reinforcements, the story begins to come undone. Not only do the terrorists swerve from being coolly strategic to firing their machine guns recklessly and at random, but the hostages, too, come very close to revolting *against* Frank and Joe as it seems less and less likely that the Hardy Boys will actually be able to over- come the hijackers. After a shootout in the main cabin, the hijackers flee to the first-class cabin and eventually into the cockpit, where it turns out that one of the henchmen can fly a plane. As the jet engines roar to life and the airliner begins to taxi toward the runway, the hostages panic and want to jump from the plane; the Hardy Boys warn against this, noting that they will likely hurt or kill themselves: "'You can't jump from a moving plane,' Frank told [them]. 'It's like jumping from a second-story window.'"[15] At this point, the hostages start to chant: "Throw them off! Throw them out!"—the cap- tives having turned against their liberators.[16] Over the course of a hundred and thirty-five pages, Frank and Joe have transformed from high school boys into savvy detectives, then into simulacral terrorists, then into heroic rescu- ers, and finally into victims of a hostile citizen mob. To silence the shouting crowd, Frank resorts to firing "a quick burst" from his machine gun into the ceiling of the plane—back to terrorist tactics, indeed. This scene shows yet again how the airport functions as an incredibly ambiguous space in which subject positions can transmogrify dynamically to the point of absurdity.

After much protest, the Hardy Boys prevail upon the hostages to throw their personal belongings, along with every detachable object in the cabin of the plane, into the air intakes of the jet engines. The engines burnout, and "[t]he airliner coasted along until it came to a stop, about two-thirds of the way down the runway"—a hostage then looks out a smashed window of the plane and observes, ". . . the most unbelievable trail of garbage you ever saw, stretched out behind us."[17] One could almost consider this a 1980s remix of the closing lines of Shelley's "Ozymandias," in which the speaker declares "round the decay / Of that colossal wreck, boundless and bare, / The lone and level sands stretch far away."[18]

In his essay "The Question Concerning Technology," Martin Heidegger describes "an airliner that stands on the runway" as "such an object . . . [of] standing-reserve, inasmuch as it is ordered to insure the possibility of transportation."[19] At stake for Heidegger in this essay, finally, is the relation between technology and the revelation of truth. Yet the essence of technology, for Heidegger, remains "in a lofty sense ambiguous."[20] In the Hardy Boys airport mysteries, it would appear that an airliner on the runway ensures nothing more and nothing less than the uncertainty of the self, wherein frameworks of identity lose coherence and become utterly "nonautonomous," to use Heidegger's word. These airport-revealed selves oscillate uncontrollably from friend to enemy, from empowered to powerless, from mobile to standing *still*. In both *Hostages of Hate* and *Tagged for Terror*, the only airplanes in these stories end up wrecked. The airport accommodates an *immaterialization* of traveling bodies: everything solid melts into air—or at least ends up as a junk pile at the end of a runway.

Unraveling The Great Airport Mystery

In many ways, the earliest Hardy Boys airport mystery represents the archetype of a terminal immaterial. In *The Great Airport Mystery* (1930), which also begins with a colossal plane wreck, Frank and Joe inadvertently stumble upon a get-rich-quick mail-theft ring operating out of their local airport. When Fenton Hardy first tells his sons about the racket, he explains that mail at the airport is both "carefully guarded" but always open to the possibility of being "left unguarded" as well.[21] This paradoxical arrangement is consistent with a corollary experience of airports as both incessantly contained yet inherently unbounded. The double imperative is also mindful of Jacques Derrida's late writings on "autoimmunity," wherein Derrida claims that vulnerable spaces such as airports are integral to the existence of democracy, *in their very vulnerability*.[22] To put it simply: by being always open to the possibility of hijackings and disaster, airports guarantee living democracy—a state based on the principle of negotiation must invite dialectics of opposition, and thus absolute security is not merely unachievable, it is also undesirable. The guarded airport that can be left unguarded is key to the nation.

   This aporetic sense of space is often reflected in a physical leveling or emptying out, such as in the dump of personal belongings strewn on the runway in *Tagged for Terror*. Yet it is also worth recalling that the scene in which Fenton Hardy explains the "great airport mystery" to Frank and Joe *does not occur at the airport*. Indeed, very little of *The Great Airport Mystery* has anything to do with the airport per se. Rather, the airport is something of a blank canvas onto which bold swaths can be painted without much attention to the materiality of the surface or the medium. In fact, halfway through the story when the Hardy Boys are framed and arrested for another airport robbery, they honestly note: "We've never been to the airport, Dad."[23] Here we are in the middle of *The Great Airport Mystery*, and the real mystery seems to be why the story *has not yet arrived at the airport*. The airport remains a mysterious, elliptical, peripheral location for practically the entire story. The airport's space in the story is *spaced out*.

The spacey spatiality of airports can be seen in crystallized form in *The Great Airport Mystery*, and it is a form that comes to have a literary futurity of sorts. As Frank and Joe first drive out to the newly built, redundantly named Bayport airport (yet never to actually arrive, keep in mind), they discuss the geographical spread of the site:

> "Wonder why they built the airport so far out," Joe said.
>
> "They have to have plenty of ground. It was the only place available . . ." Frank explained.
>
> The roadster bounced along the rutted road toward the airport. A signpost near by conveyed the information that the flying field was three miles away. A little later, as the car came over the brow of a hill the Hardy Boys could see the great flat field lying in the valley below. In front of a hanger they could see a plane with silver wings.[24]

Frank's assertions of "plenty" and "only" introduce a double bind of excess and lack: on the one hand, we are to understand airports as sites of expansive space and sublime vistas, metonymies for a land of "plenty." On the other hand, not "only" is such a suitable spread of land difficult to find, but citizens also accept limitations, restrictions, and routines that they would "only" put up with in airports. Also notable in this passage is the cascade of spatial descriptors by which the Hardy Boys' trip to the airport is vertiginously narrated: the boys drive over a hill and see a flat field in a valley, on which a hanger lies behind a plane with silver wings. The description is almost cubistic in its opening up and flattening out of the perceptual field, and this suggests perceptual difficulty: airports are hard to perceive as totalities, because their boundaries are at once material and ethereal, discernible and yet illusive, both virtual and policed.

Such approaches to airport topographies still abound in contemporary popular culture and literature. For instance, Barry Lopez's short story "Light Action in the Caribbean," published in 2000, includes a similar account of how airports can induce a particular spatial perception. Lopez's story opens with the main character embarking on an ill-fated trip: "Driving from Arvada all the way to the new Denver airport, thought Libby, was like driving to another country before you could take off. Miles and miles of these nothing fields, no houses, no mountains, no development, no roads, no trees."[25] The emptying out of landforms calls attention to how the airport figures into— and dissolves—the surrounding (narrative) landscape. The airport's borders are not exactly visible, and yet the space is apparent via negative perception: what counts is what Libby *cannot* see.

The media scholar Gillian Fuller articulates this perception in her essay "Transcapitalism and the Multiple Ecologies of an Aviopolis," where she claims:

> Airports are "terraformers." They literally make land. They flatten differ-ence into manageable contours, reconfiguring geography according to the

spatio-temporal rhythms and cross-modal standards of global capital. The airport is a world of looping horizons. It unfurls out over the city and insinuates itself into the daily activities of the dispersing world. In its endless grasping of the environment, old futures are abandoned and new ones appear.[26]

Here Fuller describes the way in which airports actually create open space, against, yet also with, the hyper-consolidations of urbanism and Modernity. In the Hardy Boys' and in Libby's accounts of airports, we see this "endless grasping of the environment" in which mental awareness of open space—the experience of "looping horizons"—is a prerequisite. This spatial opening is hardly an innocent process, either. Both *The Great Airport Mystery* and "Light Action in the Caribbean" can be read as violent examples of what Fuller calls "cross-modal standards of global capital." The Hardy Boys discover that a postal pilot has gone rouge and is stealing mailbags full of cash from airport hangers. The airport "insinuates itself" via the pretense of a mystery into the quaint high school lives of Frank, Joe, Chet, Biff, and the other Hardy Boys stock characters. In Barry Lopez's chilling story, two average American tourists depart on a scuba diving vacation only to be abruptly accosted, robbed, raped, killed, and dropped into the ocean by modern day pirates in a cigarette boat. The geographical emptiness around the airport is proleptic, anticipating the murderous episode with which the story ends. These narratives indicate a paradox at the intersection of vulnerable subjectivities and increased spatial perception: the opening of perceptual space around airports, as it were, also opens up possibilities for *unforeseeable* circumstances.

This particular airport problem is akin to what the critic Patricia Yaeger picks up on in her recent article "The Death of Nature and the Apotheosis of Trash; or, Rubbish Ecology." By way of arguing for a politicized aesthetics of trash, Yaeger discusses a moment in Don DeLillo's *Underworld* where a character drives around New Jersey looking for New York City, and instead finds a garbage dump just past the Newark Airport.[27] Where Yaeger, however, focuses on the dump, one might back up and consider the airport that precipitates the dump. In DeLillo's spatial schema, the airport *creates* the perceptual field of empty space required to then *see* a landfill. Here is the passage from *Underworld*:

> When he went past Newark Airport he realized he'd overshot all the turnoffs and their related options. He looked for a friendly exit, untrucked and rural, and found himself sometime later on a two-lane blacktop that wended uncertainly through cattail mires. He felt a bitey edge of brine in the air and the road bent and then ended in gravel and weeds.[28]

DeLillo's prose is mindful yet again of Frank and Joe's first trip to the Bayport airport, particularly in the sense of temporal indeterminacy associated with the way to (or around) an airport: "sometime later. . ." for DeLillo, "a little later . . ." for the Hardy Boys. This indefinite time pairs with flattened space and a whole host of sensory perceptions. In the opening scenes of *The Great Airport Mystery*, an errant plane swoops down upon Frank and Joe, and they note its proximity by the fact that they can hear the sonic vibrations of the plane's struts; DeLillo's character ends up in a swampy, synaesthetic ecotone, tasting the air and hearing the "gravel and weeds" crunch beneath his tires. The strange neologism "untrucked" performs a paralepsis of sorts, making space for the mind's eye by conjuring nonexistent broadsided vehicles. DeLillo's opening up of spatiality in the service of scrutiny is, in a strong sense, the same treatment of terminal immaterial that the Hardy Boys encounter again and again: airports make space for *sensing*.

By the time Frank and Joe finally arrive at the airport in *The Great Airport Mystery*, "[t]he road entering the grounds was under guard, and the big hangers were closely watched, the authorities evidently taking no chances on a repetition of the robbery"—a peculiar description, since at this point in the story the robbery has *already been repeated*; this scene occurs *after* the *second* robbery.[29] This narratological forgetfulness is entirely in line with the Hardy Boys series, which tends to replay themes and tropes across numerous episodes. However, this repetition is doubly apt around the space of the airport, which functions as a kind of architecturally embodied repetition compulsion: in order to operate, users of airports must willingly undergo incredible acts of arguably self-stripping repetition. However, these acts of repetition are precisely what give airports security and stability: the stable subject requires a space of calculable repetition. And yet, amid all the repetition of themes and schemes, the subject of the Hardy Boys airport stories remains uncertain, for one can never be certain if the mystery is about securing space, stabilizing personae, or some mixture that takes place in the elision between space and self.

The airport is open to theory

In *The Interpretation of Dreams*, Freud suggests that the way to approach the manifest content of dreams (the stuff you remember when you wake up) is to never think it can be overinterpreted. Freud points out "that it is in fact never possible to be sure that a dream has been completely interpreted."[30] Therefore, one must precisely (if also excessively) linger on interpretive conundrums in order to grasp the fathomless amounts of "condensation" that have taken place within the latent content of dreams. In this analysis, I have borrowed Freud's methodology, albeit to analyze a quite different environment. My subject of analysis is not the nebula of dreams; instead, it is the site of airports in the Hardy Boys mysteries, this rhetorical hub that condenses thematic material from far-reaching destinations. In these stories, and around this *site*, one discovers repressed spatial ambiguities and uncertain subjectivities. To continue traveling with Freud for a moment, we might even go as far to say that the light distractions of the textual life of airports involves not just an uncertain subject, but an *unconscious* subject as well.

It is worth noting that throughout many of the Hardy Boys mysteries, Frank and Joe continually carp about not wanting to go to college; they have no interest at all in higher education. In *The Great Airport Mystery*, which is set around Frank and Joe's high school graduation, Frank rhetorically pleads with his mother, "Do we have to go to college?"[31] Instead, Frank and Joe want to be private detectives like their father, the famous Fenton Hardy. The Hardy Boys series represents a sort of endless deferment of college: these "boys" never grow up, never want to grow up, and the stories keep Frank and Joe in an adventurous—if also routinely infantilized—comportment, decade after decade.

This strain recurs in *Hostages of Hate*, when at one point Frank and Joe find themselves searching the Georgetown University campus for a radical student named Pia who has been recruited by international terrorists to advertise their cause on a college campus. When Frank and Joe first encounter Pia in a student union, she is making homemade signs advocating revolution.

Finally, in *Tagged for Terror*, one of the baggage handlers suspected to be involved with the luggage theft ring (and therefore inexplicably linked to a terrorist cell) is reasoned to be tight on cash because he is trying to pay for college. Continually, the college campus is alluded to as a place that can breed terrorists and thieves—uncertain subjects, par excellence. For Frank and Joe, college is at the distant end of a theory/practice spectrum, with the Hardy Boys representing the practical, hands-on end of street smarts and deductive reasoning.

Yet the subject of the airport seems to warp this spectrum in a compelling way, simply by acting as *terminal immaterial*: that open space in which indeterminate scenarios can play out, allegiances can shift, and identities can be swapped. The airport puts pressure on the individual subject, on the very concept of "the subject," and offers itself up as subject for investigation: one might even say that the airport is open to *theory*. Amid the anti-intellectual impulse of the Hardy Boys series, Frank and Joe find themselves schooled at the airport. In other words, the airport *as subject* becomes not only a mysterious place, but also a pedagogical space—a space for thinking within and about the uncertain subjects of everyday life. The light reading of the Hardy Boys detective stories is seen to be heavy with the textual life of airports, a vortex of mysteries and loose ends.

A contemporary mystery, or, the romantic airport

To conclude this chapter, I follow the uncertain subjectivity of the fictitious Hardy Boys college student to an actual contemporary airport mystery. This is the story of a 28-year-old Rutgers University graduate student named Haisong Jiang. On January 3, 2010, Jiang slipped past the Transportation Security Administration agent at the arrivals gate in Newark Airport, in order to tarry for a few extra minutes with his girlfriend who was bound for Los Angeles.

After someone reported the transgression to airport security, the scene turned into a traveler's nightmare: the concourses were evacuated, and all passengers waiting for their flights were required to return to the terminal to be screened again. In the end, the incident resulted in a six-hour interruption that caused the delay or cancellation of about 200 flights.

Sensational photographs of the incident showed the terminal clogged with thousands of passengers in what appeared to be endless lines, some of which snaked up and down escalators at a standstill, suggesting a scene of utter pandemonium—a breakdown of multiple modern teleologies, at once.

Within days, footage from a closed circuit video camera owned by Continental Airlines was released, and promptly disseminated and analyzed. The clip shows a man "wearing light pants and a tan jacket" (as one article described him) loitering outside the secure or "sterile" zone of the terminal, and a Transportation Security Administration agent sitting at a nearby desk, watching passengers leave the arrivals gate.[32] At one point, the TSA agent stands up and walks away from his post, apparently to stretch his legs and monitor the wider area around the arrivals gate. This is the moment that the man in light pants and a tan jacket darts over the threshold; he can be seen giving someone a quick hug, and then the couple walks arm-in-arm beyond the view of the camera, back into the concourse.

Figure 3.1 The Newark Airport Security Breach (video still from *The New York Times* online)

There is something absorbing and alluring about watching the six minute and twenty-two second video feed of Jiang lingering and then suddenly transgressing the secure threshold of the airport. Suspense is of course introduced by contextual knowledge, and by the stated message beneath the video that this is a "security breach." But the vast majority of the video clip shows nothing more than the monotonous patterns of deplaned passengers leaving the gate area, presumably on their way to rides at curbside or to the baggage claim to retrieve their luggage. It is an utterly ambient video, silent and non-eventful, yet full of intricate styles and prosaic designs—this is the "social text" of the airport, replete with "secret" motives embodied in the devious Jiang and his subterfuge, and published not only by the ordinary space, but textually re-marked by the security camera.[33]

I am not attempting to draw out the indictment of the actual person Jiang, here, but merely pointing out how the airport had *already prepared for its own mystery to unfold*. The hidden camera, the immaterial yet sensitive barrier of the arrivals gate, the guard who appears to have nothing to do but sit and watch for *just this sort of person* for hours on end: in all these ways, the airport readies itself for the event, the mystery instantly made spectacular.

The discovery of Jiang's real intentions was something of a foil to the media hype and detective work that roiled around the incident; and yet, the airport was even able to absorb and recycle this shift in tone, maintaining the aura of mystery and uncertain subjectivity in spite of the news that Jiang was little more than a "romantic" at the airport. To see this shift in tone, we need only examine the weeklong progression of headlines and accompanying articles in *The New York Times* that followed the incident, from the first report of the security breach to the eventual conviction of Jiang, and beyond:

January 3: *Flights Out of Newark Airport Halted for Possible Security Breach*

January 3: *Chaos and Inquiry Follow Security Breach at Newark Airport*

January 7: *Video Shows Newark Security Breach: A Kiss before Flying*

January 8: *Man Arrested in Newark Airport Security Breach*

January 9: *A 'Romantic' Now in Trouble over an Airport Kiss*

March 9: *Consequences of an Airport Kiss*

March 13: *Airport Guard Punished*

From the initial report of a "possible" security breach, we see a rhetorical shift from airport "chaos" to systematic "inquiry"—this is supported by the suggestion of evidence garnered from the video. Curiously, the tone then stutters between matters of airport security and a far-flung romance, only to settle back in the airport, with the punishment of the airport guard at fault.

Comment threads attached to online articles quickly turned to the security agent in question. Readers asked what was so hard about watching a hallway, and demanded that the TSA worker be fired. As we have seen consistently and throughout, airport laborers can become suddenly suspect characters, possibly unreliable precisely by serving as the weak (human) link in the mechanics of flight. In other words, the as-if secure system of the airport ends up breached *not* by the imaginary (and therefore absent) rogue, but more so by the relaxed presence of an official sentry.

What this incident evinces is how the airport prepares for its own mysteries, from the ever-present closed circuit cameras to the capacious corridors ready to contain crowds going nowhere. The airport is a site open to detection: it is a field where various movements, recordings, and acts—of passengers and laborers alike—are open to interpretation. In this case, the airport mystery turned three times: from an imagined security-breaching rogue; to a bookish but "lovesick"[34] graduate student; and finally, to the airport worker whose job is tedious and yet exposed to be a high-stakes enterprise indeed.

As we saw in the Hardy Boys detective stories, airport security is a menagerie at once suspenseful and banal, utterly serious and highly entertaining. In fact, within these three works of adolescent fiction are kernels of the theoretical problems of airports that we will continue to trace throughout the following chapters. As I indicated in the above example of the Newark security breach, narratives of detection, anticipation, and mystery are ready to unfold as-if spontaneously in the most everyday airport scenarios. In Chapter 4, I press forward into the uncertain intersection of security and entertainment, specifically around the charged subject of 9/11—a critical historical node in the textual life of airports.

CHAPTER 4

9/11: POINTS OF DEPARTURE

Taking time

In Chapter 3, I explored the uncertain subject of the Hardy Boys airport mysteries. This is a subject of seemingly low stakes, couched comfortably in the realm of adolescent fiction. However, as I indicated earlier, the spectacle value of 9/11 was nascent in those works of light entertainment. Chapter 4 articulates how airports serve as reflexive intertexts in markedly post-9/11 fiction.

Regarding the events of 9/11, Jean Baudrillard asserted, "you have to take your time" when thinking about the complexities of what happened that day.[1] Alluding to this imperative, David Simpson calls his introduction to *9/11: The Culture of Commemoration*, "Taking Time." Simpson writes, "The event of 9/11 has both reproduced and refigured culture, which means that it may take more time than usual to work out how and to what ends."[2]

In a strictly material sense, Simpson's point became crystallized for me one day in the library of University of California at Davis. I had gone to the library to retrieve one specific book about 9/11, and was directed to an area of the library that I had never been to before. When I located the call number range, I scanned the nearby books and found myself amid several entire stacks of bookshelves dedicated to the events of 9/11. I wondered if there was any other single date-stamped topic that took up as much shelf space in the library.

Indeed, 9/11 spawned such a range of political investigations, conspiracy theories, critical dialogues, and personal narratives that this event can seem utterly overwhelming to research, much less write something new about. As an ad hoc example of this, one need only consider the entry for "September 11 attacks" on the online encyclopedia Wikipedia: the entry involves lengthy descriptions and intricately linked prose—and ends with an impressive and exhaustive list of 278 references (as of February 2011). In other words, even the quick and dirty version of 9/11 is (literally) a virtual tome.[3]

Of course, one does not have to do research to be reminded of how 9/11 "has both reproduced and refigured culture." One need only embark on any regularly scheduled domestic flight, and amid the security procedures required to pass from the "non-sterile" to the "sterile" zone of the airport, specters of 9/11 pop up and permeate the contemporary experience of passing through space.

Following Simpson following Baudrillard, in this book about airports I am attempting to try to take time in relation to the events of 9/11, by writing somewhat indirectly about the topic. Specifically, in this chapter I am interested in how works of literary fiction remember 9/11 through airport scenes.

On first glance, this textual trend hardly sticks out as noteworthy; in many ways, it is entirely to be expected, since airport security checkpoints are the most obvious sites where 9/11 lives on in the collective memory of U.S. travelers. Yet it seems to me that airports function in works of post-9/11 fiction not only as convenient settings for remembering 9/11, but also as key sites for complicating the mediations and memories of this event. I first look at how this works in two short stories, Sherman Alexie's "Flight Patterns" (2004) and Martin Amis's "The Last Days of Muhammad Atta" (2006). Each of these stories dwells significantly on airport scenes, and I show how such scenes allow the narratives to grapple with uneasy memories of 9/11. Then, I demonstrate how airport scenes punctuate Don DeLillo's novel *Falling Man* (2007). DeLillo's novel mentions airports three times, and somewhat briefly; nevertheless, such passing airport representations are crucial to narrative attempts to reckon with the events of 9/11. I end the chapter with a brief discussion of *The 9/11 Commission Report* and its reliance on airport figures.

The way to the airport: "Flight Patterns"

Sherman Alexie's story "Flight Patterns" is about a Spokane Indian who is a Seattle-based traveling salesman—or as the main character admits in the opening paragraph, a "bemused and slightly embarrassed owner of a twenty-first-century American mind."[4] We soon learn that William (or Willy Loman, as his wife allusively refers to him) is headed out of town on a business trip to Chicago; the story unfolds over the course of an early morning cab ride to the Seattle-Tacoma airport. The entire narrative is a drawn-out deferral of the trip to come, for the story ends precisely *at* the airport, before William takes his flight.

The airport looms as a counterintuitive destination in this story, its social dynamics also emitting a preemptive aura, of sorts. As William is preparing to leave his house in the early morning, he reflects on his young daughter's post-9/11 anxieties about air travel, which are manifest in her school drawings of fiery planes and falling buildings:

> William understood her fear of flying and of his flight. He was afraid of flying, too, but not of terrorists. After the horrible violence of September 11, he figured hijacking was no longer a useful weapon in the terrorist arsenal. These days, a terrorist armed with a box cutter would be torn to pieces by all the coach-class passengers and fed to the first-class upgrades.[5]

William makes a witty remark about 9/11, and in doing so he proves a rarely spoken truth: the commercial airliner hijackings of 9/11 took advantage of the element of surprise more than anything else. With this specific surprise tactic no longer extant, the manic security protocols of post-9/11 airports are arguably superfluous. William elaborates on this observation with a hyperbolic joke: any hijacker who tried to use similar methods of procuring an aircraft would be torn apart by coach-class passengers and eaten by the first-class passengers. While darkly hilarious, this image also conjures serious and complex class divides. William's ironic comment also suggests that everyday Americans might so easily become cannibals—a claim not all that unreasonable, given the rhetoric and effects of "shock and awe" that 9/11 reflexively produced. Even as he races willingly toward the airport in the predawn darkness, William leaks a subtle critique of the innocent patriotism associated with commercial flight after 9/11.

Embedded in the above passage is the admission that William *is* afraid of flying, but *not* because of terrorists. We never quite learn if this is a fear of flight per se—or if William's fear is associated with mortality in general, or twenty-first-century geopolitics. Like the airport that lingers on the periphery of the narrative, Alexie holds this ambient fear in suspension.

The bulk of the story centers on a conversation between William and the Ethiopian expatriate cabdriver named Fekadu, as they speed toward the airport. Fekadu strikes up a conversation, and what starts as innocuous chatting unfolds into William learning disturbing facts about Fekadu's life story. As the cab passes by Boeing Field, Fekadu somberly explains, "I flew jets for Selassie's army" and "I dropped bombs on my own people."[6] While this admission is taking place, the narrative tracks other lines of flight: "In the sky above them, William counted four, five, six jets flying in holding patterns while awaiting permission to land."[7] Links between commercial aviation and militarism are literally in the air.

William learns the full story of Fekadu's rogue escape to France where he received asylum, and of his eventual flight to the United States; Fekadu says that he cannot return to his home, a place that contains "too much history and pain, and I am too afraid."[8] This impromptu narrative rattles William, but abruptly the cab reaches the airport and Fekadu quickly wraps up his story, saying "Good-bye, William American"—at which point the normative antics of curbside drop-off take precedent, and William is thrust into the vortex of everyday air travel.[9]

The following passage marks the end of the story:

Standing at curbside, William couldn't breathe well. He wondered if he was dying. Of course he was dying, a flawed mortal dying day by day, but he felt like he might fall over from a heart attack or stroke right there on the sidewalk. He left his bags and ran inside the terminal. Let a luggage porter think his bags were dangerous! Let a security guard x-ray the bags and find mysterious shapes! Let a bomb-squad cowboy explode the bags as a precaution! Let an airport manager shut down the airport and search every possible traveler! Let the FAA president order every airplane to land! Let the American skies be empty of everything with wings! Let the birds stop flying! Let the very air go still and cold! William didn't care. He ran through the terminal, searching for an available pay phone, a land-line, something true and connected to the ground, and he finally found one and dropped two quarters into the slot and dialed his home number, and it rang and rang and rang and rang, and William worried that his wife and daughter were harmed, were lying dead on the floor, but then Marie answered.

"Hello William," she said.

"I'm here," he said.[10]

For all intents and purposes, William is just beginning his journey, his business trip—yet the airport looms as a tormented, dystopian site of excessive self-awareness and militarized surveillance. William experiences anxiety, suspense, and heavy irony in this explicitly post-9/11 terminal. The fantastical paragraph in the conclusion sends up flares of global terrorism and fireworks of national authority while simultaneously extinguishing these tropes with the mundane ephemera of outdated payphones and loose change. Transportation Security Administration agents are compared with cowboys; planes are conflated with birds. This is a twenty-first-century post-Western frontier scene at the curbside of the SEA-TAC airport: the Native American traveler, a self-proclaimed "little brown guy"[11] must pay fifty cents for the faintest semblance of ontological security in the at turns docile, paranoid, muted, and jet-roaring atmosphere of the airport.

The airport payphone in this passage serves as a secure mediating device, a communication technology that is "connected to the ground." William's utterance of "here," on the other hand, functions almost as a new media *here*—as in a nonspecific hyperlink to another location on the Internet. William's "here" signifies the airport, but it also stands for nowhere exactly: it is a point in transit, and the final word of dialogue at the conclusion of the story. This "here" is similar to Marc Augé's idea of "non-place": a site that is dedicated to transfer and passing through, never a destination in and of itself, such as a highway rest stop, an ATM, or—not coincidentally—an airport. For William "here" is not only the airport, but also a more pervasive informational condition, a way of being in a postmodern world where global realities and long histories rear up and press down hard on the (as-if) freely traveling subject.

The comportment in which William finds himself at the airport at the end of "Flight Patterns" aligns with Martin Amis's description of 9/11 as ". . . the apotheosis of the postmodern era—the era of images and perceptions."[12] William's ride to the airport, and his curbside freak-out, focus and replay the cultural productions of 9/11: suicidal violence, stories of state-sponsored atrocities, images of manic security personnel, threats of an enemy who could be anyone and anywhere, and perceptions of FAA control (or the lack thereof) over the American skies.

Yet Alexie's Seattle-Tacoma airport is precisely *not* the site of terrorist activities or even yet the moment of an identity check—this is in fact the end of a convoluted yet clear *mental* journey in a taxicab, in which the narrator William grapples with the realities of uncertain national and laboring identities in a globalized world of destabilized states. The "here" that William utters at the airport is an anywhere and a nowhere, at once a starting place and the end of the story.

Alexie's use of the airport as the endpoint of the story also serves to reverse a common temporal sequencing of the airport either being the beginning of or a midpoint within a narrative; instead, to end at the airport leaves everything on the verge of beginning. As a way to work through what William's character describes as "the horrible violence of September 11," Alexie repositions the airport as a crisis point where being is exposed, scrutinized, and paused—for again, the story ends with William immobilized at the airport. Arriving at the curbside, William fears the non sequitur death of his family by mere association, by his own presence at the launching pad of modern terror machines: the airport.

By placing the airport at the end of the narrative, Alexie asks his readers to back up, to consider all the journeys that take place before an instance—or the entire epoch—of air travel. As the Ethiopian exile Fekadu and the Spokane businessman William talk frankly about the racially charged atmosphere in the days and months following 9/11, the object correlative of air travel raises the topic of outlying lines of flight: global flight patterns that begin to put into perspective the events of 9/11. For William, airport time becomes neither the time for arrogant patriotism nor for blind progress, but a *terminal*—an ambiguous node where personal reflection and geopolitical sensitivity occur. It is as if Alexie highlights the overcompensating protocols of the post-9/11 airport precisely in order to suggest that the situation is far more nuanced—and with a far more lengthy history than can be accounted for in the time of airport security.

Dead time in "The Last Days of Muhammad Atta"

Sherman Alexie ends his story "Flight Patterns" with an embellished rejection of cavalier post-9/11 airport security protocols. The methods of airport security are a theme for Martin Amis in his story "The Last Days of Muhammad Atta," as well. However, Amis reflects on pre-9/11 security practices along the way. The story diverges into something like nonfiction commentary because of the way that Amis narrates Atta's last day at the Portland airport:

> As it happened, Muhammad Atta was a selectee of the Computer-Assisted Passenger Prescreening System (CAPPS). All this meant was that his checked bag would not be stowed until he himself had boarded the aircraft. This was at Portland. At Logan, a "Category X"' airport like Newark Liberty and Washington Dulles, and supposedly more secure, three of his muscle Saudis would be selected by CAPPS, with the same irrelevant consequences.[13]

In the midst of this story, Amis embeds a stringent critique of the realities of pre-9/11 airport security. Yet, complicatedly, it is not clear that the post-9/11 airport circumstances will fare much better. As I go on to show, the narrative structure of this story complicates how the terms *before* and *after* are hitched to the events of 9/11, and the subject of airport culture stands as a central figure through which the story undermines a sense of linear temporality.

Amis's story begins and ends with the same sentence: "On September 11, 2001, he opened his eyes at 4 A.M., in Portland, Maine; and Muhammad Atta's last day began."[14] Such a textual loop, the literal repetition of the same line at the beginning and end of this story, signals a formal break in the temporal logic of the story: the last day is a day that will repeat—possibly again and again. The linearity of this narrative is punctured and rerouted at its conclusion: the reader is returned, sent back to the beginning of the text. Through this structure, Atta is destined to a series of continual, title-worthy "Last Days" that are yet reducible to a single day at the airport—an annoying and uncomfortable one at that.

By bending the story into a circular trajectory, Amis places what happens in the circular line under Nietzschean scrutiny: the minutiae of Atta's last day, his waiting around in a hotel lobby, more waiting in the Portland airport, and yet more waiting around in Boston Logan airport—these quotidian events acquire significance by their recurrence. The text makes readers wait through scenes of waiting. The destination is the point of departure. The entire story is a circular machine by which the reader *waits* for an ending that has *already* occurred. Of course this is also true in the most literal sense: the reader most likely knows the story of 9/11 already—there is no need for a spoiler alert here. This recycling of time within a linear (and known) narrative in fact creates the feeling of what the cultural historian Alaistair Gordon calls "airportness": this is the aura of air travel attributable to certain interior designs, ambient sounds, and acts that are distinctly understood in reference to commercial flight.[15] I am suggesting that through narrative repetition, Amis formally implies the airportness involved in Atta's last day. However, the airport becomes an explicit location, as well.

As Amis imagines Atta checking in for his initial flight at the Portland, Maine, airport, the contemporaneous reader is interpellated in an uncomfortable identification with the traveling terrorist. Amis recreates the scene as such:

"Did you pack these bags yourself?"

Muhammad Atta's hand crept toward his brow. "Yes," he said.

"Have they been with you at all times?"

"Yes."

"Did anyone ask you to carry anything for them?"

"No. Is the flight on time?"

"You should make your connection."

"And the bags will go straight through?"

"No, sir. You'll need to recheck them at Logan."

"You mean, I'll have to go through all this *again*?"

Whatever terrorism had achieved in the past few decades, it had certainly brought about a net increase in world boredom. It didn't take very long to ask and answer those three questions—about fifteen seconds. But those dead-time questions and answers were repeated, without any variation whatever, hundreds of thousands of times a day. If the planes operation went ahead as planned, Muhammad Atta would bequeath more, perhaps much more, dead time, planet wide. It was appropriate, perhaps, and not paradoxical, that terror should also sharply promote its most obvious opposite. Boredom.[16]

Through this exchange and within Atta's ruminations, the text considers the utterly nondramatic, inherently unoriginal interactions of passengers and commercial airline employees at this overly wrought point of contact: the check-in counter. This moment hinges on multiple, conflicting states of being-in-waiting: the laborer's work is reduced to the repetition of programmatic lines; the passenger is cast in an endlessly repeatable situation, thus undermining the ontological status of the liberal subject; even the 'terrorist' here is rendered a thoroughly interpellated subject—subject, that is, to the monotony and boredom of air travel. The entire situation, moreover, is shrouded in the dark, repeated pun of "dead time": even before the airliner hijackings or the collapse of the World Trade Center towers, time is already exposed as being dead.

It turns out that this airport trope of "dead time" has a literary precursor: Don DeLillo's 1982 novel *The Names* articulates the repetitive stasis of airports in a quintessential definition of "dead time":

> This is time totally lost to us. We don't remember it. We take no sense impressions with us, no voices, none of the windy blast of aircraft on the tarmac, or the white noise of flight, or the hours waiting. Nothing sticks to us but smoke in our hair and clothes. It is dead time. It never happened until it happens again. Then it never happened.[17]

This passage is not about overtly violent drama, and in fact concerns little more than an ordinary moment before one of DeLillo's fictive characters boards a routine commercial flight twenty or so years prior to 9/11. And yet, this description opens up a distinct relation to airport time that resists memory. The synaesthetic qualities of the airport are looped and replayed until "the hours of waiting" elide the actual happenings of this non-place. For Amis, it is as if Atta's experience of this airport time sets the stage for horrors to come that will both demand and resist memory.

Later in "The Last Days of Muhammad Atta," Amis casts Atta in a nearly identical situation, this time at Boston Logan airport, as he is making his final connection:

> Oh the misery of recurrence . . . . It had occurred to him before that his condition, if you could call it that, was merely the condition of boredom, where all time was dead time. As if his whole life consisted of answering those same three questions, saying "Yes" and "Yes" and "No."[18]

In this daring depiction of the now infamous ghost-"terrorist," Amis constructs Atta as no more (and no less) than a bored subject of automated systems. Privileged passengers become part of an ambiance of boredom, mere biological residues of "dead time." The condition is a Nietzschean eternal return gone wrong; instead of affirmation and overcoming, Amis's Atta experiences the airport as one final, boring "recurrence" that can only end in an explosive closure. To add to the bitter irony of Atta's inconsequential security questioning, Amis reminds his readers that the terrorism of 9/11 has indeed resulted in *more* of this "dead time" that is very much alive—and even, oddly, thriving: fuel is burned, laborers are paid, passengers purchase Economy Plus seat upgrades and suck down Starbucks Grande lattes while waiting for their flights.

Even as Atta waits for American Airlines Flight 11 to board at Boston Logan, Amis evacuates all drama from the scene by filling out the gritty, everyday environment:

> Muhammad Atta took a seat outside a dormant coffee shop . . . a mechanized floor-sweeper, resembling a hovercraft, with an old man on it, beeping and sniveling around his chair . . . he sat for a few minutes on the tin chair, as he watched the mall awaken and come into commercial being, filling up now with Americans and American purpose and automatic self-belief . . . .[19]

Amis's airport indicts entire schemas of nationality, philosophy, and economics: a laborer toils with "a mechanized floor-sweeper," an anthropomorphized mall 'awakens' and comes "into commercial being," and "American purpose" looks suspiciously like a network of automaton consumers. As Atta boards the plane, "With twinkly promptitude, canned music flooded forth: a standard ballad, a flowery flute with many trills and graces. The breathy refrain joined the simmer of the engines. . . ."[20] Finally, when Atta has to use the toilet in the airplane before take off, he finds all three lavatories inaccessible:

> A frequent and inquisitive traveller on American commercial jets, Muhammad Atta knew that the toilets were locked, like all the other toilets (this was the practice on tight turnarounds), and would remain locked until the plane leveled out. He pressed a flat hand against all three: again, the misery of recurrence, duplication.[21]

At this moment in the narrative, Amis textually signals the duplication of terms and situations with the actual word "duplication"—the text thus highlights its own interest and entrenchment in cycles of material 'recurrence'— even as far as processes of human waste.

On the title page of Amis's story where it was originally published in *The New Yorker* magazine, beneath the darkly ironic heading of "fiction," there appear four black-and-white security camera still-images of Muhammad

Atta and one of his accomplices making a transaction at a gas station on September 10, 2001.

While haunting on one level, these images are also commonplace: they are the ubiquitous signatures of a surveillance saturated consumer society. Here are the would-be hijackers, caught on camera like millions of other regular American consumers on September 10, 1001. Referring to Jacques Derrida's post-9/11 theory of autoimmunity, we might note how the hijackers are "*exposed*, precisely, . . . 'in a loop,' to [America's] own cameras in its own interests."[22] Atta is recorded engaging in a simple monetary transaction, purchasing gasoline; he is caught, doing nothing wrong (yet), on video. Of course this vicious "loop" also appears in the widely publicized image of the recorded, live—and *lived*—replay of Muhammad Atta in the Portland, Maine, airport at the security checkpoint on September 11, exposing a moment of mundane passage, and the access point to the sublime weapon. In Amis's story, the airport serves at once as the eternal return, and that which seamlessly gives way to a violent, final end.

Imaginary airports in Falling Man

Don DeLillo's novel *Falling Man* focuses on post-9/11 adjustments of two main characters: Keith, a WTC survivor, whom we learn was working in the North Tower when the first plane hit; and his estranged wife Lianne, who is struggling to come to terms with her father's suicide and her mother's slide into Alzheimer's. One character, then, is dealing with the events of 9/11 directly; indeed, we learn that Keith was near enough to the blast in the North Tower to be sent "out of his chair and into a wall" and to smell jet fuel "oozing down from floors above."[23]

Lianne, on the other hand, did not experience the plane crashes first hand, but still feels their effects in an intensely personal way: she feels the aura of 9/11 through Keith's showing up at her door that day, covered in blood and glass—and also by the lingering subject of her father's unrelated suicide, which vexes Lianne's conscience and memory. In other words, DeLillo treats 9/11 as a subject that infiltrates layers of social and psychic experience. For these characters, 9/11 raises issues that cannot be dealt with easily: from suicide, to trauma, to memory itself.

There is also a third character whose perspectives occasion *Falling Man*: the hijacker Hammad, whose experiences appear in the narrative three times, twice from remote training locations (studying architecture and engineering in Germany, and studying aviation in Florida), and the third time in the hijacked American Airlines Flight 11 as it approaches and smashes into the North Tower. It is the elusive narrative perspective of Hammad that returns us to the idea of "dead time" within a critical airport imaginary.

Hammad, DeLillo's fictive terrorist-to-be, dwells on dead time exposure two times in the novel. At one point, as the novel describes it: "He watched

TV in a bar near the flight school and liked to imagine himself appearing on the screen, a videotaped figure walking through the gate-like detector on his way to the plane."[24] DeLillo's Hammad replaces ambient TV entertainment with a self-projected fantasy of his *own* dead time to come: in the figure of the TV, Hammad imagines himself passing through security at the airport. This fantasy plays out again a few pages later, "When he walks down the bright aisle [of a supermarket] he thinks a thousand times in one second about what is coming. Clean-shaven, on videotape, passing through the metal detector."[25] It is as if DeLillo's narrative dramatization of the would-be hijacker gets hung up on (or in) the familiar scene of a surveilled security line. And "what is coming"—a sublime death by air, steel, and fire—is delayed by the fantasy object of an oddly more visceral, infinitely loop-able dead time caught on video screens.

In these scenes of an anticipated mediation to come, Hammad is not speculating about what it will feel like for him to pass through the metal detectors at the airport; rather, he imagines what it will feel like for other people to *watch* images of him, *after* the violent fact, passing through the metal detectors at the airport. If Martin Amis's "dead time" is defined by monotonous airport routines, DeLillo pushes this experience one level farther, locating another sort of dead time in surveillance and spectatorship, where actual physical violence is always-already at least twice removed. In the multiplications and consolidations of airport security monitoring, dead time becomes a visual economy of removal. Even the allegedly metaphysically driven Jihadist becomes a mere reproducible image seen in the past: Hammad sees himself in an illusive, impossibly retrospective apparition in advance, on a flickering TV screen. These two airport allusions figure briefly in *Falling Man*, yet they connect to an earlier instance of airport imagery in a striking way.

The earlier airport case in *Falling Man* involves Lianne. Throughout the novel, Lianne is continually overcome with unresolved memories of her father who took his own life. At one point, nearly in passing, "She thought of her father. She saw him coming down an escalator, in an airport maybe."[26] While this is one of many fragmentary reveries concerning Lianne's father, I want to suggest that this "airport maybe" is significant—precisely for its interpretive uncertainty given the post-9/11 context of the novel's plot. The airport figures in the novel as an insecure site, a place of transit as well as a space for unsure ontology.[27]

The three airport allusions in *Falling Man* are brief and made in passing. Yet the minimal presence of airports in this novel is precisely one of the factors that make this site worth considering in terms of *Falling Man's* explicitly post-9/11 register. As I have indicated throughout this book, airports are a regular obsession throughout DeLillo's oeuvre, with many of his works lingering on these sites frequently and overtly. The events of 9/11 brought airports into the foreground of American popular culture in myriad ways, from being experienced as sites of common fears and sincere patriotism, to being lampooned as "theaters of the absurd" and exposed as uselessly strict in terms of upholding arbitrary regulations that do not ensure the safety of travelers.[28] Adept readers of DeLillo might have expected the author to have had a field day with the subject of airports in a novel explicitly about 9/11. And yet, we only get three fleeting airport scenes, and all of them take place *in the mind's eye*, as it were. There are *no* airports per se in *Falling Man*; this effective absence makes the airport a spectral figure—and perhaps a formally guiding figure for exactly this reason.

Like "The Last Days of Muhammad Atta," *Falling Man* relies on a circular narrative structure. In this case, though, DeLillo's returning narrative is drawn out over many more pages than Amis's story. The novel opens with Keith wandering away from the maelstrom of the WTC as the towers fall. The second paragraph of the first chapter describes the scene as such:

> The roar was still in the air, the buckling rumble of the fall. This was the world now. Smoke and ash came rolling down streets and turning corners, busting around corners, seismic tides of smoke, with office paper flashing past, standard sheets with cutting edge, skimming, whipping past, otherworldly things in the morning pall.[29]

The reader is plunked directly into a relentless narration of the confusion and chaos of what would become known as "Ground Zero." As we walk with Keith "away from it and into it at the same time" we are barraged with a flurry of images and sounds; one particular sight gets its own paragraph, in a sort of slight narrative pause: "There was something else, then, outside all this, not belonging to this, aloft. He watched it coming down. A shirt came down out of the high smoke, a shirt lifted and drifting in the scant light and then falling again, down toward the river."[30] In this paragraph the repetition of the word "shirt" is curious, given the singularity of the subject(s)—both the shirt and 9/11. One might be tempted to forward a symbolic reading of this doubly cited shirt as a refracted sighting of the Twin Towers. Yet I wish to propose that there is a more compelling reading of this visual stutter of the shirt on an "airport maybe" level. Such a reading arrives from the structure of this novel as it is made clear in the last chapter.

The final section of the book returns us to the scene of Ground Zero, initiated by the viewpoint of Hammad as the hijacked American Airlines Flight 11 speeds into the Hudson Corridor en route to its unsuspecting target. Hammad keeps watch over the passengers held in coach-class cabin from his position "facing a bulkhead, with the toilet behind him, first-class only."[31] Like a sinister version of Sherman Alexie's joke about first-class passengers eating terrorists, DeLillo embeds an understated comment on the architecture of class privilege that remains even in the midst of a hijacking: the first-class toilet is still the first-class toilet, even once an airliner is converted into an armed missile.

From Hammad's position looking back on the coach-class cabin,

> He believed he could see straight into the towers even though his back was to
> them. He didn't know the aircraft's location but believed he could see straight
> through out the back of his head and through the steel and aluminum of the
> aircraft and into the long silhouettes, the shapes, the forms, the figures coming
> closer, the material things.[32]

This warping of perception is consistent with the earlier descriptions of
Hammad imagining other people seeing himself on a security camera feed,
after the event. In the above scene, Hammad consciously refutes his actual
perspective, and "the material things" become both immaterially more real
and physically *closer*, as the plane approaches its final destination.

The closing pages of the novel perform a break in the narrative structure
maintained throughout; up to this point, the three main characters are treated
as discrete subjectivities, each allowed their own blocks of prose for their distinct observations and experiences. As American Airlines Flight 11 sharks over
Lower Manhattan, Hammad's narrative perspective from within the plane
morphs into Keith's subjective experience of the blast in the North Tower:

> A bottle fell off the counter in the galley, on the other side of the aisle, and he
> watched it roll this way and that, a water bottle, empty, making an arc one
> way and rolling back the other, and he watched it spin more quickly and then
> skitter across the floor an instant before the aircraft struck the tower, heat, then
> fuel, then fire, and a blast wave passed through the structure that sent Keith
> Neudecker out of his chair and into a wall. He found himself walking into a
> wall. He didn't drop the telephone until he hit the wall. The floor began to slide
> beneath him and he lost his balance and eased along the wall to the floor.[33]

The "he" in this paragraph shifts from referring to Hammad to referring
to Keith, as if in this moment of sublimation the terrorist literally becomes
the victim. This idea is elaborated upon earlier in the novel when a doctor,
removing particles of glass from Keith's body, explains how the "little pel-
lets of flesh" from suicide bombers is often found embedded in the bodies of
survivors—this phenomenon is called "organic shrapnel."[34]

The remainder of the novel accounts for Keith's hallucinatory march
out the North Tower and away from Ground Zero: "He took one step and
then the next, smoke blowing over him. He felt rubble underfoot and there
was motion everywhere, people running, things flying past."[35] The novel
has returned to the beginning, to the horrors of Ground Zero—and the last
lines return to us a familiar image: "Then he saw a shirt come down out of
the sky. He walked and saw it fall, arms waving like nothing in this life."[36]
Keith sees something "like nothing in this life"—yet this shirt has already
been seen, in fact has already been seen *twice* the first time. *Falling Man* falls
over on itself, seeing itself—the narrative stumbles into its own repetition

that occurs again at the end. The falling shirt represents no more and no less than the experience of experiencing something singular, again.

This repetition of the twice seen shirt falling down from the sky marks (and re-marks) a formal logic of repetition that comes to life in the figure of airport waiting. Thus we are returned to Hammad imagining himself twice being seen in the security line at the airport, and to Lianne imagining herself waiting in the airport for her father to come down an escalator. Sherman Alexie's twenty-first-century Willy Loman experiences the airport as an insecure destination at which point he cannot wait to phone home and establish a grounded sense of (mediated) being. And of course, Martin Amis's fictive Muhammad Atta becomes the figure of this particular figuration, mulling over his own complicity in the "dead time" effects of airport waiting.

9/11 the adventure

In this chapter, I have shown how the events of 9/11 are fictionalized, but also how these events are put in the context of real or realistic airports. Amid these attempts to understand or mediate 9/11 through fictive tales, the airports exist as unstable referents, at once the external real and the internal ambiguity—as points of departure, and as ground zeroes where everyday life collides with (potential) high adventure. I wish to end this chapter by looking at one more example of how 9/11 has been narrated in prose, with the imaginative aids of airports fully at work.

The poet and critic Joshua Clover has argued that novels

> may no longer be the place where adventure goes to find its expression, and that in the wake of modernism—with Joyce's restructuring of the adventure narrative into the space of a single day of daily life—and in the wake of post-modernism's ironizing of every form of traditional literature—that adventure lit should be sought elsewhere.[37]

Clover goes on to suggest that this "elsewhere" may be found in a somewhat surprising place: *The 9/11 Commission Report*. Clover exposes the *Report* "as drawing on that tradition, finding the content and thereby the style of the adventure novel in 'reality,' in an everyday life which was itself as adventurous as anything an eighteenth-/nineteenth-century novel could conjure."[38]

To support this bold claim, we need only turn to the opening paragraphs of *The 9/11 Commission Report*. Note the atmospheric description of the first sentence: "Tuesday, September 11, 2001 dawned temperate and nearly cloudless in the eastern United States."[39] By the almost Homeric evocation of the dawn, an incredibly strong tone of irony is set—for as the title of the *Report* belies, this story is not about temperance nor is it a celebration of clarity in any sense of the term.

The *Report* moves on to a grand articulation of the masses:

Millions of men and women readied themselves for work. Some made their way
to the Twin Towers, the signature structures of the World Trade Center complex
in New York City. Others went to Arlington, Virginia, to the Pentagon. Across
the Potomac River, the United States Congress was back in session. At the other
end of Pennsylvania Avenue, people began to line up for a White House tour. In
Sarasota, Florida, President George W. Bush went for an early morning run.[40]

This paragraph establishes a plot of political economic intrigue, cinemati-
cally drawing attention as if by aerial view to the sites of the Twin Towers,
the Pentagon, Washington D.C., and finally, zooming in to the solitary figure
of the President on an "early morning run." It is worth noting how this
passage conjures the masses as subjects first and foremost of *work*. Their
national value and identities are discernable via their status as workers; in
this view, none of the "millions of men and women" readied themselves for
play, or simply lingered in eddies of ennui that morning—the implicit suggestion is that *everyone* was living on purpose, in line with a mainstream
of progress. This rhetoric creates a seamless collective of individuals all oriented in the same political-economic direction: this is a "matrix of power"
(to adapt Walter Mignolo's phrase) in which all subjects are expected to
value *work* above all else.[41]

This zooming function of the *Report* carries through the next short
paragraph: "For those heading to an airport, weather conditions could not
have been better for a safe and pleasant journey. Among the travelers were
Mohamed Atta and Abdul Aziz al Omari, who arrived at the airport in
Portland, Maine." Again, the dry tone of irony is noteworthy. The hypo-
thetical "safe and pleasant journey" is the opposite of what happened for air
travelers that day, from the extreme of passengers who died, to the dispersed
throngs of people stranded here and there around the world once all flights
in the United States were grounded.

I want to stress the odd insistence on irony in the opening two paragraphs
of *The 9/11 Commission Report* as evidence for Clover's suggestion that the
style of the adventure novel has been recycled and rediscovered in the materials of everyday life. This ostensibly official informational document should
have no need for such a literary convention—and yet the narrative seems to
call for the interpretive ambiguity that irony demands. My hunch is that the
heavy irony with which the *Report* begins is mandated by the materiality of
the airports, for which certain practices can only be processed by recourse
to speculative imagination.

Consider the *Report*'s description of Mohamed Atta at the Portland
airport:

When he checked in for his flight to Boston, Atta was selected by a computerized prescreening system known as CAPPS (Computer Assisted Passenger

Prescreening System), created to identify passengers who should be subject to special security measures. Under security rules in place at the time, the only consequence of Atta's selection by CAPPS was that his checked bags were held off the plane until it was confirmed that he had boarded the aircraft. This did not hinder Atta's plans.[42]

Recall Martin Amis's remarkably similar description of this same scene in "The Last Days of Muhammad Atta." The symmetric description of CAPPS in Amis and in the *Report* is indicative of the textual life of airports: this security system is a standardized, computerized process linked with virtual realms of speculation and randomization.

If *The 9/11 Commission Report* turns to everyday life as source of high adventure, it is worth noting how the narrativized adventure of 9/11 begins almost immediately at the airport. As we have seen in the three instances of 9/11 fiction discussed above, narratives of 9/11 depend on airport figures as mysterious spaces, as sites that demand interpretation—and yet, these spaces also come bundled with certain assumptions and ideas of airports that are supposed to be clear and distinct.

We have seen how airport settings work to structure narratives and skew time; these operations complicate the mediations and memories of 9/11. While 9/11 is widely maintained to have been an utterly singular event, its literary appropriations—both in fiction and politics—challenge such singularity by casting the materials of this event as imaginable, predictable, and based on the formal logic of repetition. In the works discussed above, airports function as both portals and obstacles for remembering 9/11. Each work demonstrates how imaginary airports recall 9/11—and each airport textually complicates acts of remembering, retelling, and replaying the details of the event. In other words, airports are not merely convenient settings for post-9/11 fiction; the culture of flight provides integral structures that subtend how post-9/11 stories are told in general, in which the singular subject is always subject to perpetual (and perceptual) repetition. The structures of flight, then, complicate the very subject that post-9/11 narratives work to memorialize.

In Chapter 3 we explored the seemingly low stakes of semiotic instability in the Hardy Boys stories, and Chapter 4 examined the high stakes of this investigatory ambience in everyday airport culture and the fiction that recycles this culture. It is now time to focus on the point in airports where the imperatives to detection and intrigue converge: at the security checkpoint, where *screening* becomes a necessary and fraught practice.

CHAPTER 5

THE AIRPORT SCREENING COMPLEX

Confessions of a cross-utilized agent

After September 11, 2001, my job at the airport took on unforeseen aspects. As an airline employee making $7.25 an hour, I was suddenly expected to serve double duty as a sort of ad hoc security guard. The routine act of checking passengers' identifications at the time of check-in (and later, at the boarding gate) took on a heavier, politicized significance. Screening passengers' IDs had always been a minor part of the job, but after 9/11 it became a highly charged—and for some, even an entertaining—part of the job. Several of my coworkers seemed to take perverse satisfaction in the act of consulting the cumbersome three-ring binder called the "No Fly List" whenever they thought a passenger appeared suspicious; this was a totally subjective exercise, based entirely on the passenger's appearance or the level of pronunciation difficulty that a passenger's name posed. During this time, when national security surveillance seemed to merge unflappably with conscious stereotyping and crude prejudices, I began to tune into the vexed practices and problems of what I call *the airport screening complex*.

The airport screening complex has a long history, and is not limited to U.S. culture. However, for the sake of this chapter I focus on a few brief moments in the recent history of this nexus. Rather than provide a definitive portrayal of the airport screening complex, my goal here is to sketch a range of appearances and strange continuities around this emergent cultural form.

The "No Fly List" had arrived at our airport soon after the hijackings, and it was an awkward document to say the least. It was a hodgepodge of names, often redundant or with numerous spelling variations on a theme, and completely physically unwieldy due to its size. The list lived in the office behind our check-in counter, where we airline employees could pore over it in secret to see if we had a match, as the waiting and unsuspecting passengers drummed their fingers on the counter in the terminal. No matter that this was a tiny airport in the middle of the Northern Rocky Mountains—we were constantly reminded that several of the 9/11 hijackers had originally boarded flights in Portland, Maine, whose airport was about the size of ours.

Another new duty was to test the actual security personnel at the checkpoint. We were given rubber knives, toy guns, and simulacral hand grenades, with the directions to try to sneak them through the checkpoint at random intervals as we were making our way to the departure gate to board our flights. The aim of this workaday subterfuge was to keep the security teams on their toes—for we were to report them whenever they missed these concealed replicas. I remember that some of my colleagues took great pleasure in devising elaborate ways to sneak the fake weapons past the checkpoint—for instance, dunking the small fake gun in a large Styrofoam cup of soda and attempting to pass it around the metal detector as they walked through.

The media scholar Lisa Parks has commented on this odd practice in her incisive article "Points of Departure: The Culture of US Airport Screening" (2007). Beyond the instigation of informal security checks performed by ordinary airline employees like myself, there were also official undercover agents responsible for checking the performance of the security screeners. As Parks rightly points out, "there must be profound ontological confusion at the checkpoint. TSA agents are regularly subject to a variety of secret tests by undercover officers and to experiments by citizen vigilantes."[1] In other words, the screeners are always potentially being screened themselves, and sometimes passengers are also screening their own material from view, as a form of covert recreation. Indeed, I recall one time that I was on a flight from Bozeman to Denver and the passenger sitting next to me pulled a very large knife from his jacket pocket, grinning and telling me exactly how he slipped it past security. He was not out to injure or kill anybody; he just liked the idea of sneaking his knife past security and into the sky.

Who can be accurately identified as nefarious when airport workers and undercover officers are paid to *act* like terrorists, and some passengers with no violent intent simply like to test whether they can outsmart the security personnel? How many layers of screening can occur at the checkpoint? In this space of intense scrutiny, what are the operative (if never completely fixed) distinctions between reality and representation? The post-9/11 airport became a slippery zone where subject positions could slide suddenly between those being screened and those screening, between innocent trickster tactics and real/imagined terror threats.

Anatomy of a phrase

The phrase "airport screening" has become synonymous with security. However, the word screening carries a varied set of connotations that intertwine concealment, exposure, entertainment, distraction, and physical sorting. The airport screening complex emerges out of this nexus of meanings.

The *Oxford English Dictionary* entry for the verb form of "screening" reflects the range of meanings that converge around airports. According to the *OED*, screening is defined as:

1. The action of sheltering or concealing with or as with a screen. 2. As a sorting or sifting carried on by means of a screen. 3. The posting of an offender's name upon a screen or public notice-board. 4. A particular showing of a film. 5. The process of exposing a photosensitive surface or forming an image through a screen.[2]

Over the course of this definition, screening comes to encompass two oppositional acts: concealment and exposure. Screening signifies an act of keeping out (sheltering), sorting out, or sifting through material. Screening can also suggest a penal system at work. Or screening can stand for an instance of cinematic entertainment. Additionally, screening denotes the technical reproducibility of an image. The *OED* definition shows screening to be a wonderfully flexible term. And around airports, these many meanings often overlap and intertwine in curious ways.

The most concentrated example of airport screening, as I have indicated above, takes place at the security checkpoint. Here, airport screening effectively conceals the sterile or safe zone from non-passengers (or airport employees whose job does not extend to gate-side). Yet this site also reveals the very transition zone between the sterile and non-sterile parts of an airport: the security checkpoint has become a recognizable image, a cultural trope for anxieties about fixed identity, and for relative expectations of personal safety and global danger. Furthermore, the security checkpoint works to capture images of belongings, to expose the identities of passengers, and potentially to act as a place of public notice for mischievous would-be passengers. Finally, for the sake of this preliminary survey, the security checkpoint sorts out passengers and sends them onto their flights—or not, depending on the contents of one's carry-on bag and the items carried in one's pockets.

Screening becomes something that a body does: a security agent screens passengers and things as they pass through the checkpoint. But screening also becomes something done to a body: passengers are screened by metal detectors, overseen by surveillance gazes, and detected by full-body scanners that process their bodies into analytic images. Screening is also performed by a more abstract "body"—the TSA or even the larger post-9/11 security regime: this is a collective gaze at once more ubiquitous and less visible than any individual agent brandishing a magnetic sensing wand or wearing blue latex gloves. An anatomy of the phrase shows bodies to be in a complex relation to airport screening: humans both administer and are subjected to many acts of screening.

Screening (in) The Terminal

The dimension of screening involving "a particular showing of a film" need not have anything to do with airports, per se. And yet films *about* airports can bring the screening complex into sharp focus, with all its intricate layers of mediation, (in)visibility, and embodiment.

The most sustained example of this reflexive treatment of airport screening occurs in Steven Spielberg's 2004 film *The Terminal*. This movie stars Tom Hanks as the stateless, airport-incarcerated character Viktor Navorski. While in flight to the United States on a personal pilgrimage of sorts, Viktor's homeland government is overthrown. Now without citizenship, he is unable to leave JFK's International Terminal because of his liminal status. Two scenes in particular linger on the airport screening complex.

Near the beginning of the film, Viktor stares intently at the exit doors of the International Terminal. Viktor is not sure whether he should leave the airport; he has been warned by the director of security not to leave. He hesitates. Suddenly Viktor hears the electronic hum of a surveillance camera above him and sees, out of the corner of his eye, that it is tracking his every move. Further in the background, screens displaying departures and arrivals information are visible, blinking in the mezzanine. The scene then cuts to a point-of-view shot from directly above and behind the security camera; then to the same view as seen from the security control room. The security director is startled when Viktor turns abruptly and looks back at him on the closed-circuit television screen.

Figures 5.1–5.4 Stills from *The Terminal* (© 2004 DreamWorks)

Over the course of this scene, the meanings of screening overlap and enfold one another, turning the airport into what the media scholar Gillian Fuller, in her essay on motion aesthetics at the airport, calls "a perceptual machine."[3] Viktor's movements inside the airport are *screened* in the sense of being carefully examined by watchful guards. Viktor is also physically blocked or *screened* by the airport's exit doors; he cannot access the outside of the terminal, where America lies. These same doors filter or *screen* a controlled flow of arriving and departing passengers. In the background, media screens produce a steady stream of departures and arrivals information, images in place-names and time-stamps. And further in the background, out of view, TV monitors display the covert video feeds from of the surveillance cameras, and the security personnel are seen to be hard at work. Finally, the film itself is a big screen production—above all, this is a Hollywood spectacle. This last level of mediation and entertainment reflexively highlights the mediations and entertainment within the plot of the film: as the story unfolds, Viktor becomes an object of *enjoyment* for the security personnel, who watch his various moves and even go as far as to bet on his fate in the airport. (This recalls the very real situation of airport laborers for whom security matters become an object of distraction: playing tricks on the screeners and profiling passengers become ways to pass time during one's work.)

The above scene reveals the airport screening complex in all its aspects, impossibly grasped as a bundle of perceptual technologies, layers of visibility (including the subject of surveillance and the object of the camera), and bodily movements all working simultaneously in dramatic concert. In "Points of Departure," Parks demonstrates how airport security screening is at once the visual exposure of traveling bodies, the manual labor involved therein, and somatic "close sensing"—a mix of hands-on touching and looking at passengers' bodies and belongings. Parks notes how the airport checkpoint is cited as a highly technologized and security-sensitive space; yet the site also requires physical labor that is exhausting, haphazard, low paid, and even injurious. Parks explains how ". . . the most common injuries are muscle and back strains due to heavy lifting, tendonitis, hernias, and cuts and lacerations sustained while reaching into bags for sharp objects."[4] In a space allegedly dedicated to sophisticated methods of mediation and visual perception, screening detours into brute physicality.

In a later scene, Viktor is invited to play a midnight game of poker with the apparently tireless airport employees—but only after he submits to being hoisted into and run through the X-ray machine. One of the airport workers is convinced that Viktor is really an undercover C.I.A. agent, and that Viktor could in fact be trying to root out illegal immigrant airport workers—screening the airport's own, as it were. Thus the airport laborers become suspicious *not* that Navorski is a terrorist threat but that he might in fact expose *their own* questionable backgrounds.

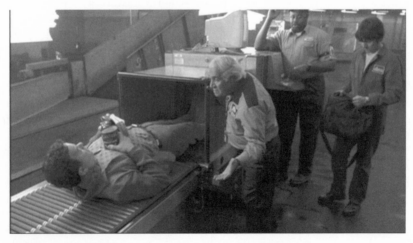

Figure 5.5 Still from *The Terminal* (© 2004 DreamWorks)

This scene of *The Terminal* reflects the haptic overload of the airport screening complex, where the bodies must submit to an over-determined onslaught of being seen, seeing, seeing into, and touching. As we see in *The Terminal*, the airport is an abyss of screens, an architectural matrix of reflexive and (re)productive visualization practices for working, scanning, and filtering bodies in anticipation of flight. And the paradoxical demands of the airport screening complex are not matters of mere fiction; these paradoxical demands are carried out in everyday life, as well.

Video resistance

The airport screening complex became a contested public matter in November 2010, as the Transportation Security Administration (TSA) rolled out "advanced imaging technology" (or AIT) devices at airport checkpoints nationwide. These full-body scanners produce images of passengers' bodies, resembling (depending on the specific device) either "an image that resembles a fuzzy photo negative" or "a chalk etching"—the body is to be fully exposed and yet also made obscure, and thus rendered momentarily anonymous.[5]

These new screening devices produced a range of strong reactions from passengers, from one website that called AIT "porno-scanners,"[6] to another site that decried the new security protocols for impinging on passengers' privacy, encouraging passengers to "opt out" on November 24: one of the busiest U.S. travel days of the year.

The valence of screening that connotes "a particular showing of a film" was activated in a slightly different way around this event. The website "We Won't Fly" encourages "members of the resistance" to video record their experiences with the TSA agents on their mobile devices; indeed, the site even recommends downloading Qik, "a neat little app that instantly uploads your video to their servers"—this, to deter TSA agents who might want to "lie and destroy evidence."[7]

In anticipation of National Opt Out Day, one *New York Times* article reported the following:

> "I hope to see deserted airports," James Babb, a co-founder of We Won't Fly, a protest group that opposes use of the scanners, wrote on his Web site. "But if you want to do it, I say, have some fun with it. Be creative. Wear the kilt. Leave your phone on record. You could be the next YouTube star."[8]

The flippantly mentioned possibility of becoming "the next YouTube star" in fact hits closest to the mark in terms of what is finally at stake for the airport screening complex. This is about being seen, seeing in secret, resisting being seen, and secretly recording what one sees. And also, having fun with it: video resistance is linked with the thrills of exposure through the mass circulation of video, and the allegedly political project is aestheticized—and potentially depleted, having been converted into a media form that Walter

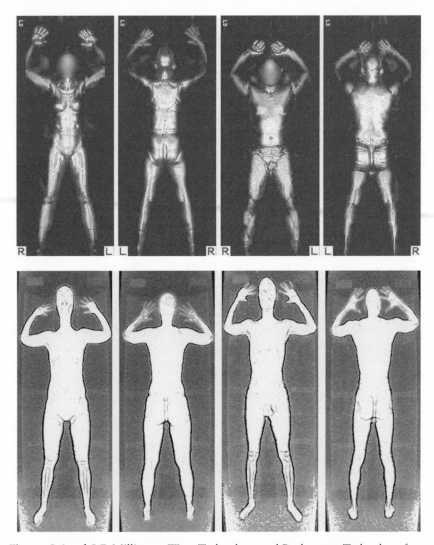

Figures 5.6 and 5.7 Millimeter Wave Technology and Backscatter Technology from www.tsa.gov

Benjamin might have pointed out "requires no attention."[9] On the other hand, the call to video resistance is a familiar move toward useful distraction: like the airport employee security games, weary and patted-down passengers converting the airport security checkpoint into a movie-making pleasure dome effectively turns *work* into *entertainment*. It takes work to submit oneself to the gaze of the TSA; but a little video espionage turns the experience into play.

This is a still frame from John Tyner's covertly recorded encounter with TSA on November 17, 2010:

Figure 5.8 Still from YouTube video posted by John Tyner, San Diego airport

On his way to a routine flight at the San Diego airport, Tyner was selected for extra screening at the security checkpoint. Tyner opted out of the full-body scan and also refused to submit to an enhanced pat down; he was awkwardly detained while various security personnel determined his fate. Tyner recorded the entire episode on his mobile phone; the video clips are mostly of the airport ceiling, with argumentative conversations overheard in the background, including the now infamous moment when Tyner warns a TSA agent not to touch his "junk." In posting his video to YouTube, the TSA screeners became screened, and the debates around security were whipped into fresh turmoil—for a little while, at least.

As for actual security screeners, the work that day in the San Diego airport went on—and this work continues, laborious and largely uneventful. Meanwhile, as if responding to a demand for quantifiable results (and publicly visible ones), the TSA website posts a "TSA Week at a Glance" summary with statistics, such as these for the week of December 6, 2010 through December 12, 2010:

- 5 artfully concealed prohibited items found at checkpoints
- 14 firearms found at checkpoints
- 5 passengers were arrested after investigations of suspicious behavior or fraudulent travel documents.[10]

By creating a visible space online to account for the tantalizing objects of discovery, the TSA participates in the entertaining aspect of the airport screening complex. The objects of discovery are tantalizing precisely by being so vague: what *did* the "artfully concealed" items look like? And what exactly *were* the "prohibited items" in question, after all? What entails "suspicious behavior" in the pantomime of an airport, and what were these five individuals actually arrested for? Security itself, as a reified mode of power and as a practice of discovery, becomes in turn an object of visibility on the TSA website, available for everyday Internet browsers.

The pleasures of airport screening

As my work experiences at the post-9/11 airport indicated, seemingly tight matters of security reveal layers upon layers of deception and trickery—often with no malicious intent, and sometimes even with pleasure. Airport screening functions as an infinite regress of possible official and unofficial screeners, within which various points of interest, intrigue, and entertainment are irreducible.

Then there is Tom Hanks's Viktor Navorski of *The Terminal*, who gradually learns to see through the regime of security, only to be further immersed in the broader scopic economy of the airport. Viktor functions as an object of labor *and* as an object of entertainment for the characters in the film—as well as for the film audience.

The latest debates around full-body scanners likewise conjure the pleasures of airport screening. The call to travelers to video record their enhanced pat downs exposes a double screening imperative: full-body scans are opted out in favor of physical contact; at the same time, video resistance is employed to document the intimate touching. Video imaging is deployed to secure mobility and to aid the labor of screening; but video feeds to other screens also work to document the secret recordings of what happens between the bodies and screening practices in question—and so to serve as a corollary outlet for visual excitement, and the distinct feelings of empowerment and agency that come with posting one's own video to the World Wide Web.

I would now like to suggest that the airport screening complex hinges on *pleasure*. On the one hand, we seem to be amid an old metaphysical conundrum: the question of whether one can apprehend reality by *seeing* it, or whether one needs to see *through* appearances to get to reality. The presupposition of airport screening in all of its guises seems to be that visual evidence is a firm access point to reality, one way or another. On the other hand, like Plato's prisoner who is dragged from the cave only to realize the numerous layers of light sources, shadowy forms, and murky reflections—realizations that do no good when back down in the dark cave—one must admit that in airports too, reality is always more than meets the eye. But in airports, metaphysics is hardly at stake. Rather, what seems to occur is a kind of generalized scopic excitement that overwhelms the banalities of security and the seriousness of flight. As in Plato's cave, one never knows where exactly one *is* in the airport screening complex: at any moment, the screener can be exposed as having been screened. It is an elaborate funhouse of seeing and being seen—and deriving pleasure whenever possible.

Screening is consistently about the pleasures available to screeners, travelers, and spectators alike. This lingering preoccupation was reflected on a timely *New Yorker* magazine cover illustration by Barry Blitt, entitled "Feeling the Love."[11] The illustration shows a TSA agent making out with a passenger who is being subjected to an enhanced pat down. In the background, another TSA agent leans into the frame and looks on, his hand suggestively positioned just off the page. Meanwhile, readers of *The New Yorker* can enjoy the clever portrayal of an exaggerated image of pleasure at the security checkpoint. The airport screening complex is in full effect, a sprawling yet concentrated menagerie of power dynamics and pleasure principles in play. (A similarly themed *Saturday Night Live* skit likewise made ironic fun of the pleasures of airport screening, suggesting that TSA agents could be compared to phone sex workers, offering the service of enhanced pat downs as an added bonus to the mundane routines of holiday travel.)

Airport security relies on numerous modes and methods for seeing and being seen, and this arrangement results in myriad successful flights each day. The physical movement of bodies across vast geographic reaches, connoted by the presence of contrails in the sky, is perhaps the sign par excellence of modern progress. But eerily like Plato's allegorical cave, airports also stand as zero-level sites where bodies are brusquely sorted out, media forms flicker away illusively, and, seen from the right (if unsettling) perspective, all the labors of mobility can appear a vast charade, with no stable referent or reality principle in view. And yet amid all this "ontological confusion," pleasures emerge in reflexive acts of concealment, strategic visibility, video entertainment, and public exposure. These layers work together to comprise the airport screening complex.

A screen in every seat

If screening hinges on pleasure, this in no way means that screening practices are superfluous. Indeed, even at their most pleasurable and seemingly distracting, screens are functional apparatus, administering and facilitating the everyday operations of airports.

For instance, Gillian Fuller helpfully outlines the screening function of airport windows in her essay "Welcome to Windows 2.0: Motion Aesthetics at the Airport." As Fuller explains,

> Airports do not merely sort and sequence our bodies, they also guide our perceptions. Airports work our feelings, as well as our baggage and identification

data. They move us in many ways. We glide on moving walkways in air-condi-
tioned comfort, shielded from the heat of the tarmac and the chill of the rain
that exits and entrances. Cocooned from the smell of avgas and uncontrollable
weather, the sound of planes is barely discernable—the threatening roar of jet
power dampened by thick layers of clear glass. Within the glassy sheath of the
airport, we can hear the chatter of the movement and calm calls of announcement systems. . . . Sensually there is a lot going on, but at the airport the visual
dominates. All senses are diverted to a sublime vision of transparency . . .[12]

Fuller sees airport windows as contributing to a more general screening
matrix, where bodies are inclined toward a scopic economy that privileges a
sense of transparency. In this scenario, physical distance is both called attention to and elided by window screens. Fuller calls attention to the "air condi-
tioned comfort" of the interior space, and the verbs "glide" and "cocooned"
speak to the pleasurable sensations of passing through an airport. Everyone
moving in the space takes part in an event that is projected on or by a three
dimensional screen, of sorts: "the glassy sheath of the airport."

Even as Fuller insists that "the visual dominates" the airport, it is worth
exploring the synaesthetic registers of screening. After all, Fuller's "sublime
vision of transparency" is supplemented by the apophatic references to "the
smell of avgas" and "the heat of the tarmac and the chill of the rain." Indeed,
as Fuller later argues: "One no longer just looks at the screen, one operates through it."[13] As we have seen throughout this chapter, screens always
acquire multiple levels of meaning, and semiotic transgressions are integral to their myriad functions. Therefore, as Fuller indicates, the visual can
usher in (while still dominating) a whole bundle of sensory operations.

Probing further into this synaesthetic airport screening media ecology,
Anna McCarthy, in *Ambient Television: Visual Culture and Public Space*,
discusses the sonic aspect of the CNN Airport Network. Ceiling suspended
TVs distributed throughout terminals and concourses are perhaps the most
innocuous seeming and pervasive evidence of airport screening, in the
entertainment sense of the term. McCarthy points out that the TV screen
as a visual apparatus gives way to an audio component piped throughout
ceilings such that viewers (and non-viewers) can *hear* the sound regardless
of whether the screens are in their line of vision. McCarthy shows how
the CNN Airport Network, with audio levels that adjust automatically to
ambient sounds in the concourse, "places commercial speech precisely at
the threshold of consciousness, a fact that is presented not as the evidence
of the network's insidiousness but rather of its user-friendliness, no different
from any other form of airport communications."[14] The TV screen acts as
a deflective shelter, as it were, for a more pervasive acoustic environment:
the visual screen coordinates with a broader assimilating communications
matrix in the airport.

The absorptive screen also takes flight, as we noted in Don DeLillo's
play *Valparaiso*, wherein the main character watches his own plane take

off, virtually on the screen while feeling it actually happen to his body. A Qantas airlines advertisement (in an Alaska Airlines in-flight magazine, no less) reads: "Relax with personal screens in every seat." The ad features two giddy passengers who are equally and separately fixated on their respective glowing seatback screens—the grinning man plays a video game with both hands, while the woman sips white wine, absorbed in some other program.

Figure 5.9 "Relax with personal screens in every seat" (© Qantas)

Such airline campaigns for personal screens, embraced ever more widely, suggest a confused baseline of desired communication and happy solipsism inherent in flight, and the priority of the visual collapsed into an airborne host of bodily comportments and sensations.

As I have shown in this chapter, networks of screens and practices of screening encompass the culture of flight: screening spreads beyond the checkpoint, and penetrates all aspects of air travel. The closer we look at this tangle, the more elaborate and loose-ended it appears. In Chapter 6, I widen the view in order to consider the subject of airports at large—how airports themselves can be rethought of along lines of aesthetic and philosophic experimentation. Airports are more than just transition zones: they are spaces for study.

CHAPTER 6

AIRPORT STUDIES

Public art tour

In May 2005, a friend and I drove to the Sacramento airport. We were not going to fly anywhere that day, nor were we planning to pick anyone up. In fact, we were headed to the airport to go on an art tour conducted by the Sacramento Metropolitan Arts Commission. The airport had just completed the installation of two new pieces of public art, and the free tour was in honor of these latest additions to the landscape.[1]

Over the course of the tour, we were led around the various parts of the terminal, and we even lingered before the daunting security checkpoint underneath a glowing, sound-emitting art installation hanging from the ceiling.

Figure 6.1 "Chromatic Oasis" by Christopher Janney at the Sacramento airport (author's photo)

It felt strange to be somewhat interrupting the hustle and bustle of the airport in order to experience this dazzlingly interactive artwork. "Chromatic Oasis," by Christopher Janney, is a sound and light sculpture. It casts a magenta glow on those who pass beneath; motion sensors trigger precision light beams as well as local sounds such as chirping native birds and cottonwood leaves rustling in wind—but not roaring jet engines or relayed security announcements, interestingly. At this point, we noted how the airport posits itself as a place-specific presence while at the same time placing its own natural sounds under erasure. And curiously, we were being subjected to the high-tech monitoring devices of an art object, in close proximity to the security checkpoint, where further methods of exposure were taking place.

To view this piece of art, we had to travel up the escalator from the main check-in area, which is open to the public; however, to ascend this escalator without a boarding pass is to transgress—for a sign at the bottom of the escalator clearly warns that the upper level is for ticketed passengers only. Here we were, caught in a camera phone shot snapped by my friend, as we headed up the escalator without tickets and with no plans to fly; we were on our way to look at art:

Figure 6.2 Escalator to security checkpoint in Terminal A at the Sacramento airport (photo by Dan Thomas-Glass)

This sculpture was thus positioned in an area supposedly off-limits to us, since we were neither traveling passengers nor airport employees. Therefore, its status as "public art" is debatable. And yet under the auspices of admiring art, we were allowed to tarry under the eerie radiance of "Chromatic Oasis."[2]

We observed fixed art installations scattered around the airport, and we also saw so-called plop art: these were temporary pieces set up by the Sacramento Metropolitan Arts Commission throughout the airport that could be moved around or replaced at will. Such art, contained in glass cases and positioned innocuously around the terminal, can end up creating curious visual juxtapositions, as this stand-alone piece in Sacramento did:

Figure 6.3 "Plop art" at the Sacramento airport (author's photo)

Over the course of this tour the airport opened up as a place for study. The art called for contemplation and speculation; but gradually, the entire space began to feel observable, a space itself to be studied. We were not thinking about departure times, the weight of checked baggage, or where the arrivals area was—we were reflecting on art.

As we experienced the airport as an art space, this bled into how we viewed all of the normal operations of flight happening all around. Airport studies began to emerge everywhere we looked: they were not contained by frames or glass cases, unless these frames were the fences at the perimeter of the airfield, or the glass cases were the very windows and walls of the terminal.

At a certain point the docent who was leading the tour made a bold proclamation: "Art means different things to different people." This idea of art being open to interpretation may sound obvious, and yet such a statement seemed eerily incongruous with the normative protocols and procedures of the airport; for airports to function effectively, after all, they really cannot be *too* open to interpretation. And yet, as we discovered that day, public art could convert the highly functional node into a site of open study. This suggested an elastic threshold of understanding: airports *could* in fact remain functional while also being open to interpretation. (We saw this in Chapter 5 with security screening.)

Throughout the remainder of this book, I return to particular artworks around the Sacramento airport, as several of the pieces represent critical semiotic thresholds in the textual life of airports. In this chapter, however, I focus on a range of airport studies that evince just how elastic the threshold of interpretation can be; that is, I want to show how airports can be rethought simultaneously to their active presence. In this chapter I explore a variety of literary, acoustic, and visual texts that call on airports to do a variety of different things besides facilitate travel. This chapter assembles a textual life that is at turns ironic, aesthetic, therapeutic, and philosophic— these are airport studies.

Hell, horses, and horsemen

One thing that has always struck me as odd is how people tend to talk about airports as dreadful places, particularly after a long delay or a lost bag incident—but when I suggest that perhaps air travel will cease because of how dreadful airports are, the same people become appalled and refuse to entertain this notion. Indeed, people are often all too willing to reassert the fixed status of airports and air travel as irrevocably essential to modern life. In short, many people seem to hold an ambivalent opinion about airports, at once hating them and needing them to exist.

This spatial ambivalence can be exploited in interesting ways, as evinced by the public art tour at the Sacramento airport. The extreme attitudes concerning airports—as at once awful and absolutely necessary—leave space in between for critical thinking. The following three examples hint at the range of possibilities for airport studies.

Annie Proulx's satirical story "I've Always Loved This Place" narrates a hilarious postmodern Devil who rides around Hell on a golf cart and comes up with the idea "to upgrade the current facilities."[3] One of the Devil's big plans is to renovate "the Welcome to Hell foyer" to include the "combined features of the world's worst air terminals, Hongqiao in Shanghai the ideal, complete with petty officials, sadomasochistic staffers, consecutive security checks of increasing harshness, rapidly fluctuating gate changes and departure times"—and all of this is to end with, "finally, a twenty-seven-hour trip in an antiquated and overcrowded bucket flying through typhoons while rivets popped against the fuselage."[4] In this glib assessment, Proulx employs airport tropes for ironically evil ends, suggesting that normal operations of flight, when taken cumulatively, might suitably add up to the entrance way to eternal damnation.

"I've Always Loved This Place" is one of Proulx's iconic "Wyoming stories," and the Devil is cast as a sort of latter-day cowboy. But what does this story have to do with Wyoming? Hardly anything. Yet by a point of contrast, and nestled within the frontier imaginary of the Wyoming stories, airport commonplaces function as phenomenological antitheses to the individualist and rural ideals of the American West—and it is these tropes of Wyoming that Proulx is so effective at complicating and exposing for their ideological pitfalls. By recasting the frenzy of air travel as a form of eternal damnation, Proulx challenges the basic teleology of American frontier narratives: what we think of as the leading edge of progress might just be the makings of our own suffering.

Across the state line, an interesting corollary case study emerged, this one around a real airport. In February 2008, Louis Jiménez's sculpture "Mustang" was installed at the gateway to the Denver International Airport. The sculpture is a 32-foot blue horse, replete with red LED eyes, in the pop-Western motif that Jiménez is known for. Airport art is often intended to tranquilize the space/time of travel; or as one *New York Times* article about this sculpture put it, airport art is commonly used "like visual Dramamine to soothe travelers' nerves."[5]

However, Jiménez's "Mustang" provoked outrage from many residents of Denver, who felt as though the horse was a bad omen of sorts, a downer in too-close proximity to what should be the uplifting ambience of flight. As one *Wall Street Journal* article reported:

> "It looks like it's possessed," says Denver resident Samantha Horoschak. "I have a huge fear of flying anyway, and to be greeted at the airport by a demon horse—it's not a soothing experience."[6]

This worry about possession and demons returns us to Annie Proulx's satirical airport, but in real time. On the one hand, the airport is acknowledged as a frightening place; on the other hand, the artwork does something to tip the experience into transcendent terror. "Mustang" is by all accounts authentic Western art: Jiménez is an acclaimed artist whose works play on intersections of tradition (a horse) and postmodern culture (LED lights). Yet there was something about this intersection *at the airport* that seemed to implicitly turn regional aesthetics *against* the airport. It was not received as a piece of soothing art, but as an *airport study*: it brought too much awareness to the space and unsettled fliers and citizens. Something akin to Proulx's proto-Western Devil, Jiménez's "Mustang" calls on traditions of the West only to make tremble broader narratives of progress and expansion—everyday airport life.

Curiously enough, like Proulx's story, "Mustang" also spurred an Eastern allusion. A Denver resident organized a campaign on behalf of the outraged, to compose and collect "protest haiku" against the sculpture. One reads as such:

> Because of this thing
> People think they are in hell
> Instead of Denver.[7]

This recourse to a Japanese literary form exhibits an almost reflexive textual and aesthetic impulse: it was as if the airport art had to be countered by *more* study, inspired from another part of the globe. Never mind the absence of seasonal imagery, or the rather bland evocation of "hell"—most interesting is how the airport gets so easily entangled in matters of religious language and literary form. The airport art prompts an explosive (if not exactly rigorous) *study* in language and culture.

It is as though Proulx's fantastical yarn and the real politics of Denver airport art go hand in hand. Each airport is yoked to an idea of the East: for Proulx it is "Hongqiao in Shanghai the ideal" worst airport; in the case of "Mustang," haiku are adopted as an aesthetic antidote to the rearing horse of the West. In both cases, wide-reaching affects of airports are studied, and attention lingers on the dark matters of flight. Flight itself becomes an afterthought or a sideshow (as in Proulx's tacking on of a 27-hour flight in a dilapidated airliner), and the heavy feel of life in and around the airport takes priority.

As if to make this final point clear, one airport employee expressed her feelings about "Mustang" this way: "When they unwrapped it, I was just horrified . . . It makes me feel like I'm looking at something out of a science-fiction movie."[8] This claim is fascinating given the specific context of the airport: amid jets thundering into the sky and descending to land, and all manner of machines operating on the ground in the service of flight—how exactly does a *horse* come to induce the feeling of science fiction? It is worth noting that this employee was not just any random airport worker: she was an air traffic controller. In other words, from the perspective of the control tower, the feeling of science fiction arrives neither from the elevated vantage point nor from the intricate tracking technologies of flight; it was a Western artwork that threw the site into a realm of interpretation and speculation—an airport study. Art exposed the textual life of airports, exploding across genres and challenging any easy reading.

Another literary example further outlines the range of airport studies. In Joseph O'Neill's novel *Netherland* there is a very literal case of an airport being reconceived, and studied for an alternative use. In this scene, the main character and his friend Chuck tour a potential site where they might create a cricket field:

> We turned south onto the unpopulated, quasi-rural section of Flatbush Avenue, where the road was lined with barren trees. Half a mile or so down, Chuck swung left through a wide gateway and onto a concrete private road. This led to a no-man's-land of frozen bushes and scrubland. Another turn, leftward, led to an immense white emptiness. The snow had not been plowed from this portion of the road, and like a wagoner, Chuck steered and bumped us along in the hardened ruts of old tracks. A desolate, complex of buildings— warehouses, a tower—was now in view on the left. The sky, aswirl with fleet, darkening clouds, was magnified by the flat null steppe that lay to the east. If a troupe of Mongolian horsemen had appeared in the distance I would not have been shocked.
>
> "Jesus," I said, "where are we?"
>
> Chuck, both hands on the wheel, spurted the Cadillac forward. "Floyd Bennett Field, Brooklyn," he said.
>
> As he spoke, the tower assumed a familiar outline. This was once an airfield, I realized. We were on an old taxiway.[9]

In the rambling first paragraph of this passage, the airfield lurks and looms at both the periphery and eventually as the center of the scene: the airport serves as a "barren," open space that actually startles the narrator into uttering "Jesus"—and we are thus thrust back into the quasi-theologies circulating around Proulx's airport hell and Jiménez's Western art.

For O'Neill, the obscure airfield stands as a long, detouring pathway to introducing the character Chuck and his obsession with the sport of cricket. The leveling out of landforms, and the stock masses of the old airport, create empty space and yet firm structure for developing the character of Chuck. The airport is simultaneously a blasted wasteland and fertile narrative ground. The airport is counterintuitively cast as an organic zero level: an "immense white emptiness"—almost a blank page. Idyllic, individualistic fantasies and the hard realities of cosmopolitanism are in friction throughout this post-9/11 novel; in this oblique airport scene, Western civilization is at once wiped away and exposed in stark, skeletal form.

This imaginary airport scene follows the logic of what I called *terminal immaterial* in Chapter 3: this happens when literary representations of airports are put to use in such ways that the actual operations of flight vanish—the airport simply creates a flattened, open space for other observations and reflections (and usually grim ones, at that). The other observation in *Netherland* is, once again, an Orientalist hallucination: the "Mongolian horsemen" riding into the open terrain suggest an anxiety about distant spaces and political relations. Like Proulx's Hongqiao, and like the haiku prompted by the sculpture "Mustang," an imagined Far East is projected around the airport. Interestingly, in O'Neill's geographic mirage there is a glimmer of something like *ecology*: O'Neill seems to be tapping into how airports make manifest migration patterns and material obsolescence. I take up the subject of airports and ecology in Chapter 7 of this book; for now, there are more airport studies to consider.

Music for airports

In *The Global Soul*, the travel writer Pico Iyer writes:

> A modern airport is based on the assumption that everyone's from somewhere else, and so in need of something he can recognize to make him feel at home; it becomes, therefore, an anthology of generic spaces—the shopping mall, the food court, the hotel lobby—which bear the same relation to life, perhaps, that Muzak does to music.[10]

This rich description holds many clues to the textual life of airports—perhaps most obviously the phrase "anthology of generic spaces." This suggests that airports are first and foremost places to *read*, as I argued in Chapter 1. For the purpose of this chapter, I focus on the sonic parallel that Iyer posits here. What would it mean to think about airports as "generic" musical spaces? What meanings do airports take on or emit when studied with ambient sound in mind?

Iyer means the comparison of airports to Muzak to serve as just that: an analogy. And yet, I think there is more to this than a simple comparison. After all, Brian Eno's album *Ambient 1: Music for Airports* was composed specifically with the uninspiring sound of airports in mind—according to Eno, the point was to resist the comfortable predictability of Muzak in favor of more truly "environmental music"—music that would work with the "tint" of particular surroundings.[11] The four tracks of *Ambient 1* were originally installed in the Marine Air Terminal at New York's LaGuardia Airport; rumor has it that Eno's piece was decommissioned because the music unsettled passengers, making it all too clear that they were indeed in an airport. Eno's aesthetic project succeeded entirely, working with and enhancing, as it were, the peculiar feel of airport life: being in between. But consequently, the generic and unconscious aspect of air travel was reasserted, as if the kind of cultural reflection made by Pico Iyer makes it available only from a certain distance.

If the airport became a staging ground for Eno's experiment with ambient music, in a surprising reversal the high-end accessory store Brookstone® harnessed and repurposed airport sounds in one of their sound machine models designed to aid travelers' sleep: the setting called "Jet Lag" reproduces the muffled sounds of safety announcements, beeping passenger carts, and calls to boarding.[12] In the removed sphere of a hotel room, one might recreate the somnolent aura of airport interiors.

At another remove, the interior acoustics of airports have been given a strong textual value in literary works. Consider this scene in Don DeLillo's *Underworld*:

> Matt Shay sat in the terminal at the airport in Tucson and listened to announcements bouncing off the walls. . . . There was a man being paged known only as Jack. . . . There was a man in a wheelchair eating a burrito. . . . Whenever the ambient voice asked someone to pick up the white courtesy phone, a small girl made a fist and spoke into it.[13]

The airport in this scene is not a passive setting. Rather, the character Matt Shay is barraged with a cacophony of sights and sounds that seem at once normal and utterly bizarre. Causal relations are evacuated between burrito and wheelchair, and between the ambient voice and the pantomiming girl— the music of airports becomes a phantasmagoric world in the middle of the desert. The terminal is a labyrinthine construction: it is a dense techno-social confluence that requires hyper-attention.

As if to reinforce this point, disjointed but familiar airport sounds are sprinkled throughout the novel: "Wait-listed passenger Lundy please present yourself at the podium."[14] Such fragments function as the contemporary white noise that DeLillo likes so well: the airport is reconceived as a boom box of (post)modern life.

The poet Maxine Kumin likewise appropriates such sounds in her poem "Getting around O'Hare," which quotes Chicago O'Hare airport's recorded voice that commands from the ceiling, "*look down. The walkway is ending.*"[15] Kumin evokes the ambient airport noises as an implicit critique to heaven-oriented theology: the more urgent concerns lie in front of us, on the ground.

The sounds of airports have inspired other avenues of study. Consider the philosopher Stewart Cohen's "Three Approaches to the Airport Case":

> Mary and John are at the L.A. airport contemplating taking a certain flight to New York. They want to know whether the flight has a layover in Chicago. They overhear someone ask a passenger Smith if he knows whether the flight stops in Chicago. Smith looks at the flight itinerary he got from the travel agent and responds, "Yes I know, it does stop in Chicago." It turns out that Mary and John have a very important business contact they have to make at the Chicago airport. Mary says, "How reliable is that itinerary, it could be a misprint, they could have changed the schedule at the last minute." Mary and John agree that Smith doesn't really *know* that the plane will stop in Chicago on the basis of the itinerary. They decide to check with the airline agent.[16]

Cohen employs this model to explore how "knowledge ascriptions [seem to] involve some kind of standards variability."[17] As an airport study, this narrative simulation draws from the ambient sounds (overheard conversation specific to the culture of flight), whirring machinery (the possibility of a misprinted itinerary), and general flux of a terminal setting ("last minute" schedule changes). Cohen's inquiry into knowledge conditions depends on the uncertain space/time of the airport, particularly as mediated through "overheard" reports. A philosophical investigation springs forth from the music of airports.

Another instance of study prompted by airport sounds—this one from the outside, at a distance—hints at metaphysical connections between noise, meaning, and silence. This is from John Cage's aphoristic essay "Indeterminacy":

> Suzuki never spoke loudly. When the weather was good the windows were open, and the airplanes leaving La Guardia flew directly overhead from time to time, drowning out whatever he had to say. He never repeated what had been said during the passage of the airplane.[18]

Here, Cage reflects on the airport and its airborne prostheses as environmental obstacles of sorts. The aircraft leaving La Guardia get in the way of Suzuki's teachings, creating lacunae in the lessons. For Cage the noise of aircraft on ascent interrupts and cancels out "what had been said" by Suzuki: one set of meanings (the decipherable noise of air travel) is able to override another (Suzuki's speech), which becomes indecipherable. However, Suzuki's words seem to take on more meaning by being muted: they become "never repeated" and thus stand against the repetitive sounds of aircraft taking off. Cage studies the noise of airports in order to fashion a Zen koan of sorts.

To round out this section on the textual layers of music for airports, consider David Kranes's short story "The Wishbone," in which a terminal is imagined as a hideaway spot for two young lovers:

> One Sunday, on about our third weekend, we took a bus out to International Airport. It was because we couldn't stay apart. I remember we kissed at four twenty-one on the observation deck. There were jet trails going peach in the sky above us, and we danced (very quietly) to the music they were playing in the United terminal.[19]

In this passage, airport music functions as far more than a mere background effect. Rather, the narrator of this story experiences airport music as one part of a whole synaesthetic ensemble, involving an exact sense of time by which to recall kisses, and absent planes whose condensation traces remain, deliciously aglow on the depthless ceiling. This airport scene both consolidates and expands the whole project of flight, converting all the noise of progress into a quiet dance under the sign of an airline brand that might also stand for a feeling of intimacy: United. Here again, the airport studied for its own ambience attains an almost ecological register, perhaps causing the reader to rethink the meaning of a simple corporate logo, and to reconsider reaches of airspace under the rubric of romantic time. To see the airport in this alternative light is to hear airport music differently—to imagine destinations beyond those reachable by air, yet closer to hand.

Destination terminal

As I have shown, airport studies draw subjects other than flight into the foreground of perception and thought. Music for airports is one form of art that can achieve this cognitive shift. I want to look at the lyrics of an actual song as a way of moving even more fully into the topic of creatively (re) inhabited airports.

Ani DiFranco's 1999 song "The Arrivals Gate" is about going to the airport to people watch—in this song, actual planes exist on the periphery of consciousness, if anywhere. This is a markedly pre-9/11 tune, at once celebrating an innocent form of entertainment and insinuating the airport as an inherently creepy site.

As the song begins, we might note a familiar feel. Vaguely melancholy and undulating tones are set to an ambient electronic beat. We are in the vicinity of music for airports: it is atmospheric and slightly off-kilter, not quite memorable. When DiFranco's syncopating banjo strumming suddenly arrives, an upbeat tone offsets the melancholy, as if anticipating the ambivalent lyrics to come. The first verse introduces an explicit airport study:

> Gonna go out
> to the arrivals gate at the airport
> and sit there all day
> watch people reuniting
> public affection is so exciting
> it even makes airports o.k.
> watching children run
> with their arms outstretched
> just to throw those arms
> around their grandpas' necks
> watching lovers plant kisses
> old men to their misses
> at the arrivals gate

Rather than functioning as a point of origin or transit to be passed through on the way to far-flung destinations, this song imagines the terminal *as* a destination, existing "out" in a nonspecific borderland, a place to see things happening. This is an all-day event, and DiFranco immediately imbues the airport with a voyeuristic potential that certifies the site as an "o.k." space. The emphasis on "watching" ranges across romantic and domestic connections, situating the airport as a simultaneously public and private place, and one rife with affections of all types.

The second verse continues the theme of watching, and interestingly converts this act into that of *being watched*. While this airport context is absent the post-9/11 security regime, the lyrics of this song nevertheless gently nudge us in the (multiple) direction(s) of the airport screening complex:

> watching a mother
> with a mother's smile
> don't tell me to move
> I just wanna sit here for a while
> I have determined
> it's a sure cure for cancer
> watching excitement turn family dogs
> into dancers
> at the arrivals gate

As we note the singer's slow-motion perception of facial expressions, our reading becomes surveillance: suddenly the singer is being asked to leave, to stop loitering—which is precisely what DiFranco wants to do, to "sit here for a while" and watch. And yet, as if reflecting the ever-changing landscape of the terminal, the song suddenly switches subjects. DiFranco abruptly and whimsically suggests a medicinal value for the airport: "it's a sure cure for cancer." This claim perhaps demonstrates the tenacity of the airport as a non-place, as it is effectively translated into another kind of non-place: the modern hospital or pharmacy. The actual "cure" in question here arrives in the form of a circus scene of sorts, with airport reconnections seen through a canine lens; in this contact zone, DiFranco notices an interspecies web that Donna Haraway might call the "natureculture" of airports.[20]

This attentiveness to the wide-ranging affects and encounters at the arrivals gate continues in the next verse, which takes on a somber, almost sinister tone:

> I got me a white bread sandwich
> with some shredded lettuce
> and I got me a ringside view
> for my quaint little fetish
> I just wanna drain my little pink heart
> of all its malice
> and kick back for the afternoon
> in this fluorescent palace

Behind this verse one might hear sounds reminiscent of Brian Eno's piano chords in *Music for Airports*, as if signaling how the all too ambient feel of the airport has infected the song. DiFranco notes her sandwich as a "strange stranger" of sorts, an uncannily familiar object that, in the space of the airport, becomes weirdly objectified.[21] These mass-produced consumer food objects—white bread and shredded lettuce—become overdetermined in the space of air travel, as if reflecting the whorls of production and consumption that define the culture of flight. The airport itself gradually blurs over the course of this verse, overwhelmed as it is by metaphoric analogs, including a boxing ring and a "fluorescent palace." DiFranco's perspective becomes darker in these lines, and she admits to having to drain her "little pink heart / of all its malice." The airport again arrives as a kind of therapeutic zone, where one can "kick back"— all of this takes place at a remove from the immediate cycles and flows of flight. In other words, DiFranco's song studies the airport in a multiplex fashion, enjoying it via observation, and yet exposing it as a site rife with strange values, from the violent connotation of the boxing ring to the quasi-religious mention of airport loitering as a "fetish," as something with its own internal social life.

The closing lines of the song draw out a vaguely theological reading of airports, evoking yet another layer of non-placement:

> everyone's in a hurry
> here in purgatory
> except for me
> I'm where I need to be
> here at the arrivals gate.[22]

DiFranco's song reinstates the airport as non-place again and again by serving as a shimmering interpretive surface, comparable with a host of other non-places, not unlike Pico Iyer's "anthology of generic spaces."

What I find striking about this song is how it participates in a sort of mainstream textual life of airports, and yet also serves as a platform for studying the eccentricities of airports. DiFranco engages in active interpretation of the airport as a social text, and in the process the song becomes tacky, as it were: as this song about the airport unfolds, it spirals out and becomes about a range of familiar but unrelated objects, narratives, and feelings. The song starts off jubilant and quirkily collective, and gradually becomes melancholy and singular: in the end, the singer is alone and where she needs to be, at the arrivals gate with no plans to fly, at an uncertain ending.

Lingering in non-places and writing about it

Ani DiFranco's song "The Arrivals Gate" in fact falls in line with an explicit aesthetic project: the idea of going to the airport explicitly to observe everyday life is what the psycho-geography influenced *Lonely Planet Guide to Experimental Travel* calls "Airport Tourism." This ironic form of travel consists of spending "24 hours in an airport without getting on a plane."[23] As the guidelines explain: "This experiment offers the opportunity to turn a place of transit into the actual destination."[24] Like DiFranco's tune, this situationist form of travel studies the airport as an interesting location in and of itself, and thus attempts to reorient the traveler's perspective such that the minutiae of flight take on fresh appeal. And like DiFranco's song, airport tourism results in a *text*, an interpretive lens through which the subject of flight can be studied.

The chapter on airport tourism goes on to narrate a cheap adventure, in which a sort of ethnographic "airport tourist" by the name of Michael Clerizo wanders around the Heathrow airport observing the flows of mobility, making friends, and watching "the show" of departures and arrivals.[25] Already, we should be tuning into familiar themes concerning the spectacle value of flight: no mere transit zone, the airport is conceived as an entertainment space.

Also like DiFranco's song, the airport becomes a reservoir of the mundane. Clerizo shares what he learned during his extended stay at the airport:

> Unlike my previous journeys to airports, I had not once glanced at my watch. Time didn't matter. Nor had I constantly performed my usual nervous ritual of fumbling through my pockets, making sure I had my passport, ticket and credit cards. All that was for people who were actually going somewhere. Me, I was just going to hang out. I didn't even have my passport with me—just a toothbrush, toothpaste, lots of stuff to read, a notebook and several pens.[26]

Clerizo's textual record of this experiment resembles and expands on DiFranco's "quaint little fetish." While just there to "hang out," as time slips away Clerizo finds the airport to require a personal inventory of affects— recalling DiFranco's "white bread sandwich / with some shredded lettuce." And this inventory ends with materials for *reading* and *writing*: the experimentally inhabited airport resembles the regularly inhabited airport through its maintained *textual* life.

Curiously, the suggestion that "time didn't matter" is complicated in the Lonely Planet guide by the heavy presence of temporal markers that frame Clerizo's ethnographic paragraphs: each note is given a time-stamp, so that we know, for instance, that somewhere around 4:00 P.M. Clerizo discovers in Terminal 2 "a few rows of comfortable seats overlooking its arrival area."[27] This form of experimental travel is time-bound indeed; the goal, as Clerizo explains it, involves "*spending time* away from workaday cares and responsibilities, exploring places, observing people and indulging your inner child."[28] Whereas DiFranco's song understands the airport as a potential spectacle, and airport tourism as a spontaneous hobby of sorts, the Lonely Planet guide imposes quite strict rules whereby a full twenty-four hours of airport inhabitance must be "spent." And as Clerizo has hinted, a large portion of this involves textual expenditure: reading and writing.

Almost at the outset of his adventure, Clerizo's textually enmeshed project is already exposed:

As Douglas Adams observed in *The Long Dark Tea-Time of the Soul,* "It can hardly be a coincidence that no language on earth has ever produced the expression, 'As pretty as an airport'" . . . My plan is to pass some of my 24 hours searching for something 'pretty.'[29]

In this passage the airport tourist doubles as a literary reader, as Clerizo resorts to an outside text as a way of constructing a plan for his time in the airport. Flight is rendered all but irrelevant; matters of citation and questions of aesthetics take priority. Clerizo's noble "plan" gets somewhat derailed as the night at the airport unfolds; by the end, he is exhausted from playing around in the airport, "floor-skating" in his socks down the tunnels between parts of the terminal. The airport fades into an ambient background and Clerizo's narrative episodes take priority. Being present in the airport is supplemented by the need to document the journey, to write about being in the ironic destination.

An expanded version of airport tourism took place in 2009, when London's Heathrow airport employed the writer Alain de Botton to spend "a week at the airport," in order to write the eponymous book. The intention was to inaugurate the new Terminal 5 by inviting a writer-in-residence to observe and document what he saw—to create a textual airport study. As de Botton describes it, his task was "to conduct an impressionistic survey of the premises and then, in full view of the passengers and staff, draw together material for a book at a specially positioned desk in the departures hall between zones D and E."[30] This idea of transparency is fascinating, for it seems to suggest that there is something otherwise *hidden* in the textual life of airports. Indeed, de Botton's findings are often less than upbeat; at one point, he ruminates: "There is a painful contrast between the enormous objective projects that we set in train, at incalculable financial and environmental cost—the construction of terminals, of runways and wide-bodied aircraft—and the subjective psychological knots that undermine their use."[31]

As the week unfolds, de Botton finds that his centrally located writer's desk "turned out to be an ideal spot in which to do some work, for it rendered the idea of writing so unlikely as to make it possible again."[32] The airport stands opposed to writing, and therefore invites it. De Botton goes on to consider how "the presence of a writer occasionally raised expectations that something dramatic might be on the verge of occurring, the sort of thing one could read about in a novel."[33] And of course this is precisely what happens as de Botton writes his book—which is not quite a novel but nevertheless follows a carefully structured arc—and records his various meetings with travelers and airline employees alike. The airport lends itself to the text, even as the spectacle of a text-in-progress heightens the sense of the airport's own narrative possibilities.

Toward the beginning of the book, De Botton articulates his rationale for the project as such: "In a world full of chaos and irregularity, the terminal seemed a worthy and intriguing refuge of elegance and logic. It was the imaginative centre of contemporary culture."[34] There is a tension implicit in this sentiment: the airport is at once the "refuge" and the "centre"—the state of exception *and* the point of reference for contemporary culture. Walking this fine line, de Botton does equal justice to the normal and the bizarre residing in the airport. But over the course of the week, de Botton's speculations become more and more existentially inflected. By the end, de Botton comes to see airport inhabitants as "creatures of appalling fragility and vulnerability."[35] While there are certainly opportunities for philosophical reflection at the airport, de Botton concludes inconclusively: "We will need to go back and learn the important lessons of the airport all over again soon."[36] In other words, the knowledge conferred by airports is not cumulative or translatable beyond one's trip; these "lessons" slip past consciousness once we leave the airport. This is a subtly scathing report on our ability to think critically about airports—as if they somehow evade our intellectual grasp. This also makes de Botton's book a paradoxical document, in which he strives to communicate or transport difficult truths that are quite site-bound.

Like DiFranco's song "The Arrival's Gate," de Botton's book starts out by celebrating the culture of flight, and ends up rather hesitant about the uniform hurry and teleological drive of human progress. At one point, de Botton goes on a predawn drive around the runways with an airport worker, looking "for stray bits of metal."[37] When he sees a field mouse scurry onto the runway, de Botton pauses to reflect: "Its presence this night on the moonlit tarmac served optimistically to suggest that when mankind is finished with flying—or more generally, finished with *being*—the earth will retain a capacity to absorb our follies and make way for more modest forms of life."[38]

As we have seen, airport studies offer ways to think about how these spaces connect to vaster timescales and profound sensations of being; de Botton discovers at the airport a humbling ecological perspective, one that radically diminishes human activities and emphasizes the tenacity of life conceived more broadly. And yet paradoxically again, the airport is central to this realization.

Ani DiFranco, Michael Clerizo, and Alain de Botton seem to be approaching similar questions concerning what happens when airport studies take priority over flight. These experiments in misuse render the spaces and processes of flight at once strange and familiar—airports become exposed as uncanny objects. Throughout this chapter, we have seen a variety of attempts to integrate and account for how these sites have become part of the fabric and weave of everyday life on our planet. In Chapter 7, I want to turn more fully to this eccentric line of inquiry: how airports figure as environmental topoi in the culture of flight.

Chapter 7

Ecology in Waiting

I'll Never Make It

I wish to begin this chapter by looking at a *New Yorker* cartoon by Leo Cullum, published in 2008.

Figure 7.1 © Leo Cullum, The New Yorker Collection at www.cartoonbank.com (reprinted by permission)

This cartoon depicts a man in tattered clothing crawling across a desert landscape. Cacti and rocky buttes line the horizon. From the left edge of the frame, an announcement emanates: "FLIGHT 22 TO J.F.K. NOW BOARDING . . . GATE 46"—and above the man's badly sunburned visage, a thought bubble appears: "I'LL NEVER MAKE IT." In what sort of airport do we find this forlorn traveler? Does this expansive and rough terrain sardonically conjure the miserable distance between departure gates? Or is the airport such a clamorous site that its interpellations can be heard from miles away, far out in the wilderness? I must admit that I still struggle to fully understand the humor of this cartoon. Is it funny because our traveler is suffering *in* an airport, or because he is suffering *outside* of an airport in order to *get there*? These two possibilities house very different implications in terms of how we interpret the arid landscape around this unfortunate soul.

If we are to interpret the desert in this drawing *as* the airport, a further question arises: Why satirize airports as "natural" environments in the first place? It sounds counterintuitive; common sense would tell us that airports infringe on, interrupt, or even poison ecosystems (think of the rivulets of de-icing fluid that pour into drainage canals at the edge of tarmacs all winter long). And yet, people do inhabit airports, whether for work, in transit, or due to indefinite delays. We might say that airports are a human habitat—no metaphor required.

In his book *Naked Airport: A Cultural History of the World's Most Revolutionary Structure*, Alastair Gordon claims that the idea of "airport-ness" emerged as a cultural concept in the 1950s. According to Gordon, as airports became increasingly familiar to people, this space took on its own legibility: travelers learned how to *read* airports as a space at once oriented toward jet flight and also grounded in specific architectural and interior motifs. Airports not only became increasingly inhabited cultural nodes; they also became places that one could experience and evoke out of context as a distinct type of bracketed space. For instance, in the 1968 film *2001: A Space Odyssey*, Stanley Kubrick represents a futuristic space station as a completely mundane airport. The idea of airportness suggests a basic form of environmental awareness, through which people take note of how space *feels*, and how species move in a particular system. In Leo Cullum's cartoon a boarding announcement signifies an airport, and text skews the context: a pictorial desert acquires *airportness* through just a few words.

But the airport in the cartoon is absurdly discontiguous with this land-scape. It is as if by metaphorizing a parched desert as an airport, attention to detail is precisely *lost*. Airportness, as a kind of environmental perception, both succeeds and fails in this particular context. This cartoon goes against the environmental writer Gary Snyder's assertion that crawling can help people get to know their bioregions. But then, this is just a cartoon: we are meant to *laugh* at the poor guy, and to shake our heads over the wild conditions of vast airports in a globalized world. Yet I want to stress this cartoon's use of airport textuality as a metaphorical aperture. The problem with this cartoon's airport humor is its environmental aesthetic: it is aware of a space that slides off the frame, away from the text, into a nagging unconscious. The *space* is out of joint.

Without world

Another voice from the desert: "Sitting around, two hours, three, in this wretched clamorous rotten and crowded fucking Denver airport. Christ, you have to wait in line for *every* damn thing here."[1] So wrote Edward Abbey in his journal on August 15, 1980. This brief passage reflects in negative Abbey's writings that celebrate the American West, inheriting and recapitulating Romantic concepts of wild nature. For instance, Abbey's classic work *Desert Solitaire* is a testament to "[t]he slickrock desert. The red dust and the burnt cliffs and the lonely sky—all that which lies beyond the end of the roads."[2] Big cultural objects such as airports hardly ever figure into Abbey's prose, except as occasional and peripheral foils to the author's experiences of rugged wilderness.

Obviously, one can assume that Abbey was content with certain forms of waiting—such as watching the slow movement of a desert sunrise, for instance. But waiting in an airport somehow escapes the immediacy of experience that Abbey so craves. It is as if Abbey anticipated the words of the philosopher Giorgio Agamben, albeit in a different context: "And what sense does it make to speak of 'waiting' without time and without world?"[3] In this view, the airport represents an evacuated world, a space bracketed so heavily by culture that no nature exists within its bounds. Abbey's statement seems to suggest that airports are, for all intents and purposes, "without world."

And yet, what if waiting around in the airport were to be rethought, and recast as a harbinger of ecology? Not only might this be possible, but in fact this rethinking of airports has already taken place: the American environmental imagination is littered with airport scenes that counterintuitively harness acts of waiting as portals for ecological awareness. Against Abbey's impulse to see the "wretched clamorous rotten and crowded fucking Denver airport" as a decidedly uninspiring built space, a convincing archive of American literary texts reveals airports to be places storing an ecological reserve. I venture to call this surprising coincidence *ecology in waiting*. I use this phrase to suggest that even in something as seemingly passive as waiting, ecology exists. In fact, I argue that seemingly unconscious or unintentional patterns of habitation can expose ecology as clearly as what would seem to be more obviously 'environmental' acts such as hiking or kayaking. If this sounds counterintuitive, it should. However, my aim is not simply to celebrate an unconscious ecology, but rather to demonstrate how, by taking the routines of everyday life more seriously *as* ecological, we can then work to consciously change the conditions of everyday life. In other words, the latent ecology in waiting might result in a manifestly *different* ecology, one that has been *waiting* to emerge.[4]

The aim of this chapter is to practice a kind of ecocriticism that, to use the literary scholar Dana Phillips's term, is *picaresque* in its approach to literature and culture.[5] I look at fictional and poetic representations of airports in order to work out ecological implications. This approach offers a twofold benefit. First, it provides an analytic rubric for what might seem to be an unexpected environmental subject: the space/time of airports. Second, this point of interest opens up the field of possibilities for how a wider range of texts can *count* as environmental literature.

My analysis involves, paraphrasing the political theorist Jane Bennett's work on *vibrant matter*, thinking slowly about a nonsubject (or big objects: airports), and focusing carefully on a topography that one otherwise might be tempted to quickly term mere background material or setting.[6] Marc Augé's influential book *Non-Places: Introduction to an Anthropology of Supermodernity* describes airports as paradigmatic of the myriad transition sites (others would be highway rest stops or ATM machines) distributed throughout contemporary geographies. Augé ends his study by suggesting that non-places such as airports call for "an ethnology of solitude."[7] The present analysis takes up this project, but changes the terms a bit: I outline an *ecology* of solitude, located around the subject of airport waiting. I focus on airport *passages*: these are brief descriptions or mentions of airports in literary texts that call attention to the architecture of transit, the physical corridors through which people pass on the way to flight.

The elimination of speed

The ecologist and poet Gary Snyder makes explicit use of airports three times in his 2005 collection, *Danger on Peaks*. Far from being superfluous transitional settings, these airport instances each initiate an "elimination of speed" that becomes key to ecological reflection in Snyder's poems. I borrow the phrase "elimination of speed" from Roland Barthes, who, in his 1957 essay "The Jet-Man," pointed out a curious inconsistency around the figure of the jet pilot:

> ... what strikes one first in the mythology of the *jet-man* is the elimination of speed: nothing in the legend alludes to this experience. We must here accept a paradox, which is in fact admitted by everyone with the greatest of ease, and even consumed as proof of modernity. This paradox is that an excess of speed turns into repose.[8]

Over the course of the latter half of the twentieth century and into the twenty-first century, this paradox has made its way out of the cockpit and into traveling populations at large, but not by everyone becoming pilots; rather, this paradox has been disseminated by the spread of commercial aviation, resulting in more collective time spent at airports, waiting. The postmodern paradox of flight still involves an "elimination of speed"—it is just grounded: one is technically still *traveling* while at the airport, even when this means standing around for hours in barely moving lines, or waiting for baggage to appear.

In *Non-Places*, Augé describes this sensation in the airport when a traveler, having checked-in for a flight and with boarding pass in pocket, has "nothing to do but wait for the sequence of events . . . ."[9] As Augé goes on to speculate,

. . . these days, surely, it was in these crowded places where thousands of individual itineraries converged for a moment, unaware of one another, that there survived something of the uncertain charm of the waste lands, the yards and building sites, the station platforms and waiting rooms where travellers break step, of all the chance meeting places where fugitive feelings occur of the possibility of continuing adventure, the feeling that all there is to do is to "see what happens."[10]

Augé's abrupt move from the pulsating airport to "the waste lands" is indicative of an ecological musing: how might airports allow for such "fugitive feelings" that connect built space with *wasted* space? In tracking the "possibility of continuing adventure" resonant in airport waiting, Augé suggests the modality that Snyder puts to poetic work in *Danger on Peaks*.

Snyder's prose poem "Blast Zone" starts in the air: "Early morning plane from Reno to Portland [to] meet Fred Swanson at the baggage claim. Out of the Portland airport and onto these new streets, new highways . . . ."[11] The poem goes on to detail Snyder's trip to visit the active volcano Mt. St. Helens. In fact, the mountain is a central image throughout *Danger on Peaks*, and in many ways Snyder uses the volcano as a way to grapple with the haunting simultaneity of slow geologic time and the fleeting bustle of human life.

At first, the airport's proximity to the city allows Snyder a unique vantage point on urban expansion, signified by the perceived freshness of the "new streets, new highways." The poem moves toward more classically ecological images, such as "fumarole wisps" in an "open-sided crater on the northside" of the mountain, and "smoking scattered vents in this violet-gray light."[12] The opening image of an airport arrival anticipates an adventure, but like Augé's chiasmic airport/wastelands, "Blast Zone" ends up casting the airport and the volcano as unlikely twins: both are linked to cycles of commotion, combustion, expenditure, and exhaust. At the same time, both sites also represent a certain elimination of speed: the profound humility invoked by the huge mountain is in fact commensurate with waiting around in the baggage claim of an airport.

This analogy might come across as audacious: a baggage claim for a mountain. In fact, the poem "Waiting for a Ride" follows up on this premonition in "Blast Zone," and fleshes it out.

The poem begins in a straightforward manner: "Standing at the baggage passing time: / Austin Texas airport—my ride hasn't come yet."[13] Snyder goes on to think about various personal connections—what they are doing these days; who he has or hasn't been in touch with—and then goes on to remember how he slept outside on a full moon night, "white light beaming through the black boughs of the pine / owl hoots and rattling antlers, / Castor and Pollux rising strong."[14] These familiar signs of ecology and astronomy provide firm anchor points in the poem: from within a drab baggage claim at the Austin airport, Snyder manages to boost the reader

□ Waiting for a Ride

Standing at the baggage passing time:
Austin Texas airport — my ride hasn't come yet.
My former wife is making websites from her home,
one son's seldom seen,
the other one and his wife have a boy and girl of their own.
My wife and stepdaughter are spending weekdays in town
so she can get to high school.
My mother ninety-six still lives alone and she's in town too,
always gets her sanity back just barely in time.
My former former wife has become a unique poet;
most of my work,
such as it is   is done.
Full moon was October second this year,
I ate a mooncake, slept out on the deck
white light beaming through the black boughs of the pine
owl hoots and rattling antlers,
Castor and Pollux rising strong
— it's good to know that the Pole Star drifts!
that even our present night sky slips away,
not that I'll see it.
Or maybe I will, much later,
some far time walking the spirit path in the sky,
that long walk of spirits — where you fall right back into the
"narrow painful passageway of the Bardo"
squeeze your little skull
and there you are again

waiting for your ride

(October 5, 2001)

Figure 7.2 "Waiting for a Ride" (© 2004 Gary Snyder, reprinted by permission of Counterpoint)

back into his Northern California bioregion—and even into the vaster universe.

Snyder goes on to muse about how stars drift, "that even our present night sky slips away, / not that I'll see it"[15]—this humility check is similar to the aura of the mountain in "Blast Zone": a sense of presence that eliminates speed, causes the human to focus on slower time. Yet then, Snyder backs up and wonders,

Or maybe I will, much later,
some far time walking the spirit path in the sky,

that long walk of spirits—where you fall right back into the
"narrow painful passageway of the Bardo"
squeeze your little skull
and there you are again
waiting for your ride [16]

The ecology of the night sky slips streams and becomes a spiritual register. Snyder jumps tracks, alluding to "the Bardo": the concept of intermediacy between lives in Tibetan Buddhism. And then jarringly, the Bardo becomes a birth canal ("squeeze your little skull"), and then the reincarnated speaker/ reader (note the shift to the second person apostrophe) is born back into the airport, where one is left—in a double-spaced lacuna—"waiting for your ride."

On one level this poem is basically a catalog of what Snyder thinks about as he waits in the airport for his ride. On another level—or rather, shot through the entire poem—it is full of ecology in waiting. "Waiting for a Ride" exposes the effects of the airport's elimination of speed on a person whose mind is wandering: the time of waiting prompts a thought process that downgrades the present journey while also enhancing the ambient effects of the space at hand. The poem suggests that the baggage claim— like a mountain—can blow one away. Of course, the danger of getting one's mind blown is that things no longer seem the same. The airport thus risks becoming a different kind of space: humbling, but also *humbled*—open to change.

The third mention of airports in *Danger on Peaks* appears in the poem "Strong Spirit," which is about Snyder hosting the Korean poet Ko Un at the University of California-Davis. In this poem the airport scene is the inverse of "Blast Zone" and "Waiting for a Ride," in which Snyder is picked up at the airport: in "Strong Spirit," Snyder is picking up somebody *else* at the airport. Midway through the poem, Snyder says he is "about to meet him at the airport" and a few lines later, specifies that he is headed "[d]own to the airport to meet [Ko Un] at Customs."[17] The brief airport scene transitions to heavier matters, with Snyer and Ko Un on a trip "to pay respects to our friend / poet, and translator, Ok-ku died last fall / her grave on the ridgetop near the sea." Snyder and Ko Un "walk a grassy knoll in the wind"; Ko Un stays at a hotel "in the flat plain valley just by Putah Creek"; and the poem begins with Snyder "[a]t the Motel Eco, with my steel cup full of latte from the Roma . . . ."[18] The airport exists as a peripheral, stark, and simple setting in this poem—a space from which *something else* can take place. The airport is a point of departure, precisely by temporarily eliminating speed.

Ecologically speaking, the airports in *Danger on Peaks* say three things: *slow down, pay attention*, and *be open to change*. Taken together, in moments of airport waiting, these three commands seem to inspire what the philosopher Elaine Scarry would call "perceptual acuity": an intense focus on *something* that is then freed to amble over the various thoughts, interactions, and patterns of everyday life, in all its mundane and magnificent forms.[19] Snyder's airports serve as "building sites," to evoke Augé's phrase, as spaces of imagination, (re)connection, and "intensity of experience."[20] The elimination of speed within airports depends on—and calls for—an ecology in waiting.

The ache of stunning ruins

Barry Lopez is another contemporary environmental writer who has put airports to use in literary landscapes. The short story "Light Action in the Caribbean" pays close attention to the geography of airports, picking up on several constitutive matters of ecology in waiting. A brief moment early in the story relates a cab ride by the two main characters, Libby and David, who are on their way to the Denver airport to depart on an ill-fated vacation: "Driving from Arvada all the way to the new Denver airport, thought Libby, was like driving to another country before you could take off. Miles and miles of these nothing fields, no houses, no mountains, no development, no roads, no trees."[21] This emptying out of space in anticipation of the airport is a common sight, and Libby's observation is consistent with numerous other literary airport scenes, as I hinted at in Chapter 3. I now wish to explore a wider range of sparse airport geographies in literary texts.

For example, Don DeLillo's novel *Players* describes one character's escapist limousine ride to a New York airport as such: "When the land began to flatten and empty out, [Pammy] knew they were in the vicinity of the airport. It was a landscape that acceded readily to a sense of pre-emption."[22] Another character in that same novel, Lyle, makes a similar observation from the vantage point of the airport interior, after checking-in for his flight:

> He checked his bag and went looking for a place to get a drink. It was early evening by now and across the runways Manhattan's taller structures were arrayed in fields of fossil resin, that brownish-yellow grit of pre-storm skies. The buildings were remarkable at this distance not so much for boldness, their bright aspiring, as for the raddled emotions they called forth, the amber mood, evoking as they did some of the ache of stunning ruins.[23]

This passage reinforces the binary dance of Augé's airport/wastelands, and hinges on a moment of waiting and gazing out over the tarmac. Airport landscapes appear simultaneously as "nothing" and yet as "new" (recall Snyder's rhetoric of "new streets, new highways" in the poem "Blast Zone"), as empty but preemptive, and as dynamic hubs of transport that then allow for views of "stunning ruins." In "Light Action in the Caribbean" David and Libby make their way through a series of airports—"[t]hey were flying United to Miami, then Air Carib to St. Matthew, then Bahía Blanco to San

Carlos"[24]—only to arrive at an utterly ruinous destination. Suffice it to say, David and Libby do not make their return trip through these airports.

Yet airports belie the violent conclusion of this story, and instead exist amid sprightly currents of consumer trends and capital flows. After their first flight to Miami, "[w]hen they landed, David made cell phone calls from the United gate all the way to the Air Carib gate."[25] At one point in flight, Libby recalls how "[a]t the gate he'd casually thumbed fifty $100 bills in a bank envelope at her."[26] And "[w]hen they cleared customs in St. Matthew and were waiting at the Bahía Blanco gate, she got out a copy of *Allure*."[27] Like DeLillo's Lyle "looking for a place to get a drink," Libby turns to a women's beauty magazine as a way to stave off the annihilating boredom of airport waiting.

The above DeLillo citation suggests directions well beyond a coincidence in perspective. DeLillo has become increasingly recognized for his novelistic reflections of the contemporary American environmental imagination, and while his works do not necessarily have the same outdoorsy quality as texts by Snyder and Lopez, their airport scenes reveal a shared ecology in waiting.[28]

In DeLillo's *White Noise*, the main character Jack Gladney has to pick up his daughter from the airport. What should be a punctual, passing episode becomes an existential morass: "At the airport we waited in a mist of plaster dust, among exposed wires, mounds of rubble."[29] Waiting exposes the airport as only partially intact, the frayed edge of a hyper-organized suburbia. It turns out that some deplaning passengers have nearly died due to a power failure mid-flight; the terminal is in disrepair; Jack's daughter smells like jet exhaust. According to Jack's ex-wife, "Getting out of airports is every bit as important as the actual flight."[30] This utterance occurs as Jack and company are inching through a traffic jam on the way back from the airport, thus raising questions about what counts as a trip to the airport—or, to rephrase Shel Silverstein, where the airport ends. Later in the novel, DeLillo describes a character in terms of airport waiting: "He was sprawled in the attitude of an air traveler, someone long since defeated by the stale waiting, the airport babble."[31] *White Noise* shows ecology in waiting to be a vexed field of study: the airport as a pinnacle of modernity reflects the crumbling of progress taking place, taking space, and taking lives.

What makes the sight of *ruins* ecological is that ruins reflect *history*: DeLillo's airport is indicative of a host of human decisions concerning fossil fuels, migrations, and sprawl. Considered this way, history becomes another word for ecology. Thus, when DeLillo's novel *Underworld* deploys enigmatic, out-of-context airport aphorisms—such as "Wait-listed passenger Lundy please present yourself at the podium"[32]—the text actually presents material history, and forwards the "ethnology of solitude" that Augé has advocated. Yet as I have suggested, perhaps *ecology* of solitude would be a more accurate phrase, as the ruinous vistas and isolating interpellations granted by airport waiting disclose not only living cultures, but dead things as well.

Recall how DeLillo lingers on this matter in his novel *The Names*, and unambiguously defines the feeling of airport waiting as "dead time." Here is the main character of the novel, ruminating on what it feels like to be in the airport, waiting:

> This is time totally lost to us. We don't remember it. We take no sense impressions with us, no voices, none of the windy blast of aircraft on the tarmac, or the white noise of flight, or the hours waiting. Nothing sticks to us but smoke in our hair and clothes. It is dead time.[33]

For DeLillo one key feature of airports is their ability to evacuate time, and thereby erase "sense impressions"—or at least winnow them down to their bare minimum, such as a "windy blast" here, some "white noise" there.

This idea of airport waiting as "dead time" provides a segue back to Lopez, who begins his short story "Pearyland" in a familiar vein:

> . . . at the airport at Søndre Strømfjord, in Greenland . . . . We were all standing by, long hours at the airport. Some people went into town; but the notion that the weather might suddenly clear for just a few minutes and a plane take off kept most of us around, sleeping in the lounges, eating at the restaurant, using the phones.[34]

In the delayed space/time of the airport, the narrator meets Edward Bowman, a *taphonomist*. Taphonomy is a field of biology that studies how dead organisms decay over time, or how bodies are "funneled back into the ecological community."[35] It turns out that Bowman, during his fieldwork in Pearyland, has encountered a sub-arctic afterlife of sorts, where ghostly caribou and an Inuk "caretaker" haunt the landscape. The realistic *dead time* of the airport is grafted onto a speculative story of living–dead creatures.

The story unfolds over a period of three days of waiting ethereally in the inoperative airport, after which ". . . the fog lifted suddenly, as if it had to go elsewhere. Bowman's plane, which had been there on the ground for eight days, left for Copenhagen and an hour later I flew with my friends back to Frobisher Bay, on Baffin Island."[36] Airport waiting makes space for "dead time" in this story, as the narrator is captivated by Bowman's tale, which must then be retold—as if "Pearyland" were a postmodern recasting of Samuel Taylor Coleridge's poem "The Rime of the Ancient Mariner."[37] In Lopez's "Pearyland," zombie animals haunt the ruined space/time of airport waiting—an overabundance of *dead time*, indeed.

Ecology in waiting shows airports to be increasingly mercurial sites, in dynamic relation to incongruous locations (urban wastelands, blast zones, a zombie wilderness), and always capable of converting bustling cosmopolitan hubs into the emptied out shells of civilization. In the works of Lopez and DeLillo, the staging grounds for flight create an aperture through which *history* appears: "the ache of stunning ruins" becomes part of the airport waiting assemblage. At this node where life and death tarry, planes take off or are delayed, and where landforms can be flattened into nothingness . . . ecology in waiting emerges.

The certainty of airports

When we expand the field of the American environmental imagination, through recourse to ecology in waiting, we also open the way for readings of unexpected texts. For instance, Colson Whitehead's 2001 novel *John Henry Days* is based on an African American legend of railroad construction, and tells the story of a New York City reporter, J. Sutter, who finds himself on assignment in the rural town of Talcott, West Virginia. Importantly, before the plot gets underway, the novel begins at an airport. The first chapter, "Terminal City," considers airports as sites for slow observation, naturalist wonder, and even quasi-mystical blessings. The opening lines describe J.'s sense of this eccentric ecosystem:

> Now he blesses the certainty of airports. His blessings, when he has occasion to perform them, are swift and minimal, thoroughly secular, consisting of a slight nod to no one present, a chin dip that no witness will mark. He nods to luck mostly, to express gratitude for whatever sliver of good fortune drops before his shoes. The day's first blessing is occasioned by a solemn white rind, a little feather, that J. Sutter notices a few yards away on the carpet and imme-diately recognizes, without a shade of doubt, to be a receipt.[38]

What first appears as a spontaneous blessing unfolds to reveal an ecological point of reference: a discarded receipt lying on the floor of the departure lounge, which J. will collect and submit for reimbursement at the end of his trip. This simple receipt houses an image twice metaphorical, first a "rind" and then a "feather." To linger on this double image is to consider the strange fruit that is enfolded by a thick skin of receipts, and then to imagine the bird whose plumage is a skein of receipts. The certainty of airport waiting has spurred an uncertain perception, an aura of multiplex metaphoricity.

J. reflects on this image further: "Airports bloom receipts as certainly as standing water bubbles up mosquitoes."[39] As the novel elaborates on this image of the receipt, it is described almost as a species: receipts are not simply detachable outer material, but are understood to *grow*, organically, from the peaty floors of the space. This is an odd and convoluted simile, with intransitive verbs turned into transitive animators. Throughout this description, the airport is seen to be *alive*, in a biological, ecological, and densely cultural sense: the airport as a singular plant, the airport as an entire swamp, and the airport as a "Terminal City." Here we observe the airport's ability to metaphorically transmogrify around a single object, and within the context of a relatively simple image: ordinary receipts lying around on the floor. Whitehead's writing becomes a magnifying glass through which we might pay attention to the materiality of things: to how objects accrete, and to how culture flips into nature—all in a brief scene of airport waiting, replete with its atmospheric, everyday glut of the paper products consumed therein. And yet, out of this glut, Whitehead rethinks airport waiting as *living time.*

After his flight, J. leaves the airport and is waiting for a ride:

> In the passenger loading and unloading zone the carbon monoxide, so terrible after the careful atmosphere of the terminal, hangs low around his heels, heavier than air. A gang of dirty clouds loiters over there. J. says, "What a dump," and for the second time that day he blesses the certainty of airports because he can always turn around and go someplace else.[40]

The airport in this passage inverts the inside/outside dichotomy, and stands as a pure, "careful" biosphere—an environment unto itself that is threatened by the "gang of dirty clouds" loitering in a nondescript "over there." For J., the airport is a place for endless possibilities of mobility, worship, and purity. This quirky sense of space challenges easy oppositions of nature and culture, accumulation and waste. J.'s destination is a "dump," and the airport a network of shiny green cities left behind. Yet J.'s second blessing is of course myopic, as airports do not exist without a corollary troposphere of carbon monoxide and outlying destination towns on the surface of the globe. The certainty of airports is yet again related to a vast landscape of ruins. J.'s airport is a fantasy zone, then, but nevertheless the waiting conjures a kind of surreal awareness of how inorganic objects grow, and how pollution assembles. The infinitely open "someplace else" that airports allow access to is nothing more and nothing less than ecology in waiting.

The anthropologist Kathleen Stewart's book *Ordinary Affects* might seem like an odd candidate for ecology in waiting, but one section concerns what Whitehead's J. might have fondly called "the certainty of airports." *Ordinary Affects* reads like something that Edward Abbey might have appreciated if he had let himself be as enchanted with Western sociality as he was with Western wilderness. *Ordinary Affects* is teeming with attention to detail and philosophical wonder—even when (or precisely when) the object of analysis is a west Texas Wal-Mart or the subtle mysticism of a gambling binge in Las Vegas. The book articulates a constellation of ideas, trends, queries, and myths that circulate around and define what Stewart calls the "affective subject." Not exactly based on chapters, Stewart organizes her text around aphoristic snapshots of familiar moments and micro-narratives; each section begins with its own heading, such as "RV Freedom," "Blue TV Nights," or "Tracking Nuclear Waste."

Stewart explores how the affective subject is comprised by everyday situations and flashpoints, and one section called "A Raindrop Falls in Houston" revolves around the Houston airport after a heavy rainstorm.

Flight cancellations cause lines of passengers that "stretch hundreds of yards outside the terminal" and "[i]nside the terminal, the working monitors show all flights as 'delayed.'" After a day of confusion and mayhem, "[t]he next morning the news reports that Houston airport is back to normal, and we try to forget, as if nothing happened. Just move on."[41] For Stewart, the airport is one such place where the ordinary flares up into a state of near crisis, and then everything gets absorbed back into the normal flow of things.

Yet I want to suggest that such airport cases are constitutive not merely of a general, spontaneous affective phenomenon; rather, airports must manage a perpetual proximity to crisis—and this management takes shape through elaborately orchestrated waiting imperatives, such as Stewart evinces by the endless lines, "monitors" and "news reports" in the airport that demand constant alertness. Stewart's critical anthropology suggests how the tense certainty of airports is sustained by saturated media ecology.

In a similar reflection on the mediations of air travel, the main character of DeLillo's epic novel *Underworld*, Nick Shay (a toxic waste consultant), at one point contemplates this certainty of airports in a quasi stream-of-consciousness, run-on sentence that tracks with the inflow and outflow of a baggage claim:

> Coming home, landing at Sky Harbor, I used to wonder how people disperse
> so quickly from airports, any airport—how you are crowded into seats three
> across or five across and crowded into the aisle after touchdown when the
> captain turns off the seat belt sign and you get your belongings from the over-
> head and stand in the aisle waiting for the hatch to open and the crowd to
> shuffle forward, and there are more crowds when you exit the gate, people
> disembarking and others waiting for them and greater crowds in the bag-
> gage areas and the concourse, the crossover roars of echoing voices and flight
> announcements and revving engines and crowds moving through it all, people
> with their separate and unique belongings, the microhistory of toilet articles
> and intimate garments, the medicines and aspirins and lotions and powders
> and gels, so incredibly many people intersecting on some hot dry day at the
> edge of the desert, used underwear fist-balled in their bags, and I wondered
> where they were going, and why, and who are they, how do they all disperse
> so quickly and mysteriously, how does a vast crowd scatter and vanish in min-
> utes, bags dragging on the shiny floors.[42]

This passage acts as another instance of Scarry's "perceptual acuity" such as we glimpsed in Snyder's outward oriented airport utterances. Here, however, we are closer to Whitehead and Stewart, where the intense focus is turned on the details and processes of airport life, or an ecology in waiting. DeLillo's narrative montage is at once a totally convoluted and yet an absolutely realistic representation of airports in their full, postmodern sense: these spaces are cosmopolitan compression points, dense with the excessive stuff of consumer culture, and caught in vicious cycles of momentum and the elimination of speed. As the eco-theorist Timothy Morton has suggested, "[p]ostmodernism was the moment at which global capital and the totally administered world made it impossible (in a highly toxic, negative, destructive way) not to detect the mesh."[43] Indeed, in the passage from *Underworld*, the "microhistory of toilet articles and intimate garments, the medicines and aspirins and lotions and powders and gels," and "the crossover roars of echoing voices and flight announcements and revving engines and crowds moving through it all"—this is precisely what Morton would categorize as *the mesh*: an inescapable, utterly apparent web of isolate feelings and intricate interdependencies, migratory patterns and spontaneous dispersions, sentient beings and other vibrant things.

The certainty of airports is their ability to connect wildly disparate things, and make them make sense—or not. DeLillo's *The Names* highlights this in one brief passage: "I stood waiting at the baggage conveyor in the airport in Amman. The king would be arriving later that afternoon after seventeen days abroad. When the king returns to Jordan after a trip abroad, two camels and a bull are slaughtered at the airport."[44] In swift order, DeLillo links sovereignty and sacrifice with banal waiting, and traditions and rituals become inextricable from the hyperculture of the airport. As in Snyder's "Waiting for a Ride" above, DeLillo's baggage claim scenes construct chains of connections and associations—but chains that have no discrete or logical end. Ecology in waiting is *unending* ecology, and the certainty of airports proves to include their uncertainty, as well.

Still, some people work in airports

Ecology in waiting would hardly be sufficient if we were to ignore one of the key features of the habitat: namely, airline workers, and all the networks of labor and capital flows that take place in airport spaces. Recall how in his follow-up book to *Non-Places*, Augé clarifies this critical point: "What is a place for some may be a non-place for others, and vice versa. An airport, for example, does not have the same status in the eyes of the passenger who hastily crosses through it and an employee who works there everyday."[45] Indeed, airport workers always exist on the other side of airport waiting, a porous division maintained between subsets of people.

Similar to DeLillo's description in *The Names* of airport waiting as "time totally lost to us," the contemporary novelist Lucy Corin defines such time as "forgettable time." In her short story "My Favorite Dentist," Corin writes: "I've been thinking about forgettable time, like in an airport . . . . Still, some people, I have to remember, work in airports."[46] In having to remember the forgettable time of airports, Corin suggests a deeper layer of activity that is difficult to perceive, and even more difficult to keep in mind: the *work* of airports. Ecology in waiting draws attention to the material base of airports, including all the forces and relations of production that subtend humans in flight.

The work of airports is often alluded to or mentioned askance in literary works. For example, in Nicholson Baker's densely annotated, inner-subjectively tangential novel *The Mezzanine*, one of the details of postmodernity into which the narrative tunnels is the ubiquitous baggage claim. In the midst of a tedious train of thought, the narrator imagines:

> . . . airport luggage-handling systems (those overlapping new moons of hard rubber that allowed the moving track to turn a corner, neatly drawing its freight of compressed clothing with it; and the fringe of rubber strips that marked the transition between the bright inside world of baggage claim and the outside world of low-clearance vehicles and men in blue outfits) . . .[47]

This parenthetical tour of the baggage claim, projected and protracted through the perspective of a waiting passenger, hints at an ecology of labor just barely visible—and only via a glimpse before the parenthesis blocks the view. The "low-clearance vehicles and men in blue outfits" signal a turn in consciousness, as if the narrator is yanked out of his passenger ontology for a moment to realize, like Corin, that some people *work* in airports. Baker's attention to airport work follows the elimination of speed to its extreme: structurally speaking, these airport inhabitants—the workers—cannot ever leave the ground. The certainty of airports requires a blasted and gray landscape of labor beyond and yet attached to "the bright inside world" of the traveler.

Another instance of this labor force ecology in waiting appears in Carol Muske-Dukes's poem "De-icing the Wings." In this poem a passenger speaker, from inside an airliner on the tarmac, observes airport laborers as masked and yet (oddly) clearly gendered: "They are de-icing the Eastern Shuttle. / Men in yellow masks stand on the wings / in the hard sleet and hose gold smoke / over the hold. The book on Cubism / in her hands shakes when they rev the jets."[48] The book on Cubism functions as the speaker's form of distraction (the form of entertainment known as *airport reading*), and this academic text overdetermines the abstract appearance of airport workers who are discernible in patches of primary color, and by their labor-coded affects: Muske-Dukes's "men in yellow masks" are analogous to Baker's "men in blue outfits."

At certain points in history, airport work becomes more apparent and less abstract. In his poem "Airport Security," Sherod Santos comments on "a fussier / Staff of ticket agents, and the usual if now / Beefed-up legions of security personnel" in the wake of 9/11.[49] Santos goes on to tease an impossible question out of the mayhem of airport waiting: "And something else about this milling ruckus / Of wary selves backed up and forming / Into broken lines asks us to consider this: 'Why does anyone ever leave home?' / And the answer is suddenly hard to find."[50] This may seem like a profound metaphysical question, yet all the more pressing in this context is the ecology in waiting: not why people leave home to go to the airport, but *how people work there.*

In her article "Points of Departure: The Culture of U.S. Airport Screening," the media scholar Lisa Parks develops this ecology by analyzing the practices and protocols of U.S. airport security checkpoints, pre- and post-9/11. Parks arrives at the conclusion that, "[m]uch more than a non-place, the airport has become a vital place where security, technology and capital collide, and spur the U.S. social body to recognize its terrorizing interiority." Indeed, this "terrorizing interiority" is what Santos notices in "Airport Security."[51] This is not Baker's "bright inside world" at all, but rather a realm of "milling ruckus" where "wary selves" wait for arrivals and departures.

Episodes of airport waiting are always in dialectical relations to airline employees working. In a personal essay entitled "Standing By," the humor writer David Sedaris reflects sardonically on the tensions that take place between travelers and airport workers. The bulk of the essay describes the experience of waiting in line for customer service in the Denver airport, after Sedaris's flight to Portland is canceled. Sedaris considers whether when airline employees say, "I'll be right back," what they really mean is, "Go fuck yourself."[52] Sedaris goes on to wonder about the stored up resentment and fury that can suddenly spurt out of delayed passengers. Sedaris overhears as one frustrated passenger's complaints become startlingly ramped up:

> He had been passed over for a standby seat earlier that morning and was not happy about it. "The gal at the gate said she'd call my name when it came time to board, but, hell, she didn't call me." [. . .] "I should have taken her name," the man continued. "I should have reported her. Hell, I should have punched her is what I should have done!"[53]

Sedaris outlines the potentially violent dialectics of airport waiting and airport work—and this becomes a diagram of *progress,* an ironic testament to the achievements of modern civil society.

Toward the end of the essay, Sedaris hazards a daring assessment:

> We're forever blaming the airline industry for turning us into monsters: it's the fault of the ticket agents, the baggage handlers, the slowpokes at the newsstands and the fast-food restaurants. But what if this is who we truly are, and the airport's just a forum that allows us to be our real selves, not just hateful but gloriously so?[54]

By treating directly the disparities of airport labor and the behaviors of travelers, Sedaris turns the lens on humanity in general: the airport, Sedaris suggests, is "a forum that allows us to be our real selves." Or as Jane Bennett notes in *Vibrant Matter*, "[t]o be alive is to be waiting"—and airports make public and political this constituent of life.[55]

Sedaris's glib speculation concerning airport waiting gestures toward a species being in its built up (and at least partially ruined) habitat. The inescapable *elimination of speed* derides the subject of flight. Airport waiting exposes depressing views, and can evoke *the ache of stunning ruins*. Yet *the certainty of airports* persists in their metaphorical plenitude: waiting in these sites reveals a mesh of things and people that can be inspiring, overwhelming, or debilitating. *Still, some people work in airports*. The phrase *air rage* has become associated with passengers who become aggressive in flight or in airports, when they do not get what (or where) they want. Ecology in waiting reveals such violence, and investigates the complex of materials— the airborne assemblages—that give rise to such violence. And in the wake of flight attendant Steven Slater's irreverent emergency-slide exit from a JetBlue plane on August 9, 2010, after a passenger allegedly gave Slater too much grief and pushed him over the edge, we might pause to consider seriously the politics of labor around ecology in waiting.

This picaresque foray through the American environmental imagination to foreground airports—and specifically, airport waiting and airport labor— widens the lens through which we might observe how ecology awaits (in) the densest centers of culture. Considered seriously, ecology in waiting might turn out to contain, paradoxically, the arrival of a more rigorous and flexible ecology. As Robert Sommer wrote in *Tight Spaces*, addressing the confining aspects of air travel: "Things are only going to change when waiting is considered a serious activity instead of dead time . . . ."[56] Sommer suggests that by taking waiting seriously, we might consciously and conscientiously re-inhabit our so-called *non-places*, and thereby imagine and work toward other spaces, in a future to come.

CHAPTER 8

BIRD CITING

Vital materialists will thus try to linger in those moments during which they find themselves fascinated by objects, taking them as clues to the material vitality that they share with them.

—Jane Bennett, *Vibrant Matter*

The first flash of a bird incites the desire to duplicate not by translating the glimpsed image into a drawing or a poem or a photograph but simply by continuing to see her five seconds, twenty-five seconds, forty-five seconds later—as long as the bird is there to be beheld.

—Elaine Scarry, *On Beauty and Being Just*

Recording starlings

I knew an artist who told me an intriguing story: She said that one evening she dressed in camouflage and drove out to the Sacramento airport, in order to record the deafening sounds of birds flocking at dusk.

I had witnessed this phenomenon at the airport, when I once stood in the rental car lot and saw a skein of thousands of starlings explode from a cluster of trees and fly in undulating patterns before suddenly alighting again. Indeed, the massive flocks of starlings are part of the elaborate ecosystem that is the Pacific Flyway, which runs through the Central Valley of California.

The artist whom I was talking to wanted to record the deafening birdcalls for an installation she was working on. I forget the details of the actual artwork; what stuck with me was the garb she donned for this project. The Army surplus fatigues were intended to conceal her presence from airport personnel. The artist feared that recording starlings at the airport would appear suspicious or subversive—I suppose because this act was effectively misusing the space at hand. But was she really a threat to the airport? Did this consist of unlawful loitering? Whatever the motivating factor, the artist's precaution struck me as illuminating: as if the artist could have been cited for being at the airport with birds—*not planes*—in mind.

As I have suggested, eccentric airport studies can tend to uncover unexpected aspects of air travel, including playful, philosophical, and gloomy elements within the culture of flight. But such studies can also expose the ecological mesh that human flight is a part of. In this chapter, I develop one such airport study by considering a wide range of intersections between birdlife, avian imagery, and human flight. This is a rather far-fetched onto-story, and it involves many twists and turns. But through a series of illus-trative snapshots I demonstrate how the textual life of airports involves intimacies with birds that complicate human exceptionalism. I show how bird forms evince immanent critiques within the real and imaginary materi-als of air travel; I call this *bird citing*.

Literary citations

Wallace Stevens's poem "Thirteen Ways of Looking at a Blackbird" begins with the following three lines:

> Among twenty snowy mountains
> The only moving thing
> Was the eye of a blackbird.[1]

These lines initiate bird citing. Stevens *cites* the blackbird as a poetic subject. The bird is *sited* or situated in the mountains. The bird is *sighted*—as in viewed—as a solitary figure in a panoramic landscape. The blackbird's own sighting is then cited, in a terrific zooming-in gesture to a single small eye, moving. Stevens's poem goes on to propose thirteen "ways" that the black-bird can be seen to infiltrate and interpenetrate human activities. "Thirteen Ways of Looking at a Blackbird" seems to suggest an ecological maxim: wherever you look, traces of birds appear.

First published in 1917, Stevens's multiple register of the blackbird sets up an airborne schema, a soaring experiment in perspective coincidental with the emergence of human flight. While "Thirteen Ways of Looking at a Blackbird" has nothing to do with human aviation per se, its recourse to avian imagery offers an analytic framework for thinking about the intersec-tions between birdlife and technological flight.

Bird citing becomes complicated when avian forms collide or collude explicitly with human motion/perception. As a poetic example of inter-sectional bird citing, consider T.S. Eliot's 1942 poem "Little Gidding," which notes how "the dark dove with the flickering tongue / Had passed below the horizon of his homing."[2] Eliot's "dove" is an ironic figure for the Junkers Ju 87 (or "Stuka") dive-bomber that conducted German air raids on Great Britain during World War II. This complex image evokes the plane as a perceptual machine ("homing"), and as an animal equipped with a flame-emitting, machine-gunning "tongue." In other words, the speaker of the poem imagines the plane as a distant object (bird), and as an inhabitable point-of-view (plane).

The poem later returns to this image, as if to reinforce the perceptual crisis of bird citing: "The dove descending breaks the air / With flame of incandescent terror."[3] Eliot's dove houses a naturalizing mechanism, thus conceptualizing military air power as an avian ecology. At the same time, the birds become weaponized.

Perceptually for Stevens, and metaphorically for Eliot, bird citing triggers a cognitive threshold where the human subject loses its center.

Neat little home for birds

Bird citing also involves how airports have been imagined in the culture of flight. In *The Airport Book* (1979), Martin Greif cites an article from 1920 written by the American journalist William G. Shepherd:

> The Audubon Society knows every domestic whim o[f] every desirable American bird, and no farm home is complete without its neat little home for birds. What we need today is an Audubon Society of American cities and towns for the cultivation of the welfare of our linen-winged, aluminum-lunged, unfeathered friends.[4]

This passage reflects how ornithology and air travel have been historically intertwined: to promote airports is, in a way, to promote something related to the aesthetically oriented mentality of the bird fancier. Shepard suggests equivalence between bird sighting and plane watching. Via this analogy, Shepherd also implies how air travel disseminated across the nation: artificially, as it were, by a "society" that might cultivate airports—as well as organically, through biological dispersion of "linen-winged" and "aluminum-lunged" aircraft. In other words, the call to birdlife is both a grasp at a natural order of things, as well as an enculturation of new technologies.

Martin Greif cites this case as unique: "Never before nor since, one imagines, has the airport been likened to a bird house."[5] Yet it turns out that this ornithological impulse haunts the culture of flight. Even on a purely colloquial level, it is not a stretch to think of airports as birdhouses; it is common knowledge that planes are often referred to as "birds."[6]

Furthermore, actual birds also converge around airports, and this has led to the increasingly alarming phenomenon of "bird strikes," or when aircraft hit birds on takeoff or while in flight, potentially causing damage and accidents. A wildly famous case of this type of bird citing took place in January 2009, when U.S. Airways Flight 1549 made a miraculous water landing on the Hudson River after hitting Canada Geese shortly after takeoff out of La Guardia. Since this incident, mass exterminations of Canada Geese have taken place in the vicinity of New York airports.[7] Bird strikes are a bleak reality that warp but nevertheless echo Shepard's pastoral wish image for an Audubon Society of American cities and towns.

On another level, artistic bird forms adorn airport spaces. Avian imagery is a common aesthetic strategy for airport symbolism and aerospace technologies, as I go on to show.

Eagles for airports

One only need turn to the crest of the U.S. Department of Homeland Security to see the familiar patriotic form of a spread-winged eagle on various displays throughout air terminals, like this one in Sacramento, suspended before the security checkpoint.

Figure 8.1 Sacramento airport Terminal A security checkpoint (author's photo)

Birds are not only evoked as inspiration for flight, then, but also as mythic protectors of air travel. This relatively recent deployment of eagle imagery (with the Homeland Security Act of 2002) is somewhat in friction with the threat posed by surrounding ecosystems, à la bird strikes. Nevertheless, the sign of the eagle continues to ornament airport passages, promising vigilance and security in the spaces of commercial aviation.

The sign of the eagle has a longer history at the juncture of airport nationalism. Built in 1941, Berlin's neoclassical Tempelhof Aerodrome was created to look like a mighty eagle, familiarly spread-winged, when seen directly from above. A Google Earth view shows the outward (and by a flight of imagination, upward) curving concourses, which would be the wings of the bird:

Figure 8.2 Tempelhof as seen on Google Earth

This bird citing challenges notions of scale and point of view: an airport *on the ground* is supposed to look like it is a *flying* creature—but we can only see this from an *already elevated* aerial view. Such bird citing in airport architecture tends to play with scale by magnifying or amplifying birdlife, thus diminishing or altogether evacuating the human subject. For where is the human subject who can view the patriotic eagle evoked by Tempelhof? This subject position exists in an impossibly sustained bird's eye view, hovering above the earth and able to decipher the (grounded) sign of the (soaring) eagle.

The flight of a great bird

In another instance of architectural bird citing, Eero Saarinen's 1962 TWA Terminal in New York has also been described in terms of its bird-like contours, if more abstractly conjured.

Figure 8.3 Eero Saarinen's TWA Terminal, at www.nyc-architecture.com

In *Naked Airport*, Alastair Gordon describes this piece of modernist architecture in reference to avian morphology: "The larger sections were like the wings of a bird that stretched laterally in daring cantilevers to the north and south."[8]

Likewise, in *The Airport Book* Martin Greif suggests, "The terminal's soaring central structure suggests the flight of a great bird."[9] The "flight of a great bird" in this description is no less than an airport on the ground. Such oscillations between ground and air become a standard feature of bird citing, at once mimicking the nimble flight of birds and rendering indeterminate the culture of flight. Never mind that Saarinen's original concept for the TWA Terminal came from playing with grapefruit sections; the point here is that the building took on the imaginary appearance of a bird in the minds of critics. The textual life of the airport becomes a matter of bird citing.

The art of bird citing

Bird citing penetrates the interiors of airports, as well—and not just in the common sightings of rogue swallows who makes their nests in the support beams of vaulted concourses. The artist Ralph Helmick has created art installations in several airports that use bird forms to adorn and reflect the culture of flight. One in particular takes bird citing to extreme levels of hybridity and confusion. The sculpture Rara Avis hangs above an escalator bank in the main terminal of Chicago's Midway airport:

Figure 8.4 Rara Avis (© Ralph Helmick & Stuart Schechter, photo by Clements/ Howcroft, used by permission of the artists)

This diaphanous sculpture is a rendering of a cardinal—the Illinois state bird. The avian form is achieved by the careful arrangement of 2000 tiny metal airplanes and other flying machines. Miniature aircraft actually *comprise* this huge bird; the monstrous animal is made of toy machines—and the airport itself is turned into a surrealist aviary of sorts. From the outside, the human viewer is both larger than the airplanes, yet smaller than the great bird—a vertiginous subject position, to be sure. Internally, this sculpture twists scale one more time: contemporary airliners are made to appear the same size as early balloons, antique biplanes, WWII fighter planes, and helicopters from the 1960s.

Figure 8.5 Rara Avis (© Ralph Helmick & Stuart Schechter, photo by Clements/ Howcroft, used by permission of the artists)

Helmick's artwork suggests the conflicted nature of bird citing. On the one hand, humans look toward birds as models for flight; on the other hand, our most advanced technologies become mere models of flight, absorbed in larger systems. This reality becomes all too apparent when birds arrive in flocks around airports—and Rara Avis turns this reality inside-out by the cardinal actually consisting of a transhistorical flock of aircraft.

Among twenty jet planes

Outside airports, avian appearances can become overdetermined when the real and the symbolic overlap. Consider a photograph that I took at the Sacramento airport on a spring day in 2005.

A female Brewer's Blackbird balances on a barbed wire fence. In the background, the tail of an American Airlines Boeing 757 features a bird sign between its AA logo. The iconic bird is the inspiration for the airliner; and yet the actual blackbird dancing on the threshold of the tarmac somewhat mocks the serious and secured perimeters of human flight.

In fact, beyond this serendipitous coincidence the Sacramento airport has a highly charged relationship with birdlife. The website Birdstrike Control Program reports that "FAA data show New York's JFK, [&] Sacramento, Calif., airports have most bird strikes with damage." As the article goes on to explain: "Sacramento International, the nation's 40th busiest, lies beneath

Figure 8.6 Sacramento airport (author's photo)

the Pacific Flyway used by millions of geese, swans, ducks, cranes, raptors and other birds that migrate with the seasons and stop to feed on crops in the farms that abut the airport."[10] Another online article about bird strikes at the Sacramento airport describes it this way: "Rice fields, the Sacramento River and the Yolo bypass create a paradise for waterfowl and wading birds, like herons. And above it all is the Pacific Flyway, a major migratory route for birds."[11]

The Sacramento airport has become a hotspot for risk assessment and deterrent tactics to keep avian ecology at a distance. The airport's relationship with birds is vexed, however, because birds are commonly cited as symbolic registers for flight, as evinced by the American Airlines insignia, which overlays birds upon birds. To rephrase Wallace Stevens: among twenty jet planes, every moving thing is a bird.

Angles of banking

After exiting Interstate 5 on approach to the Sacramento airport, several huge birds come into view. These are Dennis Oppenheim's "Flying Gardens," installed at the airport in 2004. The installation consists of twelve exoskeletal, car-size bird sculptures scattered around Terminal A—most of them are hanging-off of the parking structure, actually appearing to fly out of the building:

Figure 8.7 "Flying Gardens" by Dennis Oppenheim at the Sacramento airport (author's photo)

Figure 8.8 "Flying Gardens" by Dennis Oppenheim at the Sacramento airport (author's photo)

These sculptures are a postmodern remix of the phoenix myth: colorful, futuristically articulated birds fly out of the uniform wreckage of a parking garage—sunset glow and the interior lighting can make the structure resemble a smoldering ruin.

The birds appear triumphant and sleek against the monochromatic stack of the parking structure. Originally the birds were designed to include foliage growing all over them, replete with climbing vines, as if to project and multiply an alive image: bird plants. These overgrown appendages may have also furthered a post-apocalyptic aura around the parking garage. However, the airport authority forestalled this plan: as actual gardens, these icons of wildness would have become a little *too* wild, allowing *other* birds to nest in the artworks, thus requiring airport laborers to clean up copious amounts of bird excrement on the sidewalks below.

Figure 8.9 "Flying Gardens" by Dennis Oppenheim at the Sacramento airport (author's photo)

Without any actual flora growing on the birds, the name of this installation is a non sequitur: there is nothing garden-like nor organic about these creatures aside from their avian shapes. Interestingly, there *are* plants growing beneath the sculptures, but to extend figurative logic to the sculptures we would have to imagine the birds themselves as growing out of the parking garage, their solid iron anchors serving as roots or shoots. From this perspective, the birds would become blooms and the parking structure becomes a bloated matrix in which cyborg bird-plants are grown.

A prominent feature of these sculptures is the construction materials and sutures of these artworks that have been left exposed, as if ironically to demystify any organicized ideals about commercial flight. In other words, while the homage to birds celebrates human aviation as if it is a natural extension of our species, the self-referring madeness of these sculptures serves to question the very comparison implicit in the shape. Birds can fly, and human beings can fly airplanes; but a prefabricated bird the size of a minivan and tethered to a parking garage pushes the avian metaphor into a realm of absurdity.

Figure 8.10 "Flying Gardens" by Dennis Oppenheim at the Sacramento airport (author's photo)

Looking out at these birds from the *inside* of the parking structure raises an uncomfortable question: if these birds are flying *out* of the garage, are they then flying *into* the airport, in the disturbing style of 9/11? A juxtaposition of two quickly snapped camera-phone shots would suggest so:

Figure 8.11 Camera-phone photo juxtaposition (by the author and Dan-Thomas Glass)

This serendipitous analogy exposes comparable angles of banking that denote abrupt, tactical piloting. Oppenheim's birds are not aimed skyward, but rather are headed into the built space of commerce and privileged mobility. In other words, to put it bluntly, "Flying Gardens" is eerily reminiscent of Boeing 767s banking into the World Trade Center; these hijacked birds mimic terrifying maneuvers. The installation thus reveals a double geographic imperative: the object of flight serves both as an inspired reminder of the airport's ecosystem (a bird migration zone), and also conjures other forms of anxious banking in New York City (World Trade/Global Terrorism). Designed as a pleasant distraction for passengers, these avian aesthetics in fact riff on repressed anxieties of flight and predation that leak out of a globalized unconscious.

Citing bird shadows

At this point I want to return to our original sense of bird citing: the simple noticing or mentioning of a bird. As in Wallace Stevens's perspectival poem "Thirteen Ways of Looking at a Blackbird," bird citing often turns on visual disorientation. To further illustrate the problem of disoriented visuality, I turn to Gary Snyder's 2004 poem "No Shadow," which records the ornithological impulse in terms of foreground and background views. The speaker of the poem is looking out over the Sacramento River Valley; this panoramic landscape view initiates a bird citing that ricochets off a technosphere of military aviation.

The poem begins as a narrative prose tour of the Yuba Goldfieds, an area in the Sacramento River watershed that was heavily impacted by hydraulic mining in the nineteenth century. The first paragraph of "No Shadow" focalizes a scene, "at the lower Yuba River outflow where it enters the Sacramento valley flatlands, a mile-wide stretch between grass and blue oak meadows. It goes on for ten miles."[12] The second paragraph describes "a female osprey hunting along the main river channel. Her flight shot up, down, all sides, suddenly fell feet first into the river and emerged with a fish. Maybe fooling the fish by zigzagging, so—no hawk shadow."[13] The poem proper commences shortly after this ornithological citation: two prose paragraphs give way to streamlined poetry as a new object of perception comes into view:

> Standing on a gravel hill by the lower Yuba
> can see down west a giant airforce cargo plane from Beale
> hang-gliding down to land
> strangely slow over the tumbled dredged-out goldfields
> —practice run
> shadow of a cargo jet—soon gone
> no-shadow of an osprey
> still here [14]

This poem draws uneasy parallels between a mammoth Air Force cargo plane and a solitary osprey. They both fly in the river valley, and at first glance they seem to beg comparison. Snyder, however, contrasts the "no-shadow" fishing technique of the osprey with the "strangely slow" vector of the aircraft "hang-gliding down to land"—in the end, the osprey is "still here." The jet, on the other hand, will be "soon gone"—both in the immediate context and also, to take a deep ecological view, in the longer future of the planet in geologic time. Here, the osprey is a metonymy for animality in general, while the cargo plane seems to stand in for a militarized state apparatus at large.

Upon closer inspection, however, the division is not a simple binary opposition of aggressive human and passive animal. The bird is not cited as more naturally aesthetic; nor is the air force cargo plane purely militarized. Remember, the poetic turn is triggered by the Air Force *cargo* plane, in all its silence (because "hang-gliding") and spacious (even potentially humanitarian) capacity; the stealthy tact of an *actually hunting* osprey remains, almost more ominous as the unending end of the poem (because no period). The osprey is paramilitary; the Air Force cargo plane is, in this instance, a benign object of perception—it is on a "practice run," after all.

What at first seems to be a politicized critique of certain modes of flight gets complicated, as the poem's ornithological impulse ushers in other specters of empire and militarized surveillance. Consider a zoomed-out view of the page on which this poem appears:

▫ No Shadow

My friend Deane took me into the Yuba Goldfields. That's at the
lower Yuba River outflow where it enters the Sacramento valley flatlands, a mile-wide stretch between grass and blue oak meadows. It
goes on for ten miles. Here's where the mining tailings got dropped
off by the wandering riverbed of the 1870s—forty miles downstream
from where the giant hoses washed them off Sierra slopes.

We were walking on blue lupine-covered rounded hundred-foot
gravel hills til we stood over the springtime rush of water. Watched
a female osprey hunting along the main river channel. Her flight
shot up, down, all sides, suddenly fell feet first into the river and
emerged with a fish. Maybe fooling the fish by zigzagging, so—
no hawk shadow. Carole said later, that's like trying to do zazen
without your self entering into it.

Standing on a gravel hill by the lower Yuba
can see down west a giant airforce cargo plane from Beale
hang-gliding down to land
strangely slow over the tumbled dredged-out goldfields
—practice run
shadow of a cargo jet—soon gone

no-shadow of an osprey

still here

Figure 8.12 "No Shadow" (© 2004 Gary Snyder, reprinted by permission of Counterpoint)

The page's two predominant shapes—prose paragraphs and line-broken
poetry—mimic the aerial viewing patterns of the two flying objects in question, and their corollary topographies below: the Air Force plane affords
a uniform, "strangely slow" scanning view of the miles of "dredged-out"
terrain; the osprey's airborne perspective, on the other hand, jumps around,
"zigzagging" above the "river channel." The poem conjures multiple points
of view: the vantage point of the poet looking down into the valley; the
bird's eye view of a riparian ecosystem; a plane's trajectory, homing in on
the airfield. These points of view are at once shared and held apart, allowing
the bird citing to flip between foreground and background throughout the
poem, the osprey and cargo plane appearing to exist on the same scale.

Another Blackbird

If Snyder's poem "No Shadow" seems launched from a complicatedly elevated view, this has a regional value, one referred to explicitly in the poem.
This is Beale Air Force Base, where the cargo plane is both "from" and
where it will land.

Figure 8.13 Beale Air Force Base as seen on Google Earth

Google Earth's satellite view of Beale Air Force Base, zoomed all the way in, contains a surprising bird citing: the word "Blackbird" cuts across the tarmac and into a grassy lawn:

Figure 8.14 Beale Air Force Base as seen on Google Earth

The black figure in the diamond-shaped, white center of this aerial view turns out to be the Lockheed SR-71 Blackbird, previously stationed at Beale. The Blackbird is a supersonic, high-altitude spy plane developed secretly in the early 1960s and subsequently used for reconnaissance missions over North Vietnam; David Pascoe suggests that the SR-71 Blackbird "emerged out of paranoia."[15]

To really linger on this image is to adopt a disoriented and somewhat paranoid subject position. The downward gaze implicit in aerial perception has been twisted, and rearranged horizontally: we look into a computer screen in order to view the ground as if from high above. The viewer essentially swaps subject positions with the Blackbird, such that the personal computer user now spies on the grounded spy plane. Yet this leads to a query inspired by Snyder's "No Shadow": is the plane in the satellite image really a plane, or might it more accurately function as the *shadow* of the very plane from which the Google Earth user is spying? In the view of this base as rendered through high altitude imaging technologies, we are seeing a techno-cultural shadow of sorts—the military airbase on the ground.

Google Earth's view of Beale opens up a visual puzzle that includes a palimpsest for textual traces; thus the spy plane is remarked by its name, "Blackbird." As Snyder's "No Shadow" cites a visual overlap between the osprey and the cargo plane, so too does Google Earth register a corollary overlay at Beale Air Force Base, between sighting planes and citing birds. Each text cites collusions between militarized flight and ornithological reference–perception: Snyder's poem sights a bird, and then sees how an Air Force plane is like and unlike a bird; Google Earth overlays the word "Blackbird" on the visual field of a military air base, inviting animality into to the scene.

On the Grid

To find a clearer picture of the SR-71 Blackbird I resort to Google Images, and I enter the word "blackbird" into the search bar. What comes up is a tangle of bird citing, yet neatly arranged on a new media grid:

Figure 8.15 Blackbird image search at www.google.com

Contra Wallace Stevens, Google suggests that there are "about 1,630,000" ways of looking at a blackbird—and this is an ocular amalgam in which planes and birds are thoroughly commingled. On the grid, we see the SR-71 spy plane from different angles intermixed with images of various species of blackbirds.

I select the first image of the SR-71, a "wallpaper" download that again redirects the focus to the screen in front of my eyes.[16] A bird's eye view and the comportment of the ordinary computer user are conflated in this search:

Figure 8.16 Lockheed SR 71 Blackbird Wallpaper at www.wallpaperpimper.com

We see the aircraft from a meta-aerial perspective, a bird's eye view of the plane that includes the rugged terrain unfurling below. It is as if Stevens's "twenty snowy mountains" continue to frame and subtend the movement of the Blackbird. Both the spy plane *and* the underlying topography are shown to be quite literally *on the grid*: they lie beneath the surveillance gaze of a spy plane one level removed—these are the roving eyes of the new media subject, the plugged-in Googler. In the culture of flight, among twenty snowy mountains, everything is on the grid.

Hawaiian birds

This multiply nested grid form of bird citing in fact has an antecedent in the culture of flight. As if borrowing from the logic of a Google image search,

Hawaiian Airlines produced a magazine advertisement sometime in the early 2000s that placed its own aircraft in another grid of bird citing:

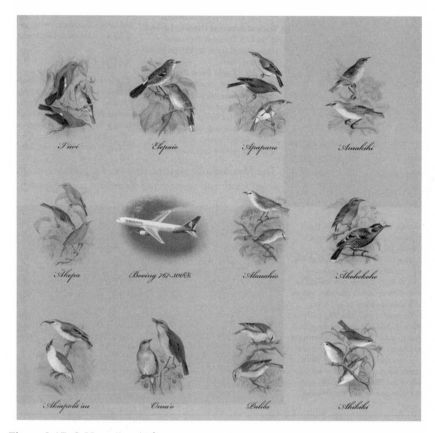

Figure 8.17 © Hawaiian Airlines

In this diagram, a commercial airliner is cleverly folded into a grid of Hawaiian birds. The Boeing 767-300ER is set amid painterly illustrations of resident bird species, and thus the wide-body jet is figured into a native framework by way of catalogued birdlife. The plane is off-scale and out of place, and yet the grid works through the metaphorical turn of bird citing: from the right perspective, a plane is another airborne object to watch.

We might probe further inconsistencies in this ad. The practically weightless birds rest on tree branches, while the 400,000-pound jet full of human beings is not at its arrivals gate—it is *in flight*. The birds captured at rest suggest the vantage point of a birder, or an armchair enthusiast reading an Audubon book; the airliner, on the other hand, requires the viewer to be *above*, to gain an almost impossible bird's eye view—we get this view, in fact, from within the SR-71 Blackbird spy plane. This advertising matrix depends on multiple levels of bird citing: the grid is redoubled, at once a playful, associative assemblage of flying objects—and a militarized, aerially monitored order of things.

Bridge back to the airport

We never strayed too far from the Sacramento airport. A Hawaiian Airlines 767-300ER departs to Honolulu from Sacramento each morning at 9:00 A.M. If we were taking this flight, upon arriving at the airport we would have to cross from the parking structure to Terminal A, traversing a pedestrian bridge that spans the pick-up and drop-off lanes in front of the terminal. Looking out of the floor-to-ceiling windows of this enclosed bridge, we might see Dennis Oppenheim's "Flying Gardens" blasting out of the parking structure. We might not look down in this space, but if we were to, we would see another art installation: Seyed Alavi's "Flying Carpet."

Figure 8.18 "Flying Carpet" by Seyed Alavi at the Sacramento airport (author's photo)

This art piece consists of a high-density wool carpet rendering of an aerial view of approximately 50 miles of the Sacramento River valley. The bird citing in this instance happens to be *us*, human passengers who may glance casually down and see a strip of California from a bird's eye view. Like Snyder's osprey—or perhaps more like Snyder's cargo plane—we glide above the river as we make our way from the garage to check-in.

Alavi suggests that the artwork can be "read" as a "welcome mat" for visitors arriving in Sacramento.[17] The installation thus contains a *textual* prompt. Alavi goes on to explain the siting of this piece eloquently:

> A bridge is a connection between two destinations; it is not a destination in and of itself; it is neither here, nor there. In this way it is similar to an airplane, or a river connecting one place to another; here to there; a moment of flight frozen in mid air; a flowing river that takes us along with its current to another destination. In this way, the piece also creates a koanic relationship between a river and a bridge, since their ordinary positions have been turned around, and it is now the river that is on/above the bridge.[18]

This is a beautiful interpretation of "Flying Carpet." And yet, there is another koanic relationship implied by this piece. The perspective adopted by the passenger is also akin to the blackbird—the actual bird, but also the spy plane based out of Beale. The civilian traveler becomes a militarized subject, or a soaring animal (and to recall Snyder, perhaps a *hunting* animal). As we have seen, the flights of birds, commercial airliners, and military aircraft are thoroughly entangled in the Sacramento River valley. Flight cannot be reduced to nature or culture—it is a mesh full of vibrant *actants*.[19] Added to the play between river and bridge, nowhere and somewhere, "Flying Carpet" also 'turns around' the subject positions of flying and walking as well as bird's eye view and human navigation. This art piece is a bird citing in that it aestheticizes a comportment at turns the most technological (the SR-71 Blackbird) and the most "natural" (the osprey). The human becomes animal either way.

Waiting in Sacramento

Let us continue to follow this onto-story. Having checked-in for the flight to Honolulu, we may have time to kill before boarding. Luckily, Sacramento is one of the airports that features "free WiFi."

Airport waiting invites the very sort of bird citing that we have been conducting through Google Earth sighting and Google image search. This becomes another valence of the airport screening complex, a textual loop that has been lurking throughout this chapter: the way that the screen and aerial vision can share a bird's eye view. Indeed, this form of airport reading—Internet browsing—is increasingly commonplace, even when it seems to have nothing to do with bird citing. In other words, the textual life of airports brings us into intimate contact with our own strange animality:

Figure 8.19 Free WiFi at the Sacramento airport (author's photo)

Googling is a kind of species behavior, another form of flitting about. And yet, I want to suggest that there is another layer of bird citing to consider at this juncture of wireless information systems and airport waiting.

Consider the human subject in the midst of airport waiting:

Figure 8.20 Waiting in the Sacramento airport (author's photo)

I have shown throughout this book how airport reading—whether in the form of the novel, the magazine, or free WiFi—staves off boredom; but such textual proclivity also evinces the looming presence of boredom, threatening at every instant, at the click of each overhead announcement for boarding that might announce a delay. As we have seen in the bloom of dead time, and through ecology in waiting, airports produce massive amounts of what Giorgio Agamben, following Heidegger, might identify as "profound boredom."[20]

Agamben articulates how "the man who becomes bored finds himself in the 'closest proximity'—even if it is only apparent—to animal captivation."[21] In this formulation, airport waiting might comprise *the most* animal experience known to humans. In a counterintuitive turn, the apex of human progress (digital technologies notwithstanding) becomes the place where humans confront their animality. Bird citing, in this light, becomes not only a conflicted semiotic zone where the inspiration of flight is also its nemesis (as in "bird strikes"), it also becomes symptomatic of a more general paranoia about the cage that humans have created for themselves, the grid that humans have constructed: they call it *freedom*.

As a closing example of bird citing, I want to turn to a passage from Don DeLillo's novel *The Names*:

> Air travel reminds us who we are. It's the means by which we recognize ourselves as modern. The process removes us from the world and sets us apart from each other. We wander in the ambient noise, checking one more time for the flight coupon, the boarding pass, the visa. The process convinces us that at any moment we may have to submit to the force that is implied in all this, the unknown authority behind it, behind the categories, the languages we don't understand. This vast terminal has been erected to examine souls.
>
> It is not surprising, therefore, to see men with submachine guns, to see *vultures* squatting on the baggage vehicles set at the end of the tarmac in the airport in Bombay when one arrives after a night flight from Athens.[22]

For DeLillo, "men with submachine guns" are juxtaposed all too easily with the inexplicably italicized *"vultures"*—a bird citing once again signals the collusion of animality and technology that troubles any clear sense of priority in the textual life of airports. Bird citing is no simple matter. The culture of flight both "removes us from the world" and examines our souls; the collision of birds and aircraft is the semaphore of modernity, and a species indicator of a particular kind of mortal life, one that involves an abundance of waiting before flight.

CHAPTER 9

CLAIMING BAGGAGE

Other Twin Towers

In the baggage claim area of Terminal A at the Sacramento airport, sparrows flit in and out of the sliding glass doors, pecking crumbs of Cinnabons off the floor and troubling the inside/outside boundary. In between the carousels, two columns of suitcases swell out of baggage carts and reach up to the ceiling, as if precarious piles of long lost luggage.

Figure 9.1 "Samson" by Brian Goggin at the Sacramento airport (author's photo)

This is Brian Goggin's brilliant art installation "Samson." The sculptures consist of over 700 pieces of donated vintage luggage; these items spill absurdly upward, reaching a ceiling joist and appearing to prop up the space. The artwork is a sort of paean to all the belongings that circulate through the airport. It may provoke a chuckle, or a gasp—passengers have been known to mistake these twin towers for actual heaps of checked luggage that they then must sort through to find their own bags. The installation thus serves as another instance of "the ache of stunning ruins," in which an airport produces a vision of progress at its end. In the case of passengers who mistake "Samson" for actual unclaimed luggage, the baggage claim prompts a sudden feeling that the airport has ceased working—as if all the baggage has been left unsorted in a mass exodus of airport workers. This somber sensibility is also implied in the name of the artwork, with its allusion to the mythical subject who commits an at once liberating and destructive act of suicide, bringing down the very structure that confines him.

In the real time hustle and commotion of the baggage claim area, however, deplaned passengers often seem barely to be aware of the art that both mocks and pays tribute to their travel. These other twin towers are part of the textual life of the airport: they make up an innocuous art piece meant to distract and sooth travelers at the end of their journeys, but they can just as easily slip into the background inventory of terminal affects.

This book ends in the baggage claim. This is the endpoint of air travel, a space rife with emotion, uncertainty, relief, and exhaustion. It marks the threshold where the textual life of airports bleeds out into everyday life: it is where all the stories of flight are told to those whom we meet or with whom we are reunited. It is a place of excitement and anticipation—but it can also be a place of low energy and feelings of impatience. Claiming baggage marks a final interpretive zone (and an act) where the culture of flight both congeals and disperses.

That endless jumble

As Alain de Botton describes the baggage claim in *A Week at the Airport*,

> . . . in the end, there was something irremediably melancholic about the business of being reunited with one's luggage. After hours in the air free of encumbrance, spurred to formulate hopeful plans for the future by the views of coasts and forests below, passengers were reminded, on standing at the carousel, of all that was material and burdensome in existence.[1]

De Botton contrasts the unencumbered time of actual flight with the heavy realities of life on the ground. For de Botton, the baggage claim marks the zero level of air travel, the point where the romance is over and physical belongings remind travelers of all their tedious obligations and fraught everyday lives.

This sentiment seems to be echoed and amplified by the poet W.D. Snodgrass in his poem "Baggage Claim," which is staged in the eponymous area of the airport.[2] In this poem, the speaker observes as a cycle of luggage is "dropped suddenly into place: / that endless jumble slithering past— / suitcases, golf clubs, backpacks, bags— / yanked off the belt to be checked out."[3] At first this resembles little more than a catalog of what Don DeLillo called the "microhistories" that scatter at the end of any single flight.

However, this baggage is not from the speaker's flight. The speaker watches "one last black bag alone, vanishing / ten times into the rough black curtains / unclaimed." The speaker's "plane [is] down, / but still not listed for unloading;" this instance of the airport screening complex (the posted 'list' of flights in the baggage claim) punctures the space and opens up a speculative poetic moment: why the delay? It turns out that past the "rough black curtains" there is a military service taking place, for a dead marine, killed by "*a roadside / bomb blast*" whose casket "had quietly been slipped on board."

This poem comprises one 26-line stanza that describes the commonplace scene and the grim denouement; and then there is an ending couplet that returns to the banality of the scene:

Bag after bag now crawled past to be
accepted, then hauled off as our own.[4]

In other words, the shape of this poem is a contained block of line-broken text that moves out of the airport and into memories and distant wartime realities; and then there is an empty space for thought, followed by these closing two lines that somewhat redouble the closure while bringing us back into the ambience of the airport.

In Snodgrass's poem, baggage is linked to human biomass and associated with cultural practices concerning the ends of war. Baggage claims become spaces where we might glimpse—or be prohibited from seeing—the bare life of contemporary military pursuits. The poem allows Snodgrass to locate political consciousness in a specific, everyday social space: the poem discovers a hidden view in the common place of the baggage claim. The dead marine remains concealed from public sight, and yet the poem opens a brief and imaginative aperture through which we suddenly experience the baggage claim as a machine for the processing of militarized bodily remains. Mundane "suitcases, golf clubs, backpacks, bags" and "roadside bombs" have been conjoined in the poem "Baggage Claim."

How does poetry become the apt means for this expression? It turns out that claiming baggage is also a matter of aesthetics. In *On Beauty and Being Just*, Elaine Scarry explores "errors in beauty," one of which involves how "an object already within the [perceptual] horizon, has its beauty, like late luggage, suddenly placed in your hands."[5] Scarry uses this idea to analyze how certain things are "repudiated" as potential objects of beauty—only to be discovered "suddenly" to be quite beautiful indeed. Snodgrass's poem manifests this error, by which the gritty baggage claim becomes doubly ugly—not just a collection of people's stuff, but also a repository for human remains—only to become an abruptly *poetic* subject.

The high-end outdoor-apparel company Patagonia banked on this aesthetic turn in an advertisement for a piece of luggage called the MLC, or "Maximum Legal Carry-On."

Figure 9.2 MLC® (Maximum Legal Carry-On) ad © 2008 at www.patagonia.com

In one particular ad campaign from 2008, the MLC was touted as the way to "skip baggage claim"—here the familiar airport endpoint is automatically assumed to be the bane of existence, a non-place in the most quotidian and undesirable sense of the term. In this image, an avoidable realm is conjured by the textual mention—and graphic elision—of the baggage claim. The suave traveler in a crisp white shirt is poised against spray painted, corrugated metal siding, as if already traveling, while further delayed passengers wait for their bags in the negative space of the airport. Meanwhile, the MLC bag stands out as a tense signifier, caught in between the atrocious airport and sublime adventure locations: it *is* baggage, but it also *subverts* baggage. It is beauty pitted against heavier loads that defy beauty—"that endless jumble" of suitcases snaking around the carousel, those objects that, to recall de Botton's descriptor, remind us of all that is material and burdensome in existence.

Do they match?

Claiming baggage is also a psychological diagnosis of sorts; it is something we say when we seek to displace accountability: "He has a lot of baggage."

This trope was famously literalized in the opening credit scenes of Mike Nichols's 1967 film *The Graduate*. In many ways, the entire film is anticipated by Dustin Hoffman's arrival in LAX, with an ingenious cut from the character Benjamin Braddock on a moving walkway, to the eerily symmetrical image of Benjamin's suitcase progressing along the baggage conveyor.

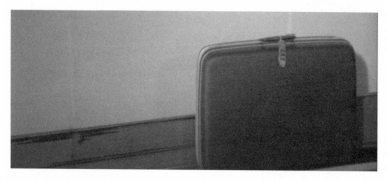

Figures 9.3 and 9.4 Stills from *The Graduate* (© 1967 Embassy Pictures Corp.)

During this scene, Simon and Garfunkel's song "The Sound of Silence" is over-laid on top of the ambient sounds of a moving walkway and the passive over-head interpellations of the baggage claim: "PLEASE HOLD HANDRAIL AND STAND TO THE RIGHT" . . . "PLEASE MAKE YOUR CLAIM CHECK AVAILABLE TO SECURITY. . . ." As Benjamin's suitcase is deposited onto the carousel, a sign calls for passengers to double-check that the bag tags square with their checked-baggage stubs; a sign flashes by asking, "Do they match?" By this move, the recent college graduate and promising "track star" is suddenly equated with mere generic luggage. This juxtaposition anticipates the alienation of Dustin Hoffman's character throughout the film: he feels increasingly like an accessory without human agency. The LAX baggage claim scene makes the space—and takes the time—for this textually re-marked correspondence.

Other films have likewise exploited how equivalences can be drawn around the subject of baggage. For example, David Fincher's *Fight Club* (1999) uses the baggage claim to stage Edward Norton's character hit-ting rock bottom: when his luggage does not appear on the carousel in a gloomy baggage claim area, Norton initiates a conversation with an airline employee who describes the shiftless midnight work of baggage handlers, who are called "throwers" (an echo of the novel's original passage, discussed earlier in Chapter 2). The work of baggage handlers is never seen in the film, but is degradingly referred to in the cavernous space of the baggage claim. Meanwhile, in the background, a spectral Brad Pitt, who carries no checked luggage, hijacks a red convertible and races away from the curbside—thus reinforcing a series of claims to aesthetics, (im)mobility, and privilege that are consolidated in the subject of baggage.

In David O. Russell's *Three Kings* (1999), Ice Cube's character has joined the military in order to *not* work at the Detroit airport as a baggage handler any longer. At one point, a momentary analepsis shows Ice Cube hauling luggage around the tarmac—this airport scene is notably *even more* chaotic than much of the cinematography that imagines a very chaotic wartime Iraq in the film.

Along these same lines, Leonardo DiCaprio's character in Martin Scorsese's *The Departed* (2006), is given an analogous airport reading: when he is sized up by the police *and* by the gangsters with whom he is to go undercover, both parties recall that his father worked at the airport as a baggage handler. This appellation does double duty, at once providing proof that DiCaprio's character is in line with the law (for the state police department), and also reflecting an individualist work ethic that can be bent *against* the law (for the Boston Irish mob). In each of these cinematic cases, there occurs an underlying textual demand to ask of people and their baggage: *Do they match?*

Many Banks Look Alike

In the A concourse of the Portland, Oregon airport, U.S. Bank advertises its services through recourse to anxieties of equivalence that stem from claiming baggage. Within the ad, an illuminated sign warns, "MANY BANKS LOOK ALIKE."

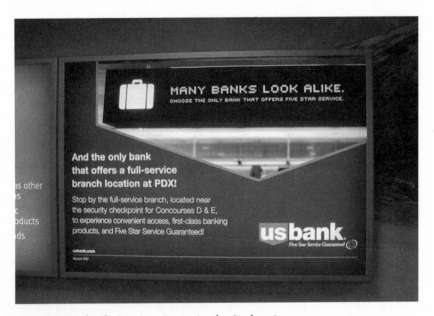

Figure 9.5 Portland, Oregon, airport (author's photo)

This message's typography appears to mimic pixels, as if to resemble the type of manipulable messaging systems mounted above baggage carousels. Indeed, an icon of a suitcase is situated to the left of this message, explicitly forcing the pun of *banks* and *bags*. Beneath the sign within the sign, a blurry baggage claim area appears. (Keep in mind, this is all framed within an advertisement that is located near the *departure gates* in this concourse—quite far away from the actual baggage claim area, therefore adding to the semiotic confusion.) The textual life of airports is teeming in this advertisement. First, the sign equates *banking* with *baggage*; as if capital itself is something that one has to check through to distant locations, and then haul off as one's own—and in a way, it *is*. But there is also the possibility of mistaking another banking for one's own—capital is murkily individual, and in fact always threatens to flatten different bankers/travelers' differences. Of course, U.S. Bank is supposed to stand out as different, in this ad; as the small print reads, "choose the only bank with five star service." Still this claim to exception is muddied by the spatial dissonance of this sign: it invokes the baggage claim *in* the airport, but out of place—as if five star service does not translate to clear navigation. In fact, the sign does a sort of risky symbolic damage to the sterile/non-sterile designations of the airport: one is supposed to be in the *secure* zone within the concourse, and yet the U.S. Bank advertisement suggests that one has wound up in the baggage claim, an insecure, non-sterile site, where one's individuality is ambiguous at best, and an inescapable burden at worst.

Strictly speaking, one can never bank on the security of one's baggage—or *banking*, for that matter, as the film *Up In the Air* demonstrated, with its recession-era gloom casting a cynical shadow over the culture of flight. Walter Kirn's novel *Up In the Air* celebrated the almost endless possibilities of frequent flying in the euphoric glow of the late-90s; Jason Reitman's film adaptation, from the vantage point of a decade later, seemed to suggest that the textual life of airports cannot be read without claiming the baggage of economic speculations and bubble bursts. Many banks look alike, but they all come with baggage.

Notice of Baggage Inspection

Anxieties about claiming baggage are hardly restricted to these more abstract dimensions of banking and capital. An indicator of anxiety that literally gets into one's stuff can be found on the three-inch by eight-inch pieces of paper slipped into many passengers' bags, usually discovered and discarded far from the airport. This is the disposable document known as the "Notice of Baggage Inspection."

Figure 9.6 Notice of Baggage Inspection distributed by the U.S. Department of Homeland Security

This slip of paper provided by the Transportation Security Administration is a fascinating text; it both promises security and yet evinces insecurity—we find ourselves thrust back into the puzzle of airport detection. I proceed here to read this document slowly, with all the lessons from the textual life of airports well in mind. The first paragraph of the notice reads:

To protect you and your fellow passengers, the Transportation Security Administration (TSA) is required by law* to inspect all checked baggage. As a part of this process, some bags are opened and physically inspected. Your bag was among those selected for physical inspection.

This paragraph tries to be reassuring—the skies are safe, it is just you and your fellow passengers. And yet, the text betrays the language of a fascistic paranoia: *anyone* and *everyone* might be an enemy, and therefore *all* bags must be inspected—indeed, by the time you are reading this slip of paper, *your bag has already been ransacked.* The rhetoric in the paragraph proffers a deeply troubled partiality: *all* bags are to be inspected, but only *some* are chosen for "physical inspection." One wonders, then, what an inspection entails that is *not* physical; is this a metaphysical inspection, an ineffable *sensing* that certain bags are okay, and others not? What are the guidelines for this intuition, and how are they written into the legalities invoked by the asterisk: "*Section110(b) of the Aviation and Transportation Security Act of 2001, 49 U.S.C. 44901(c)–(e)*"?[6]

Practically speaking, the nonphysical inspection of baggage most likely refers to the monitoring of baggage flows from a distance, based on passenger background information provided by the airlines. Certainly, there is a vast system in place, and its mechanisms of supervision are being constantly improved and tested (as we saw in Chapter 5). And yet, one cannot help but note how the rhetoric of the notice sustains in the popular imagination a worst-case scenario wherein TSA agents discover (and possibly detonate) a bomb concealed in a suitcase. And for however long, through the moments of physical inspection, they thought that bag might be *yours.* The personal suitcase can be the Samson(ite) that might tear down the structure around it. The airport hovers behind the text, as a secure(d) space verging on ground zero—and this textual drift continues as long as these slips of paper can be wedged into "some bags."

This well-known text travels beyond the walls of the airport and into homes or far-flung destinations; it may be ignored or seem innocuous. Yet even the most disinterested action of pulling out this notice and tossing it in the waste bin serves to reinforce a widespread hysteria around the culture of flight: this is a luxurious imprisonment in a matrix of mobility where *some* are *all,* the most secure is the most vulnerable, the physical blurs into the nonphysical, and inspection has no bounds. Last, the "you" of the notice is not *you* if you are the real target of the notice, a so-called terrorist. In other words, the *you* of the notice is a present absence, a somebody who turned out to be nobody, because the inspectors found underwear instead of uranium in your bag. Your "fellow passengers" are similarly slippery, promised to be friends but just as easily imagined as foes. Everyone is claimed to be a patriotic flying fellow, but *you* have been singled out as suspect. The baggage claimed by this notice is heavy, and it goes way beyond individual pieces of luggage.

The second paragraph of the notice is short but even more troubling: "During the inspection, your bag and its contents may have been searched for prohibited items. At the completion of the inspection, the contents were returned to your bag." The text suggests a possibility that has in fact already been guaranteed: one *knows* that one's bag has been searched by the very fact of reading the document at hand, otherwise the notice would (presumably) not be present. Does this language in fact hint that certain bags are searched *without* notice? And if so, how might the present notice function as a red herring of sorts, distracting the passenger from more covert methods of inspection that cannot be validated or interpreted by a TSA-stamped notice?

Aside from a bomb, what other items are prohibited to be "checked" (and therefore must be *checked for*) in baggage? Here we might recall the bloody incident in the baggage claim area of Tel Aviv's Lod International Airport on May 30, 1972: three deplaned passengers picked up their checked luggage, opened their Samsonite suitcases, removed machine guns and hand grenades, and proceeded to wreak havoc on a crowd of around 300 people. In *Airspaces*, David Pascoe highlights this event to signal a shift to "strategic time," a phrase coined by Paul Virilio in his writings on terrorist attacks in international airports. For Pascoe, via Virilio, airports come to instantiate a new type of geographical territory where many time zones converge and overlap, creating particularly rich targets for violent acts of extremism—this also reflexively does conceptual violence to the "civilian" aspects of airports, since they become sites for (inter)national defense.[7] In the TSA notice, "strategic time" comes through a perplexing textual surface that translates the manifest baggage claim as a latent bloodbath.

A glaring irony of the notice occurs where it states, "at the completion of the inspection, the contents were returned to your bag." Wait—this makes it sound as if it includes the return of any prohibited items that were found: they are simply inspected, then replaced? Clearly not. Yet strangely, this *would* be the case with acceptable items such as handguns, hunting rifles, and ammunition: they would most likely be inspected, and then replaced. Guns, then, are not prohibited, and indisputably can result in terminal disaster. The differences between "prohibited items" and the "contents" of baggage can be semantically confused, actively elided, or simply overlooked.

The next two sections of the Notice explain the protocols for locked baggage:

> If the TSA security officer was unable to open your bag for inspection because it was locked, the officer may have been forced to break the locks on your bag. TSA sincerely regrets having to do this, however TSA is not liable for damage to your locks resulting from this necessary security precaution.
>
> For packing tips and suggestions on how to secure your baggage during your next trip, please visit: www.tsa.gov

Through these two sections, an infinite regress precedes a paradox. Who forces the officer to break the locks? Is there a TSA Security Officer Enforcer who surveils and screens the TSA security officers? But then who would watch over the TSA Enforcer? In short, can the supervision of security ever really end? Who can safely exist outside of an all-encompassing airport inspection? Security has left the Panopticon. Speaking of security, this concept is alluded to six times in the seventy-one words of the above paragraphs: two times exactly, three times implied in the acronym TSA (Transportation SECURITY Administration), and once by the word "secure." It is as if the idea of security is instated through sheer repetition, while also radically taken away in order to insist on ambient conditions of insecurity all around. The counterintuitive point of these absurdly layered securities is that, in order to be secure, one's bags *cannot under any circumstances be secured*. But then, visiting the TSA website will supposedly give us tips as to how one *can* secure a piece of luggage. Security relies on our being insecure about our own baggage, uncertain about our fellow passengers, and surrounded by a plethora of security agents and implied over-agents, a veritable theology of the regime of Security.

Toward the bottom of the notice, one encounters some pleasantries of the TSA: "We appreciate your understanding and cooperation. If you have questions, comments, or concerns, please feel free to contact the TSA Contact Center:"—the colon is followed by a toll-free phone number and an email address. But what precise "understandings" have been communicated in this notice? From even the most preliminary—if admittedly drawn out—reading of this document, its content appears deeply problematic, and functionally awkward. While thanking passengers for their cooperation, the document in fact declares absolute exception *from* passengers' "cooperation." If your bags are locked, tough luck: TSA agents will break them. In fact, the notice is written especially for those who *have not* cooperated—for those passengers who have locked their bags. How close, one wonders, have these uncooperative passengers veered toward the brink of illegality by attempting to secure their own luggage? Finally, travelers/readers are encouraged to "feel free" to use email or telephones to get in touch with a contact center. The expansiveness of the phrase "feel free" rings hollow on a slip of paper that has been clandestinely shoved into one's so-called personal belongings.

How does the TSA notice manage these intense contradictions? The textual life of airports mediates: the semiotics of the document present cleanly formatted text, blue horizontal lines as if demarcating runways, the familiar sign of bird citing (as hinted at above, this is an eagle carrying arrows and an olive branch, replete with a shield showing inset plates of mountains, waves, and stars), a website, phone number, and email address. Most curious, the last bit of text, slightly off-centered, reads: "Smart Security Saves Time." As we have seen, claiming baggage often turns on poetics: the alliterative S sounds give a smoothness to this slogan, in fact saving the time it takes to say the words—alliteration is efficient diction. This single declarative sentence, in all its economy and poetry, begs further questions: Is transportation security about saving time, or saving *lives*? What sort of "time" is being saved through smart security? This is Virilio's "strategic time" again, here in service of tactical security. But this strategic time also hearkens the "dead time" of reading, in which the traveler is ensnared in a web of protocols and contingencies in preparation for flight, forestalling a trip to the airport in favor of textual attempts to understand how security works.

Claiming the future

The dilemma of (in)secure baggage is indicative of how we struggle to claim presence in the culture of flight—as well as the challenge of claiming the future of airports.

The environmental theorist Timothy Morton has written about an early morning trip to the airport in the "airporter" van as a kind of uncanny event in which "the journey becomes a stimulating kind of jazz."[8] As Morton experiences his hometown streets in unpredictable ways, the trip *to* the airport foregrounds how "the sense of place is already a displacement." In other words, the secure sense of a *known* place (like one's "home") functions as a *displacement* of all the weird routes and withdrawn locations that surround.

Morton claims that, "capitalism has ruthlessly demystified the notion of place only to re-place it with other forms of interstitial place such as airport lounges."[9] And yet oddly enough, airports can be somewhat reclaimed. Morton provides an example of this in a description of one particular airport in comparison to others:

> I like San Francisco Airport. I don't usually like airports. But I do like this one—actually I really like it. I always look forward to transiting here. It's been designed carefully, you can see that. Someone thought about the not too foreboding signage. Someone really thought about the interconnected hubs. They dilute the flow of traffic and provide true way stations for you to orient yourself, as well as bringing the gates closer together. The absolute contrast for me would be Dulles or Chicago. I almost like Denver. But the libertarians who set up the wifi should never be allowed to mess with public space again.[10]

This is no mere pragmatic evaluation of comparable non-places. Rather, this is more in line with what we earlier explored as an airport study: Morton's prose reflects his position that ordinary things—from our lawns to the weather—should be reconceived as "extended phenotypes of homo sapiens." From this perspective, whenever "we acknowledge a shared neutral space," we might readjust our focus and see that wherever we are is in fact reducible to how we are living (in) it.[11] Our baggage really is our baggage.

An explicit attempt to claim the future of air travel, John Kasarda and Greg Lindsay have called their book *Aerotropolis: The Way We'll Live Next* (2011). This text expounds on the jerky and stuttered history of flight, and the authors wager on a promise of vast cities planned to accommodate a surge of air transit in the years to come—these are *aerotropoli*. A curious aspect of this book emerges in its vacillation between evolutionary logic and an insistence that humans can break out of certain "natural" patterns by sheer will. An example of this oscillation can be seen in conflicting sentences throughout the book. For example, at one point Kasarda and Lindsay insist, "the aerotropolis isn't born, it's made. It doesn't occur naturally or simply emerge from the urban cores it's supplanting."[12] And yet mere pages later, when Kasarda and Lindsay describe the very city that they previously asserted was *made*, not born, they describe it this way:

> The shape of the Memphis aerotropolis tells this story in much the same way a redwood encodes a lifetime of rains and droughts into its rings. It's the urban embodiment of an evolution from warehousing to distribution to logistics that

took less than twenty years and saw it rise from a necessary evil to the front lines in an eternal war on costs and the competition.[13]

Mixed metaphors aside, what is most crucial in this passage for the textual life of airports is the metaphor of the redwood tree that "encodes" its history into its own material: this assessment of the culture of flight is exactly right, and yet the consequences of this seem to escape the authors, who are far more interested in telling a story about a vulgar Darwinism, a teleological struggle based on economic survival of the fittest (or *fastest*, in Kasarda and Lindsay's version). *Aerotropolis* is uncertain about whether we can think about airports as 'natural' habitats—like beaver dams—or whether we must imagine them as super-natural spaces, extending *from* evolutionary networks yet somehow willed to exist *outside* these very systems, in perfected form. Indeed, the city models depicted in the book are visualized as Platonic urban grids from a familiarly detached aerial view (the perspective of a drone plane?), with no mortals in sight.

To really think rigorously about the "natural" or evolutionary aspects of air travel (or human life, for that matter), would be to pose far more pro-found—if also grounded—questions about the ways we live *now*, and what sort of baggage we have to claim in order to *have* a future. The critic Ian Bogost, in a shrewd review of *Aerotropolis*, puts it this way: Kasarda and Lindsay fail to tackle "the question of what it *feels like* to live 'the way we'll live next.'"[14] Bogost proposes that, among other things, we should wonder:

> How does the aerotropolis age work? What would living in such a situation entail? What worries would arise, and what might I want to change? What are the eco-nomic, political, and social forces that I would have to contend with? What fanta-sies or expectations about the twentieth century would I have to leave behind?[15]

It is just some of these "fantasies and expectations about the twentieth cen-tury" that we have been unpacking throughout the present study, and in par-ticular seeing the baggage we have to claim around the subject of airports. As we have seen, when we begin to consider deep time and vast space, the minutes of waiting for one's bag to appear on a black belt take on a differ-ent kind of resonance. Bogost ends his review by suggesting, "*Aerotropolis* underscores the fact that the story of the twenty-first century will not be one of stories, at all, but of systems instead."[16] Bogost has hit on a critical tension in the textual life of airports, for this reveals how the frenzy of nar-ratives spinning out of the culture of flight becomes a signifying system that cannot keep track of its own meanings.

Concrete parentheses

To bring us back to literal acts of claiming baggage, I want to end by looking at an instructional polemic concerning the culture of flight. Rachel Lehmann-Haupt and Bess Abrahams co-authored a book called *Airplane Yoga*, which wraps the entire experience of flight in practical and case-specific yoga exercises. Curiously, while the book's title is *Airplane Yoga*, more than half of the pages are concerned with *airport* spaces. To directly quote the authors, "This book is organized to parallel your airport experience."[17] Rather than elide the space/time of the airport in lieu of the more romantic spectacle of flight, *Airplane Yoga* lingers in this banal environment as if to rethink the airport as an overlooked chance for mindful presence. The airport, in other words, is metaphorized as a makeshift yoga studio.

Airplane Yoga follows the traveler through the stages of checking in, passing through security, waiting to board, being in-flight, deplaning, all the way through the baggage claim, and finally out to the curb, where the reader is left waiting for one's ride. The text, in other words, is itself a narrative journey, redoubling the metaphoric value of travel, with each scene warranting its own illustration and diagrams for appropriate poses. For our purposes here, I focus on the baggage claim.

In the penultimate section, under the heading "luggage," the reader is instructed to stretch one's arms, for "that long luggage haul to your final destination." A simple note follows: "You will need room to stretch your arms out to the side."[18]

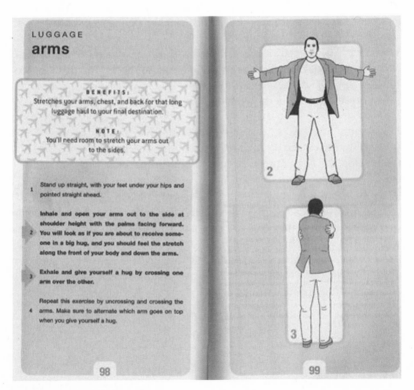

Figure 9.7 © *Airplane Yoga*

These straightforward messages contain, to rephrase Ludwig Wittgenstein, a stress ball of philosophy condensed in a single yoga pose. First off, the instructions dramatically deemphasize the distance of air travel: a thousand-mile flight is suddenly outweighed by another journey to one's car or public transit at the airport. The geography of elevated crosswalks, subterraneous escalators, and concrete parking structures becomes a veritable wilderness in and of itself; the textual inversion of expansiveness retains the airport as a transition point, but still manages to deflect perception to other spaces.

This particular yoga position designed for the end of a flight is unsettled by the anticipation of a journey still to come; the space of the airport is *anxiously* aware of other spaces. In the diagram for "luggage," note how the white frame around the traveler expands and contracts with his arm movements. The visualization of space reveals an environmental sensibility at work: the traveler/reader is called upon to really *perceive* space: as *flexible* and as *inhabitable*—but also as contained and *restricted*. To notice one's own personal space and to *expand* this space in an airport requires not only that one become aware of the room around oneself, but also that one pay attention to *others*. But the empty margins of the page belie actual airport conditions; the baggage claim would most likely be full of people. Yet imagine an entire baggage claim converted into a room where everyone really *notices* each other, not to mention the grubby space itself. Would the baggage claim become spontaneously more efficient and friendly? Or might not the whole operation cease to function entirely, because people would pay more attention to one another than to their luggage going round and round? How much awareness can an airport handle? A booklet on yoga would be entirely justified to forward a full-on critique of the speed and frantic pace of air travel; but for obvious reasons, the authors of *Airplane Yoga* must strike a conciliatory note, since their book is a utilitarian treatise of sorts. This conciliation relies on a balance of spatial preferences, through which the airport both calls for and resists interpretation, at turns.

The exercise called "arms" involves hugging oneself: this ostensibly prepares one physically and mentally for the long haul to the final destination. It appears that one is preparing to hug someone *else*—but then one hugs one*self*. In other words, *Airplane Yoga* does not advocate hugging other human beings in this space: the therapeutic hugging is always only for oneself. Arms become parentheses around the self; this is peculiarly like how airports are figured by Marc Augé as "immense parentheses"[19] around many people's day-to-day lives. But, as Timothy Morton notes, "concrete parenthesis is not just a case of vast airports, but of abandoned airports."[20] In other words, there is always more happening around the airport than the mere health or satisfaction of singular traveling subjects; this is decay at work, too. Morton's prompt to imagine the inoperative "junkspace" of abandoned airports serves to jar us into seeing that systems are grinding away: space is spent, and incredible amounts of resources are consumed. And perhaps stranger still, this is no less than "the face of the infinite."[21] Airports cannot be left unclaimed.

Some airports, like Denver's Stapleton, have in fact been abandoned—in these cases, as Kasarda and Lindsay rightly note in *Aerotropolis*, it matters very much what we do with these spaces. We might even invite these spaces into being. Anticipating the future might mean taking the lessons of *Airplane Yoga* more seriously than the authors intended: it might mean hugging more than ourselves on the ground, and it might mean embracing abandoned airports.

Late baggage delivery

After the last inbound flight would arrive at the airport in Bozeman, it was my job to coordinate late baggage delivery for those passengers whose lost luggage had finally arrived. This baggage was usually recognizable by being significantly scuffed and bereft looking, and festooned with multiple rerouting bag tags. These bags would be sitting askew on the carousel after all the passengers had left the terminal.

After I sorted out the bag tag mysteries and confirmed passengers' whereabouts, I had a list of phone numbers I was supposed to call: these were for local drivers, free agents of sorts who charged exorbitant fees to deliver late baggage to even the farthest flung locations at the bleakest hours. I remember hauling duffle bags and hard-sided cases out the sliding glass doors at the darkest hours, and loading them into dusty, souped-up Oldsmobile or Mercury sedans. The drivers had sometimes just woken up, called to duty by a phone call from United Airlines. They were often drinking cans of Red Bull or Monster Energy. The late baggage loaded, they would tear off into the night, leaving me at the curbside of the deserted airport, the inky sky pressing down.

As I would head back into the airport to finish up my shift, though, I'd see the uniformed janitor getting ready to vacuum the terminal floor, and then I'd notice the Delta workers dealing with *their* late baggage—their final flight of the night arrived an hour after the last United plane landed.

The textual life of airports carries on: even when all the airport employees go home for the night, somewhere a driver will be racing across Montana, even into the first flush of sunrise, to deliver someone's lost luggage as magpies begin to caw.

NOTES

Introduction

1 Sam Shepard, "Land of the Living," *The New Yorker*, April 11, 2009, 83.
2 Marc Augé, *Non-Places: Introduction to an Anthropology of Supermodernity*, trans. John Howe (New York: Verso, 1995), 96 (my emphasis).
3 Roland Barthes, "From Work to Text," *Image Music Text*, trans. Stephen Heath (New York: Hill & Wang, 1977), 161.
4 Donna Haraway, *When Species Meet* (Minneapolis: University of Minnesota Press, 2007), 4.
5 Ibid.
6 Lev Manovich, "Introduction to Info-Aesthetics," *Antinomies of Art and Culture*, ed. Smith et al. (Durham, NC: Duke University Press, 2008), 343.
7 Nate Silver, "The Full-Body Backlash," *The New York Times*, online, November 15, 2010: http://fivethirtyeight.blogs.nytimes.com/2010/11/15/the-full-body-backlash/?scp=1&sq =Americans%20are%20willing%20to%20tolerate%20a%20great%20number%20 of%20things%20at%20the%20airport%20&st=cse (accessed January 4, 2011).
8 F. Scott Fitzgerald, "Three Hours between Planes," *Esquire*, 1941: http://www.gutenberg. net.au/fsf/THREE-HOURS-BETWEEN-PLANES.html (accessed May 20, 2009).
9 Ibid.
10 Impressive and nuanced accounts of the culture of flight in a broader sense than I take up here can be found in David Pascoe's two books *Airspaces* (London: Reaktion, 2001) and *Aircraft* (London: Reaktion, 2004), and in Robert Wohl's *A Passion for Wings: Aviation and the Western Imagination, 1908–1918* (Yale, 1996) and *The Spectacle of Flight: Aviation and the Western Imagination, 1920–1950* (Yale, 2005).
11 Jacques Derrida, "Autoimmunity: Real and Symbolic Suicides," in Giovanna Borradori, *Philosophy in a Time of Terror: Dialogues with Jürgen Habermas and Jacques Derrida* (Chicago: University of Chicago, 2003), 95.
12 Jennifer Price, *Flight Maps: Adventures with Nature in Modern America* (New York: Basic Books, 1999), 187
13 Jane Bennett, *Vibrant Matter: A Political Ecology of Things* (Durham, NC: Duke University Press, 2010), 4, 116.

Chapter 1

1 Augé, *Non-Places*, 2.
2 Walter Kirn, *Up in the Air* (New York: Anchor Books, 2001).
3 Ibid., 1.
4 Fredric Jameson, *Postmodernism, or, The Cultural Logic of Late Capitalism* (Durham, NC: Duke University Press, 1990), 2–3.
5 Kirn, *Up in the Air*, 7.

6   Ibid., 10.

7   Erin Collazo Miller, "Bestsellers: Airport Reads" at about.com http://bestsellers.about.com/od/readingrecommendations/tp/airport_reading.htm (accessed November 20, 2010.

8   Lorrie Moore, *A Gate at the Stairs* (New York: Knopf, 2009), 77.

9   In Chapter 4, I analyze airport figures in three specific works of post-9/11 fiction.

10 The relationship between airports and screened entertainment is rife with complexities, a topic that I probe in Chapter 5.

11 Don DeLillo, *Underworld* (New York: Scribner, 1997), 827.

12 Ibid., 252.

13 DeLillo's phrase "out to the airport" raises another thematic of airport reading: perceptions of sparse geographies that make way for the concentrated space/time of departures and arrivals—and all the waiting in-between. I take up this matter in Chapter 3 as well as in the final chapter of this book.

14 For a more fantastical and dystopian take on a similar scene, see the short story "Wait" by Roy Kesey. This story is about an interminable airport delay caused by an unmovable fog, and about the absurdly wide range of activities that the passengers engage in to pass the time. Roy Kesey, "Wait," *All Over* (Westland, MI: Dzanc, 2007).

15 "The river is moving. / The blackbird must be flying." Wallace Stevens, "Thirteen Ways of Looking at a Blackbird," *The Palm at the End of the Mind,* ed. Holly Stevens (New York: Vintage, 1991), 166.

16 Marc Augé, *An Anthropology for Contemporaneous Worlds* (Stanford: Stanford University Press, 1999), 110.

17 This definition is from the *Oxford English Dictionary*, under the entry for *airport* in its attributive form: "Designating a work of popular fiction of a type commonly sold in airports as suitable for in-flight reading, and typically regarded as light or undemanding entertainment; designating a writer of this type of fiction."

18 Arthur Hailey, *Airport* (New York: Berkley Books, 1968, 2000), 5.

19 Michel Foucault, *Discipline and Punish: The Birth of the Prison,* trans. Alan Sheridan, 1977 (New York: Vintage, 1995), 202.

20 Ibid., 204.

21 Hailey, *Airport,* 533.

22 Ibid., 70.

23 Sacramento County Airport System, "The Big Build" Fly-Through Video, http://www.big-build.org/photo-media-gallery/design-overview/fly-through-video (accessed February 18, 2011).

24 Pascoe, *Airspaces,* 10.

25 Ibid., 11.

26 Augé, *Non-places,* 94.

27 Pascoe also discusses Arthur Hailey's *Airport* in a brilliant section that reads *Airport* through an allusion to the "junk novel" in Martin Amis's novel *The Information.* Pascoe goes on to forward a theory that aviation fiction makes travelers "feel more secure in their containment"— Pascoe then goes on to articulate what he sees as "an aesthetic affinity [. . .] between airspace and cinema" (251–4).

28 Joe Sharkey, "Registered Traveler Program Appears Ready to Take Off," *The New York Times* online, September 5, 2006, http://query.nytimes.com/gst/fullpage.html?res=9504E1 DF1631F936A3575AC0A9609C8B63 (accessed January 7, 2011).

29 Anthony Lane, "High and Low: Flying on the really cheap." *The New Yorker* (April 24, 2006), 60.

30 Brian Edwards, *The Modern Airport Terminal: New Approaches to Airport Architecture,* 2nd edn. (London and New York: Spon Press, 2005), xvi.

31 Jacques Derrida, "Ulysses Gramophone: Hear Say Yes in Joyce," *Acts of Literature,* ed. Derek Attridge (New York: Routledge, 1992), 309.

32 Augé, *Non-Places,* 108.

33 Alastair Gordon, *Naked Airport: A Cultural History of the World's Most Revolutionary Structure* (New York: Henry Holt and Company, 2004), 2.

Chapter 2

1   Chuck Palahniuk, *Fight Club* (New York: Owl Books, 1996), 42–3.
2   David Fincher's film adaptation of *Fight Club* (Twentieth Century Fox, 1999) repro-
    duces this scene with a similar effect, keeping Edward Norton's character (the narrator)
    bewildered and physically distanced from the airport security officer, who cracks wise
    and then waves off Norton's character, instead tuning into a phone conversation to
    which neither Norton's character nor the audience have access.
3   Pascoe, *Airspaces*, 253.
4   Mark B. Salter (ed.), *Politics at the Airport* (Minneapolis: University of Minnesota Press,
    2008), xiii.
5   Foucault, *Discipline and Punish*, 228.
6   Robert Sommer, *Tight Spaces: Hard Architecture and How to Humanize It* (Englewood
    Cliffs, NJ: Spectrum, 1974), v.
7   The title was later expanded to *The Love of the Last Tycoon: A Western*, under the edito-
    rial direction of Matthew Bruccoli (1994). While I refer to Bruccoli's edition of the text for
    all citations, I prefer to use the more streamlined title assigned by Edmund Wilson for the
    original edition: *The Last Tycoon—An Unfinished Novel* (New York: Scribner, 1941). To
    me, the earlier title reflects more accurately the fragmented and unfinished nature of the
    text.
8   F. Scott Fitzgerald, *The Love of the Last Tycoon: A Western*, ed. Matthew Bruccoli (New
    York: Scribner, 1994), 3.
9   Fitzgerald is, after all, considered to have been something of a Romantic holdover amid
    the trends of high Modernism; he also referred to this novel-in-progress as a "Romance."
    Indeed, the textual life of airports draws from certain Romantic tropes and aesthetic
    ideals.
10 *Tactical knowledge* and *airborne vision* had been culturally and technologically linked by
    the mid-1930s, as Paul Virilio has argued in "I See, I Fly" in *War and Cinema*: "When com-
    mercial flights began again in 1919, often using converted bombers like the Bréguet-14,
    aerial vision became a widespread phenomenon with a large public." Paul Virilio, *War and
    Cinema* (New York and London: Verso, 1989), 19.
11 Fitzgerald, *The Last Tycoon*, 6.
12 Ibid., 7–8.
13 See, e.g., the animated cartoon "Popeye the Sailor Meets Ali Baba's Forty Thieves," pro-
    duced in 1937 by Fleischer Studios. Wimpy the sailor sees a desert oasis with a fully
    set dinner table under a palm tree; when Wimpy attempts to leap onto it and eat, the
    scene disappears into nothing but sand. The cinematically depicted dialectic between oasis
    and mirage was thus well-ingrained in the popular mindset by the time that Fitzgerald
    described the airport as an oasis.
14 Hailey, *Airport*, 75, 88, 79.
15 Gordon, *Naked Airport*, 56.
16 Ibid., 56.
17 Ibid.
18 Robert A. Martin's essay "Fitzgerald's Use of History in *The Last Tycoon*" also mentions this
    moment of the text, albeit very briefly: "Even to 'the coastal rich ... who casually alighted from
    our cloud in mid-America' ... the airports seem depressing and sterile." *F. Scott Fitzgerald—
    New Perspectives*, ed. Jackson R. Bryer, Alan Margolies, and Ruth Prigozy (Athens: University
    of Georgia Press, 2000), 150. This explication teeters awkwardly between two ontological
    states: the glam appeal of being (or coming from) *in flight* and the stationary ennui of being *on
    the ground*. The passengers' agency is held in question in the airport, at once celebrated (liter-
    ally on display) and rendered stagnate, even depressed.
19 Martin's essay also touches on the issue of Hollywood as a hyper-real site: "... history
    becomes distorted and is turned into myth, illusion, and metaphor—the transformation of
    the American Dream and history into the dream factories of Hollywood, the triumph of

mass entertainment over reality.... Fitzgerald might well have realized that he was not only at the end of the pioneer line in time but also geographically at the end of the pioneering place, the California of Hollywood make-believe rather than the reality of a physical land of tycoons and settlers of an earlier day ...." Martin, *F. Scott Fitzgerald*, 144–5.

20 Fitzgerald, *The Last Tycoon*, 14
21 I discuss at length the subject of airport seating in Chapter 9 of this book.
22 Fitzgerald, *The Last Tycoon*, 7.
23 See Wallace Stevens, "Anecdote of the Jar," *The Palm at the End of the Mind*, ed. Holly Stevens (New York: Vintage, 1967), 46. The quotidian particulars of Modernist art are frequently reflective and manufactured—and they often prefigure or directly point out their status as disposable, as rubble.
24 Fitzgerald, *The Last Tycoon*, 4.
25 Ibid.
26 Bruno Barreto's 2003 film *View from the Top* serves as a contemporary example of this theme, with its fabulously attired flight attendants representing this work as fun, funny, and full of adventure.
27 Don DeLillo, *Valparaiso* (New York: Scribner, 2003), 27, 28, 31, 32.
28 Ibid., 86.
29 Jean-François Lyotard, "Answer to the Question: What is the Postmodern?" *The Postmodernism Reader: Foundational Texts*, ed. Michael Drolet (New York: Routledge, 2004), 236, 237.
30 DeLillo, *Valparaiso*, 68.
31 Jean Baudrillard, *Simulacra and Simulation*, trans. Sheila Faria Glaser (Ann Arbor: University of Michigan Press, 1994), 125. It is noteworthy that Baudrillard locates the model of hyperreality in J.G. Ballard's novel *Crash*, which is set in critical relation to the continuous flight patterns of London airport. (Indeed, the airport makes no less than 76 appearances in this novel.)
32 Ibid., 84.
33 Julie Bruck, "Men at Work," *Monkey Ranch* (Brick Books: London, Ontario), forthcoming 2012.
34 Ibid.
35 Ibid.
36 Ibid.
37 Ibid.
38 "The Social Text," *Henri Lefebvre: Key Writings*, ed. Stuart Elden, Elizabeth Lebas, and Elonore Kofman (New York: Continuum, 2003), 91.

Chapter 3

1 Gillian Fuller and Ross Harley, *Aviopolis* (London: Black Dog, 2004), 46.
2 Franklin W. Dixon, *The Hardy Boys Casefiles: Tagged for Terror* (New York: Archway Paperbacks, 1993), 4.
3 Ibid., 23.
4 Susan Trento and Joseph Trento, *Unsafe at any Altitude: Exposing the Illusion of Aviation Security* (Hanover: Steerforth, 2006), 47–8.
5 Dixon, *Tagged for Terror*, 155.
6 Ibid., 17.
7 Ibid., 13.
8 Ibid., 54.
9 Ibid., 126–7.
10 Ibid., 154.
11 Franklin W. Dixon, *The Hardy Boys Casefiles: Hostages of Hate* (New York: Archway Paperbacks, 1987), 9.

12 Ibid., 45.
13 Ibid., 92.
14 Ibid., 58 (my emphasis).
15 Ibid., 135.
16 Ibid.
17 Ibid., 139.
18 Percy Bysshe Shelley, "Ozymandias," *The Cambridge Companion to Shelley,* ed. Timothy Morton (Cambridge: Cambridge University Press, 2006), 202–3.
19 Martin Heidegger, "The Question Concerning Technology," *Basic Writings,* ed. David Farrell Krell, 2nd edn (New York: Harper Collins, 1993), 322.
20 Ibid., 338.
21 Franklin W. Dixon, *The Hardy Boys: The Great Airport Mystery* (New York: Grosset & Dunlap, 1930), 74.
22 See Derrida, "Autoimmunity. See also Jacques Derrida, *Rogues* (Stanford: Stanford University Press, 2005).
23 Dixon, *The Great Airport Mystery,* 110.
24 Ibid., 3.
25 Barry Lopez, *Light Action in the Caribbean* (New York: Alfred A. Knopf, 2000), 127–8.
26 Fuller and Harley, *Aviopolis,* 105–6.
27 Patricia Yaeger, "The Death of Nature and the Apotheosis of Trash; or, Rubbish Ecology." *PMLA* Vol. 123, 2 (New York: MLA, March 2008), 331.
28 DeLillo, *Underworld,* 183.
29 Dixon, *The Great Airport Mystery,* 115.
30 Sigmund Freud, *The Interpretation of Dreams,* trans. James Strachey, 1955 (New York: Basic Books, 2010), 296–7.
31 Dixon, *The Great Airport Mystery,* 71.
32 "Video Shows Newark Security Breach: A Kiss Before Flying," *The New York Times* online, January 7, 2010, http://cityroom.blogs.nytimes.com/2010/01/07/video-shows-newark-security-breach-a-kiss-before-flying/ (accessed January 17, 2011).
33 See Henri Lefebvre, "The Social Text." *Henri Lefebvre: Key Writings,* ed. Stuart Elden, Elizabeth Lebas, and Eleonore Kofman (New York: Continuum, 2006), 88.
34 Haisong Jiang Guilty: Newark Breach Security Breach Suspect Pleads Guilty" *The Huffington Post* http://www.huffingtonpost.com/2010/03/09/haisong-jiang-guilty-newa_n_491569.html.

Chapter 4

1 Baudrillard, *The Spirit of Terrorism,* 4.
2 David Simpson, *9/11: The Culture of Commemoration* (Chicago: The University of Chicago Press, 2006), 18.
3 "September 11 attacks," http://en.wikipedia.org/wiki/9/11 (accessed February 13, 2011).
4 Sherman Alexie, "Flight Patterns." *Ten Little Indians* (New York: Grove Press, 2004), 102.
5 Ibid., 107.
6 Ibid., 120.
7 Ibid.
8 Ibid., 122.
9 Ibid., 123.
10 Ibid.
11 Ibid., 108.
12 Martin Amis, *The Second Plane—September 11: Terror and Boredom* (New York: Afred A. Knopf, 2008), 5.
13 Martin Amis, "The Last Days of Muhammad Atta." *The New Yorker* (April 24, 2006), 157.
14 Ibid., 153, 163.

15 Gordon, *Naked Airport*, 170–1.
16 Amis, "The Last Days of Muhammad Atta," 157.
17 Don DeLillo, *The Names* (New York: Vintage, 1982), 7.
18 Amis, "The Last Days of Muhammad Atta," 160.
19 Ibid., 160–1.
20 Ibid., 161.
21 Ibid., 161–2.
22 Derrida, "Autoimmunity," 95.
23 Don DeLillo, *Falling Man* (New York: Scribner, 2007), 239, 241.
24 Ibid., 173.
25 Ibid., 177–8.
26 Ibid., 67.
27 Curiously, DeLillo echoes this scene in his more recent novella *Point Omega*, in a passage where one of the characters expresses confusion concerning another airport escalator, another father: "She said she got confused when she stepped onto an escalator that wasn't functioning. This happened at the airport in San Diego, where her father was waiting to meet her. She stepped onto an up escalator that wasn't moving and she couldn't adjust to this, she had to self-consciously climb the steps to move and she'd sort of half walk but not seem to be going anywhere because the steps weren't moving." *Point Omega* (New York: Scribner, 2010), 41.
28 Sharkey "Registered Traveler Program."; Trento and Trento, *Unsafe at any Altitude*.
29 DeLillo, *Falling Man*, 3.
30 Ibid., 4.
31 Ibid., 237.
32 Ibid., 328–39.
33 Ibid., 239.
34 Ibid., 16.
35 Ibid., 246.
36 Ibid.
37 Personal email from Joshua Clover to the author dated February 5, 2011; originally presented at the Stanford University Center for the Study of the Novel 2005–2006, on the "Adventure" panel.
38 Ibid.
39 *The 9/11 Commission Report*, 1. http://www.9-11commission.gov/report/index.htm
40 Ibid.
41 See Walter Mignolo, *The Idea of Latin America* (Malden, MA: Wiley-Blackwell, 2005).
42 *The 9/11 Commission Report*, 1.

Chapter 5

1 Lisa Parks, "Points of Departure: The Culture of US Airport Screening," *Journal of Visual Culture* 6(2) (2007), 189.
2 *Oxford English Dictionary*, "screening."
3 Gillian Fuller, "Welcome to Windows 2.0: Motion Aesthetics at the Airport," *Politics at the Airport*, ed. Mark B. Salter (Minneapolis: Minnesota University Press, 2008), 161.
4 Parks, "Points of Departure," 188.
5 http://www.tsa.gov/approach/tech/ait/how_it_works.shtm
6 http://wewontfly.com/
7 http://wewontfly.com/install-qik-on-your-phone-so-tsa-cant-delete-your-video
8 http://www.nytimes.com/2010/11/25/us/25travel.html?hp
9 Walter Benjamin, "The Work of Art in the Age of Mechanical Reproduction," *Illuminations*, trans. Harry Zohn (New York: Schocken, 1969), 241.
10 http://www.tsa.gov/

11 http://archives.newyorker.com/?i=2010-12-06
12 Fuller, "Welcome to Windows 2.0: Motion Aesthetics at the Airport," 161–2.
13 Ibid., 167.
14 Anna McCarthy, *Ambient Television: Visual Culture and Public Space* (Duke University Press, 2001), 111.

Chapter 6

1 My friend and fellow cultural critic on this trip was Dan Thomas-Glass, and I am grateful for his shrewd eye and quick mind as we toured the Sacramento airport. We went on to present a paper on this topic entitled: "Airport Art and the Misuses of Space" at the 2005 Western American Literature Association conference in Los Angeles.
2 The environmental philosopher Timothy Morton once recorded his experience of "Chromatic Oasis" in a spontaneous and informal personal email to me: "Now in airport waiting for ridiculously early flight. Will report back. Was bathed in ritualistic pink light at security . . ." (April 17, 2006, 5:39:25 A.M.).
3 Annie Proulx, "I've Always Loved This Place." *Fine Just The Way It Is* (New York: Scribner 2008), 36.
4 Ibid., 40.
5 "And Behold a Big Blue Horse? Many in Denver Just Say Neigh," *The New York Times* http://www.nytimes.com/2009/03/02/arts/design/02hors.html?_r=3 (accessed February 12, 2011).
6 "A Horse of a Different Color Divides Denver." *The Wall Street Journal* http://online.wsj.com/article/SB123395183452158089.html (accessed February 12, 2011).
7 Ibid.
8 Ibid.
9 Joseph O'Neill, *Netherland* (New York: Pantheon, 2008), 80–1.
10 Pico Iyer, *The Global Soul: Jet Lag, Shopping Malls, and the Search for Home* (New York: Vintage Departures, 2000), 43.
11 Brian Eno, *Ambient 1: Music for Airports* PVC 7908 (AMB 001), 1978.
12 "Travel Tranquil Moments Alarm Clock Sound Therapy Machine," by Brookstone®.
13 DeLillo, *Underworld*, 446–7.
14 Ibid., 317.
15 Kumin, "Getting Around O'Hare," 56.
16 Stewart Cohen, "Three Approaches to the Airport Case." Handout distributed during presentation on 11 May 2007, UC Davis Department of Philosophy.
17 Stewart Cohen, "Three Approaches to the Airport Case." Abstract for 2011 *Bled Philosophical Conference: Knowledge, Understanding and Wisdom* http://www.bled-conference.si/index.php?page=content&page_id=20 (accessed May 20, 2011).
18 John Cage, "Indeterminacy," *Silence* (Middleton, Connecticut: Wesleyan University Press, 1961), 262.
19 David Kranes, "The Wishbone," *Hunters in the Snow* (University of Utah Press, 1979), 15.
20 Haraway, *When Species Meet*, 16, 261.
21 Timothy Morton, *The Ecological Thought* (Cambridge, MA: Harvard University Press, 2010), 17, 60.
22 Written by Ani DiFranco, "The Arrivals Gate" © 1999 Righteous Babe Music (lyrics reproduced with permission).
23 "Airport Tourism," *The Lonely Planet Guide to Experimental Travel*, ed. Rachel Antony, Joel Henry, and Andrew Dean Nystrom (London: Lonely Planet, 2005), 42.
24 Ibid.
25 Ibid., 46.
26 Ibid., 44.
27 Ibid., 45.
28 Ibid., 44 (my emphasis).

29 Ibid.
30 Alain de Botton, *A Week at the Airport* (New York: Vintage, 2009), 10.
31 Ibid., 41.
32 Ibid., 42.
33 Ibid., 44.
34 Ibid., 13.
35 Ibid., 101.
36 Ibid., 107.
37 Ibid., 86.
38 Ibid., 87.

Chapter 7

1 Edward Abbey, *Confessions of a Barbarian*, ed. David Petersen (New York: Little, Brown & Company, 1994), 274.
2 Edward Abbey, *Desert Solitaire* (New York: Ballantine, 1968), 2.
3 Giorgio Agamben, *The Open: Man & Animal*, trans. Kevin Attell (Stanford: Stanford University Press, 2004), 47.
4 For more on what sort of ecology might be emergent, see Timothy Morton's evocative speculations, in *The Ecological Thought*.
5 Dana Phillips, *The Truth of Ecology: Nature, Culture, and Literature in America* (New York: Oxford University Press, 2003).
6 Bennett, *Vibrant Matter*.
7 Augé, *Non-Places*.
8 Roland Barthes, "The Jet-Man," *Mythologies* (New York: Noonday, 1957), 71.
9 Augé, *Non-Places*, 3.
10 Ibid.
11 Gary Snyder, "Blast Zone," *Danger on Peaks* (Emeryville: Shoemaker & Hoard, 2005), 13.
12 Ibid., 15.
13 Snyder, "Waiting for a Ride," *Danger on Peaks* (Emeryville: Shoemaker & Hoard, 2005), 56.
14 Ibid.
15 Ibid.
16 Ibid.
17 Snyder, "Strong Spirit," *Danger on Peaks* (Emeryville: Shoemaker & Hoard, 2005), 43.
18 Ibid.
19 Elaine Scarry, *On Beauty and Being Just* (Princeton: Princeton University Press, 1999).
20 Augé, *Non-Places*, 120.
21 Lopez, "Light Action in the Caribbean," 127–8.
22 Don DeLillo, *Players* (New York: Vintage Contemporaries, 1989), 88.
23 Ibid., 190–1.
24 Lopez, "Light Action in the Caribbean," 128.
25 Ibid.
26 Ibid.
27 Ibid., 129.
28 For a convincing take on DeLillo's significance in the American environmental imagination, see Yaeger, "The Death of Nature," 331.
29 Don DeLillo, *White Noise* (New York: Viking Penguin, 1985), 89.
30 Ibid., 93.
31 Ibid., 307.
32 DeLillo, *Underworld*, 317.
33 DeLillo, *The Names*, 7.

34 Barry Lopez, "Pearyland," *Field Notes* (New York: Knopf, 1994), 61–2.

35 Ibid., 62.

36 Ibid., 74.

37 For a vibrant ecocritical analysis of Coleridge's "Rime of the Ancient Mariner," see Timothy Morton, *The Ecological Thought* (Cambridge, MA: Harvard University Press, 2010).

38 Colson Whitehead, *John Henry Days* (New York: Anchor Books, 2002), 9.

39 Ibid., 13.

40 Ibid.

41 Kathleen Stewart, *Ordinary Affects* (Durham: Duke University Press, 2007), 90.

42 DeLillo, *Underworld*, 105.

43 Morton, *The Ecological Thought*, 102.

44 DeLillo, *The Names*, 138.

45 Augé, *An Anthropology for Contemporaneous Worlds*, 110.

46 Lucy Corin, "My Favorite Dentist," *The Entire Predicament* (Portland: Tin House, 2007), 22–3.

47 Nicholson Baker, *The Mezzanine* (New York: Vintage Contemporaries, 1990), 35.

48 Carol Muske-Dukes, "De-icing the Wings," *Air Fare,* ed. Nickole Brown and Judith Taylor (Louisville: Sarabande, 2004), 66.

49 Sherod Santos, "Airport Security," *Valparaiso Poetry Review* www.valpo.edu/vpr/santosairport.html (January 2002).

50 Ibid.

51 Parks, "Points of Departure," 188.

52 David Sedaris, "Standing By," *The New Yorker* (August 9, 2010), 33.

53 Ibid., 34.

54 Ibid., 35.

55 Bennett, *Vibrant Matter*, 32.

56 Sommer, *Tight Spaces*, 80.

Chapter 8

1   Stevens, "Thirteen Ways of Looking at a Blackbird." *The Palm at the End of the Mind*, 166.

2   T.S. Eliot, *Four Quartets* (Orlando: Harcourt Brace & Company, 1943, 1971), 52 (lines 81–2).

3   Ibid., 57 (lines 200–1).

4   As cited by Martin Greif, *The Airport Book: From Landing Field to Modern Terminal* (New York: Mayflower Books, 1979), 41.

5   Ibid., 41.

6   For example, consider Michael Crichton's novel *Airframe* (New York: Ballantine, 1997), in which the characters refer to aircraft as "birds" literally dozens of times over the course of the potboiler.

7   "Officials Plan to Eliminate 170,000 Canada Geese in New York," *New York Times City Room* http://cityroom.blogs.nytimes.com/2010/07/23/state-plans-to-eliminate-170000-canada-geese/ (accessed March 7, 2011).

8   Gordon, *Naked Airport*, 199.

9   Greif, *The Airport Book*.

10 *Birdstrike Control Program*, "FAA data show New York's JFK, Sacramento, Calif., airports have most bird strikes with damage," http://www.birdstrikecontrol.com/news/birdstrike_news/faa-data-show-new-york%E2%80%99s-jfk-sacramento-calif-airports-have-most-bird-strikes-with-damage/ (accessed March 7, 2011).

11 Paul Ferrell, "Clear-cut for takeoff" *Citing wildlife and terrorists, the airport wants to destroy more native oaks*, http://www.newsreview.com/sacramento/Content?oid=oid%3A47274 (accessed December 24, 2006).

12 Snyder, "No Shadow," *Danger on Peaks*, 85.
13 Ibid.
14 Ibid.
15 Pascoe, *Aircraft*, 164.
16 Wallpaper image located at http://www.wallpaperpimper.com/wallpaper/download-wallpaper-Lockheed_SR_71_Blackbird-size-1024x768-id-123142.htm (accessed March 2, 2011).
17 Seyed Alavi, description for "A Site Specific Public Art Project for the Sacramento International Airport" at http://here2day.netwiz.net/seyedsite/publicart/flyingcarpet/flyingcarpetframe.html (accessed January 20, 2011).
18 Ibid.
19 Here I am merging Timothy Morton's idea of "the mesh" with Jane Bennett's theory of "vital materialism."
20 Agamben, *The Open*, 65.
21 Ibid.
22 DeLillo, *The Names*, 253–4.

Chapter 9

1 de Botton, *A Week at the Airport*, 97.
2 W.D. Snodgrass, "Baggage Claim" (*The New Yorker*, February 19 and 26, 2007), 100. Also available online at http://www.newyorker.com/fiction/poetry/2007/02/19/070219po_poem_snodgrass#
3 Ibid., 100.
4 Ibid.
5 Scarry, *On Beauty and Being Just*, 16.
6 As if this quasi-legal language is clear and distinct: (c) CHECKED BAGGAGE.—A system must be in operation to screen all checked baggage at all airports in the United States as soon as practicable but not later than the 60th day following the date of enactment of the Aviation and Transportation Security Act. (d) EXPLOSIVE DETECTION SYSTEMS.—"(1) IN GENERAL.—The Under Secretary of Transportation for Security shall take all necessary action to ensure that— (A) explosive detection systems are deployed as soon as possible to ensure that all United States airports described in section 44903(c) have sufficient explosive detection systems to screen all checked baggage no later than December 31, 2002, and that as soon as such systems are in place at an airport, all checked baggage at the airport is screened by those systems; and (B) all systems deployed under subparagraph (A) are fully utilized; and (C) if explosive detection equipment at an airport is unavailable, all checked baggage is screened by an alternative means. (e) MANDATORY SCREENING WHERE EDS NOT YET AVAILABLE.—As soon as practicable but not later than the 60th day following the date of enactment of the Aviation and Transportation Security Act and until the requirements of subsection (b)(1)(A) are met, the Under Secretary shall require alternative means for screening any piece of checked baggage that is not screened by an explosive detection system. Such alternative means may include 1 or more of the following: (1) A bag-match program that ensures that no checked baggage is placed aboard an aircraft unless the passenger who checked the baggage is aboard the aircraft. (2) Manual search. (3) Search by canine explosive detection units in combination with other means. (4) Other means or technology approved by the Under Secretary."
7 Pascoe, *Airspaces*, 189–91.
8 Timothy Morton, "Displacement and Worlds," *Ecology without Nature* blog post, located at http://ecologywithoutnature.blogspot.com/2011/04/displacement-and-worlds.html (April 6, 2011).

9   Morton, "Hauntology and Non-Places," *Ecology without Nature* blog post, located at http://ecologywithoutnature.blogspot.com/2011/05/hauntology-and-non-places.html (May 28, 2011).

10 Morton, "Crowd Control," *Ecology without Nature* blog post, located at http://ecology-withoutnature.blogspot.com/2011/04/crowd-control.html (April 6, 2011).

11 Morton, "Emergency Room: Art and Climate Change," *Ecology without Nature* blog post, located at http://ecologywithoutnature.blogspot.com/2011/04/emergency-room-art-and-climate-change.html (April 19, 2011).

12 John K. Kasarda and Greg Lindsay, *Aerotropolis: The Way We'll Live Next* (New York: Farrar, Straus, and Giroux, 2011), 79.

13 Ibid., 82.

14 Ian Bogost, blog review of *Aerotropolis* located at http://www.bogost.com/blog/aerotropo-lis.shtml (March 27, 2011).

15 Ibid.

16 Ibid.

17 Rachel Lehmann-Haupt and Bess Abrahams, *Airplane Yoga* (New York: Riverhead Books, 2003), 3.

18 Ibid., 98.

19 Augé, *Non-places*, 111.

20 Timothy Morton, *Ecology without Nature: Rethinking Environmental Aesthetics* (Cambridge: Harvard University Press, 2007), 85.

21 See Morton, *The Ecological Thought*, 51.

BIBLIOGRAPHY

Abbey, Edward. *Confessions of a Barbarian*. Ed. David Petersen. New York: Little, Brown & Company, 1994.

—. *Desert Solitaire*. New York: Ballantine, 1968.

"Airport Tourism." *The Lonely Planet Guide to Experimental Travel*. Ed. Rachel Anonty, Joel Henry, and Andrew Dean Nystrom. London: Lonely Planet, 2005.

Agamben, Giorgio. *The Open: Man & Animal*. Trans. Kevin Attell. Stanford: Stanford University Press, 2004.

Alexie, Sherman. "Flight Patterns." *Ten Little Indians*. New York: Grove Press, 2004.

Amis, Martin. "The Last Days of Muhammad Atta." *The New Yorker*. April 24, 2006.

—. *The Second Plane – September 11: Terror and Boredom*. New York: Afred A. Knopf, 2008.

Augé, Marc. *Non-Places: Introduction to an Anthropology of Supermodernity*. Trans. John Howe. New York: Verso, 1995.

—. *An Anthropology for Contemporaneous Worlds*. Stanford: Stanford University Press, 1999.

Baker, Nicholson. *The Mezzanine*. New York: Vintage Contemporaries, 1990.

Barthes, Roland. "The Jet-Man." *Mythologies*. New York: Noonday, 1972.

—. "From Work to Text." *Image Music Text*. Trans. Stephen Heath. New York: Hill & Wang, 1977.

Baudrillard, Jean. *The Spirit of Terrorism*. New York: Verso, 2002.

Benjamin, Walter. "The Work of Art in the Age of Mechanical Reproduction." *Illuminations*. Ed. Hannah Arendt. New York: Schocken Books, 1968.

Bennett, Jane. *Vibrant Matter: A Political Ecology of Things*. Durham: Duke University Press, 2010.

Bruck, Julie. "Men at Work." *Monkey Ranch*. London, Ontario: Brick Books, 2012.

Cage, John. "Indeterminacy." *Silence*. Middleton, CN: Wesleyan University Press, 1961.

Cohen, Stewart. "Three Approaches to the Airport Case." UC Davis Department of Philosophy. Handout distributed during presentation on May 11, 2007.

Corin, Lucy. "My Favorite Dentist." *The Entire Predicament*. Portland: Tin House, 2006.

Crichton, Michael. *Airframe*. New York: Ballantine, 1997.

De Botton, Alain. *A Week at the Airport*. New York: Vintage, 2009.

DeLillo, Don. *Falling Man*. New York: Scribner, 2007.

—. *The Names*. New York: Vintage, 1982.

—. *Players*. New York: Vintage Contemporaries, 1989.

—. *Point Omega*. New York: Scribner, 2010.

—. *Underworld*. New York: Scribner, 1997.

—. *Valparaiso*. New York: Scribner, 2003.

—. *White Noise*. New York: Penguin, 1985.

Derrida, Jacques. "Autoimmunity: Real and Symbolic Suicides – A Dialogue with Jacques Derrida." *Philosophy in a Time of Terror: Dialogues with Jürgen Habermas and Jacques Derrida*, Ed. Giovanna Borradori. Chicago: University of Chicago Press, 2003.

—. *Rogues*. Stanford: Stanford University Press, 2005.

—. "Ulysses' Grammaphone: Hear Say Yes in Joyce." *Acts of Literature*. Ed. Derrick Attridge. New York: Routledge, 1992.

Dixon, Franklin W. *The Hardy Boys: The Great Airport Mystery*. New York: Grosset & Dunlap, 1930.

—. *The Hardy Boys Casefiles: Hostages of Hate*. New York: Archway Paperbacks, 1987.

—. *The Hardy Boys Casefiles: Tagged for Terror*. New York: Archway Paperbacks, 1993.

Edwards, Brian. *The Modern Airport Terminal: New Approaches to Airport Architecture*, 2nd edn. London and New York: Spon Press, 2005.

Eliot, T.S. *Four Quartets*. Orlando: Harcourt Brace & Company, 1943, 1971.

Fitzgerald, F. Scott. *The Love of the Last Tycoon: A Western*. Ed. Matthew Bruccoli. New York: Scribner, 1995.

—. "Three Hours between Planes." *Esquire*. 1941.

Foucault, Michel. 1975. *Discipline and Punish: The Birth of the Prison*. Trans. Alan Sheridan. London: Penguin, 1991.

Freud, Sigmund. *The Interpretation of Dreams*, Trans. James Strachey, 1955. New York: Basic Books, 2010.

Fuller, Gillian. "Welcome to Windows 2.1: Motion Aesthetics at the Airport," *Politics at the Airport*, Ed. Mark Salter. Minneapolis: University of Minnesota Press, 2008.

Fuller, Gillian and Ross Harley. *Aviopolis: A Book About Airports*. London: Black Dog Publishing, 2004.

Gordon, Alastair. *Naked Airport: A Cultural History of the World's Most Revolutionary Structure*. New York: Metropolitan Books, 2004.

Greif, Martin. *The Airport Book: From Landing Field to Modern Terminal*. New York: Mayflower Books, 1979.

Hailey, Arthur. *Airport*. New York: Berkley Books, 1968, 2000.

Haraway, Donna. "A Cyborg Manifesto: Science, Technology, and Socialist-Feminism in the Late Twentieth Century," *Simians, Cyborgs and Women: The Reinvention of Nature*. New York: Routledge, 1991.

—. *When Species Meet*. Minneapolis: University of Minnesota Press, 2007.

Heidegger, Martin. "The Question Concerning Technology." *Basic Writings*. Ed. David Farrell Krell, 2nd edn. New York: Harper Collins, 1993.

Iyer, Pico. *The Global Soul: Jet Lag, Shopping Malls, and the Search for Home*. New York: Vintage Departures, 2000.

Jameson, Fredric. *Postmodernism, or, The Cultural Logic of Late Capitalism*. Durham, NC: Duke University Press, 1990.

Kasarda, John D. and Greg Lindsay. *Aerotropolis: The Way We'll Live Next*. New York: Farrar, Straus, and Giroux, 2011.

Kesey, Roy. "Wait," *All Over*. Westland, MI: Dzanc, 2007.

Kranes, David. "The Wishbone." *Hunters in the Snow*. Salt Lake City: University of Utah Press, 1979.

Kirn, Walter. *Up in the Air*. New York: Anchor Books, 2001.

Kumin, Maxine. "Getting Around O'Hare." *Looking For Luck*. New York: Norton, 1992.

Lefebvre, Henri. "The Social Text." *Henri Lefebvre: Key Writings*. New York: Continuum, 2003.

Lehmann-Haupt, Rachel and Bess Abrahams. *Airplane Yoga*. New York: Riverhead Books, 2003.

Lopez, Barry. *About This Life*. New York: Vintage, 1999.

—. *Light Action in the Caribbean*. New York: Alfred A. Knopf, 2000.

—. "Pearyland." *Field Notes*. New York: Knopf, 1994.

Lyotard, Jean-François. "Answer to the Question: What is the Postmodern?" *The Postmodernism Reader: Foundational Texts*. Ed. Michael Drolet. New York: Routledge, 2004.

Manovich, Lev. "Introduction to Info-Aesthetics." *Antinomies of Art and Culture*. Ed. Smith et al. Durham, NC: Duke University Press, 2008.

Martin, Robert A. "Fitzgerald's Use of History in *The Last Tycoon*." *F. Scott Fitzgerald—New Perspectives*. Ed. Jackson R. Bryer, Alan Margolies, and Ruth Prigozy. Athens: University of Georgia Press, 2000.

McCarthy, Anna. *Ambient Television: Visual Culture and Public Space*. Duke University Press, 2001.

Mignolo, Walter. *The Idea of Latin America*. Malden, MA: Wiley-Blackwell, 2005.

Moore, Lorrie. *A Gate at the Stairs*. New York: Knopf, 2009.

Morton, Timothy, Ed. *The Cambridge Companion to Shelley*. Cambridge: Cambridge University Press, 2006.

Morton, Timothy. *Ecology without Nature: Rethinking Environmental Aesthetics*. Cambridge, MA: Harvard University Press, 2007.

—. *The Ecological Thought*. Cambridge, MA: Harvard University Press, 2010.

Muske-Dukes, Carol. "De-icing the Wings." *Air Fare*. Ed. Nickole Brown and Judith Taylor. Louisville: Sarabande, 2004.

O'Neill, Joseph. *Netherland*. New York: Pantheon, 2008.

Oxford English Dictionary. London: Oxford University Press, 2011.

Palahniuk, Chuck. *Fight Club*. New York: Owl Books, 1996.

Parks, Lisa. "Points of Departure: The Culture of US Airport Screening." *Journal of Visual Culture* Vol. 6(2) 2007.

Pascoe, David. *Airspaces*. London: Reaktion Books, 2001.

—. *Aircraft*. London: Reaktion Books, 2003.

Phillips, Dana. *The Truth of Ecology: Nature, Culture, and Literature in America*. New York: Oxford University Press, 2003.

Pound, Ezra. *Selected Poems*. New York: New Directions, 1957.

Price, Jennifer. *Flight Maps: Adventures with Nature in Modern America*. New York: Basic Books, 1999.

Proulx, Annie. "I've Always Loved This Place." *Fine Just The Way 'It Is*. New York: Scribner, 2008.

Salter, Mark B., Ed. *Politics at the Airport*. Minneapolis: University of Minnesota Press, 2008.

Scarry, Elaine. *On Beauty and Being Just*. Princeton: Princeton University Press, 1999.

Sedaris, David. "Standing By." *The New Yorker*. August 9, 2010.

Sharkey, Joe. "Registered Traveler Program Appears Ready to Take Off." *The New York Times*. September 5, 2006.

Shelley, Percy Bysshe. "Ozymandias." *The Cambridge Companion to Shelley*. Ed. Timothy Morton. Cambridge: Cambridge University Press, 2006.

Shepard, Sam. "Land of the Living." *The New Yorker*. September 21, 2009.

Silver, Nate. "The Full-Body Backlash." *The New York Times*. November 15, 2010.

Simpson, David. *9/11: The Culture of Commemoration*. Chicago: The University of Chicago Press, 2006.

Snodgrass, W.D. "Baggage Claim." *The New Yorker*. February 19 and 26, 2007.

Snyder, Gary. *Danger on Peaks*. Emeryville: Shoemaker & Hoard, 2004.

—. *The Practice of the Wild*. New York: North Point Press, 1990.

Sommer, Robert. *Tight Spaces; Hard Architecture and How to Humanize It*. Englewood Cliffs, NJ: Spectrum, 1974.

Stevens, Wallace. *The Palm at the End of the Mind*. New York: Vintage, 1991.

Stewart, Kathleen. *Ordinary Affects*. Durham: Duke University Press, 2007.

Trento, Susan and Joseph Trento. *Unsafe at any Altitude: Exposing the Illusion of Aviation Security*. Hanover: Steerforth, 2006.

Thoreau, Henry David. *Walden*. Princeton: Princeton University Press, 1989.

Virilio, Paul. *War and Cinema*. New York and London: Verso, 1989.

Whitehead, Colson. *John Henry Days*. New York: Anchor Books, 2002.

Wohl, Robert. *A Passion for Wings: Aviation and the Western Imagination, 1908–1918*. New Haven: Yale University Press, 1996.

—. *The Spectacle of Flight: Aviation and the Western Imagination, 1920–1950*. New Haven: Yale University Press, 2005.

Yaeger, Patricia. "The Death of Nature and the Apotheosis of Trash; or, Rubbish Ecology." *PMLA* Vol. 123 (2) March 2008.

Web Resources

The 9/11 Commission Report, 1. http://www.9-11commission.gov/report/index.htm.

Alavi, Seyed. "A Site Specific Public Art Project for the Sacramento International Airport." http://here2day.netwiz.net/seyedsite/publicart/flyingcarpet/flyingcarpetframe.html (accessed January 20, 2011).

"And Behold a Big Blue Horse? Many in Denver Just Say Neigh." *The New York Times*. http://www.nytimes.com/2009/03/02/arts/design/02hors.html?_r=3 (accessed February 12, 2011).

Birdstrike Control Program. "FAA Data Show New York's JFK, Sacramento, Calif., Airports Have most Bird Strikes with Damage." http://www.birdstrikecontrol.com/news/birdstrike_news/faa-data-show-new-york%E2%80%99s-jfk-sacramento-calif-airports-have-most-bird-strikes-with-damage/ (accessed March 7, 2011).

Bogost, Ian. Blog review of *Aerotropolis*. http://www.bogost.com/blog/aerotropolis.shtml (accessed March 27, 2011).

Cohen, Stewart. "Three Approaches to the Airport Case." Abstract for 2011 *Bled Philosophical Conference: Knowledge, Understanding and Wisdom.* http://www.bled-conference.si/index.php?page=content&page_id=20 (accessed May 20, 2011).

Ferrell, Paul. "Clear-Cut for Takeoff." *Citing Wildlife and Terrorists, the Airport Wants to Destroy more Native Oaks.* http://www.newsreview.com/sacramento/Content?oid=oid%3A47274 (accessed December 24, 2006).

"Haisong Jiang Guilty: Newark Breach Security Breach Suspect Pleads Guilty." *The Huffington Post.* http://www.huffingtonpost.com/2010/03/09/haisong-jiang-guilty-newa_n_491569.html.

"A Horse of a Different Color Divides Denver." *The Wall Street Journal.* http://online.wsj.com/article/SB123395183452158089.html (accessed February 12, 2011).

Miller, Erin Collazo. "Bestsellers: Airport Reads." http://bestsellers.about.com/od/readingrecommendations/tp/airport_reading.htm (accessed November 20, 2010).

Morton, Timothy. "Crowd Control." *Ecology without Nature* blog post. http://ecologywithoutnature.blogspot.com/2011/04/crowd-control.html (accessed April 6, 2011).

Morton, Timothy. "Displacement and Worlds." *Ecology without Nature* blog post. http://ecologywithoutnature.blogspot.com/2011/04/displacement-and-worlds.html (accessed April 6, 2011).

Morton, Timothy. "Emergency Room: Art and Climate Change." *Ecology without Nature* blog post. http://ecologywithoutnature.blogspot.com/2011/04/emergency-room-art-and-climate-change.html (accessed April 19, 2011).

Morton, Timothy. "Hauntology and Non-Places." *Ecology without Nature* blog post. http://ecologywithoutnature.blogspot.com/2011/05/hauntology-and-non-places.html (accessed May 28, 2011).

"Officials Plan to Eliminate 170,000 Canada Geese in New York." *New York Times City Room.* http://cityroom.blogs.nytimes.com/2010/07/23/state-plans-to-eliminate-170000-canada-geese/ (accessed March 7, 2011).

Sacramento County Airport System. "The Big Build" Fly-Through Video. http://www.bigbuild.org/photo-media-gallery/design-overview/fly-through-video (accessed February 18, 2011).

Santos, Sherod. "Airport Security." *Valparaiso Poetry Review*. www.valpo.edu/vpr/santosairport.html (accessed January 2002).

"September 11 attacks." http://en.wikipedia.org/wiki/9/11 (accessed February 13, 2011).

"Video Shows Newark Security Breach: A Kiss before Flying." *The New York Times* online. http://cityroom.blogs.nytimes.com/2010/01/07/video-shows-newark-security-breach-a-kiss-before-flying/ (accessed January 7, 2010).

Films

2001: A Space Odyssey. Dir. Stanley Kubrick. 1968.
The Departed. Dir. Martin Scorsese. Warner Bros. Pictures. 2006.
Fight Club. Dir. David Fincher. Twentieth Century Fox. 1999.
The Terminal. Dir. Steven Spielberg. DreamWorks Studios. 2004.
Three Kings. Dir. David O. Russell. Warner Bros. Pictures. 1999.
Up in the Air. Dir. Jason Reitman. Paramount Pictures. 2009.

Music

DiFranco, Ani. "The Arrival Gates." © 1999 Righteous Babe Music.
Eno, Brian. *Ambient 1: Music for Airports*. PVC 7908 (AMB 001) 1978.
"Travel Tranquil Moments Alarm Clock Sound Therapy Machine." Brookstone®. http://www.brookstone.com/Travel-Tranquil-Moments-Sleep-Sound-Machine (accessed September 21, 2011).

INDEX